Pick Up! Theme Voca

고급

류헌규

Iam books

Pick up! Theme Voca 고급

© 2011 **I am Books**

지은이	박준상, 류헌규
펴낸이	신성현, 오상욱
기획·편집	이성원, 이기은, 강다현
디자인	오미정, 장정숙, 박란
일러스트	조소영
영업관리	장신동, 조신국, 장미선
펴낸곳	도서출판 아이엠북스
	153-802 서울시 금천구 가산동 327-32 대륭테크노타운 12차 1116호
대표전화	02-6343-0997~9
팩스	02-6343-0995~6
출판등록	2006년 6월 7일
	제 313-2006-000122호
ISBN	978-89-6398-052-2 54740

고급

　모든 언어의 기본은 어휘입니다. 이 점은 영어에 있어서도 마찬가지입니다. 처음 영어 공부를 시작할 때, 그 기초가 되는 어휘력이 없다면 상대의 말을 들을 수도, 글을 읽을 수도, 문장을 이해할 수도 없습니다. 외국어는 듣기, 쓰기, 말하기, 읽기의 네 가지 영역을 골고루 공부하면서 그 실력을 키워나가야 하지만 그 근간에는 어휘가 있습니다. 어휘력이 갖추어지지 않았다면 그 다음 단계로의 발전은 불가능하기 때문입니다. 어휘는 나무가 가지를 뻗어 잎이 나고 열매를 맺기 위해 가장 처음 뿌리를 내려야 하는 것처럼 외국어 정복에 있어서 뿌리내리기 작업과 같은 것입니다.

　하지만, 어떻게 하면 생소한 언어의 어휘를 늘릴 수 있을까요? 어휘 암기의 조금 더 쉽고 간단한 방법은 없을까요? 그동안 수많은 책들이나 강의를 통해 단어 암기의 비법들이 공개되고 있지만 사실 어휘는 암기하는 것 이외에는 별다른 방법이 없습니다. 그렇다고 해서 무조건 어휘를 암기하는 것보다는, 암기의 효율성을 높일 수 있는 방법과 어휘 실력의 향상을 영어 실력의 향상으로 연계 지을 수 있는 방법을 찾아 어휘를 암기하는 것이 좋을 것입니다.

　첫째, 어휘는 문장을 통해서 암기하는 것이 좋습니다. 문장 속에서 암기하다 보면 어휘가 주는 뉘앙스를 정확하게 파악할 수 있을 뿐 아니라 어휘가 쓰인 문장을 함께 암기함으로써 영어 말하기와 쓰기 실력까지 향상시킬 수 있기 때문입니다. 이에 착안하여 **Pick up! Theme Voca**에서는 문장을 익히

면서 어휘를 암기할 수 있도록 어휘가 쓰인 가장 좋은 예문을 함께 실었습니다.

둘째, 서로 연관성이 있는 어휘들을 함께 학습하는 것이 중요합니다. 인간의 기억력에는 한계가 있으므로 서로 연관성이 있는 어휘들을 함께 학습하여 학습의 효율을 올리는 것이 어휘 학습에 한 가지 좋은 방법이 될 것입니다.

"Pick up! Theme Voca"는 중학교 수준의 다양한 단어를 35개의 주제로 분류하여 학습자들이 보다 효율적으로 단어를 학습할 수 있도록 기획하였습니다. 각 주제는 우리 일상생활에서 밀접한 의식주에서부터 정치, 경제에 이르기까지 다양한 영역을 포함하고 있으며, 단어별로 가장 적절한 예문을 제시하였습니다. 또한 한 가지 주제를 마무리할 때 마다 Check Up을 이용하여 암기한 단어를 가볍게 확인해 볼 수 있도록 구성하였습니다.

"Pick up! Theme Voca"는 중학교에 입학하기 전에 중학 수준의 어휘를 미리 학습하고자 하는 예비 중학생이나, 중학교에서 배웠던 어휘를 마무리 정리하고 고등학교로 진학하고 싶은 학생들, 또는 졸업한 이후로 영어를 놓고 지내 쉬운 어휘마저 잘 기억이 나지 않거나 새로 영어를 시작하기 위해 어휘를 늘리고 싶은 일반인들에게 쉽고 효율적으로 어휘의 핵심만을 정리할 수 있는 교재가 될 것입니다.

아무쪼록, 본 교재가 영어 공부의 근간이 되는 어휘력 향상의 올바른 길잡이가 되기를 바라며, 본 교재와 함께 공부하는 모든 학습자의 영어 실력이 좋은 열매를 맺기를 바랍니다.

주제별로 분류한 어휘

분류된 테마별로 중학교 수준의 핵심적인 어휘만을 선별하였습니다.

01	accompany [əkʌ́mpəni] to go somewhere with them

vt. 동반하다, ~와 함께 가다
accompanying a. 수반하는, 동봉한

Most children were accompanied **by their families.**
대부분의 어린이들은 가족을 동반했다.

02	acquaintance [əkwéintəns] someone who you have met and know slightly

n. 지식, 면식, 아는 사람(사이)
acquaint vt. 익히 알게 하다, 알리다

I have no personal acquaintance **with your older brother.**
나는 너의 형과는 알면식도 없다.

03	adolescent [ædəlésnt] no longer children but who have not yet become adults

n. 청소년 a. 사춘기의, 미숙한
adolescence n. 사춘기 l adolesce vi. 사춘기에 이르다

The psychology of the adolescent **is complex.**
청소년의 심리는 복잡하다.

04	adult [ədʌ́lt, ǽdʌlt] a mature, fully developed person

n. 성인, 어른
adulthood n. 성인기

Young users can't be allowed to view adult **content on the Internet.**
청소년 사용자는 인터넷 성인물을 이용할 수 없다.

발음기호와 영영 풀이

함께 실은 발음기호를 통해 단순하게 뜻만 암기하는 것이 아니라 정확한 발음을 함께 익힐 수 있도록 하였으며, 단어의 뜻을 영어로 풀이하여 심도있는 학습이 가능하도록 하였습니다.

뜻과 파생어

단어의 여러 가지 뜻 중에서 가장 많이 쓰이고 꼭 외워야 할 뜻과 함께 다양한 파생어들을 함께 실었습니다.

예문

학습자가 그 어휘의 뜻을 쉽고 빠르게 이해할 수 있도록 어휘의 의미를 가장 잘 살려줄 수 있는 예문을 선별하여 실었습니다.

| **Check up**

Check up 코너를 통해
Lesson별로 학습했던 어휘
를 한 번에 총정리할 수 있
습니다.

C h e c k   u p

A 다음 각 문장에서 강조한 단어의 의미가 본문에서 쓰
것을 고르시오.

1. I think you are mature enough to do that.

① fully grown and developed

② ready to be paid in business

2. The stern look on her face was enough to send t
hurrying back.

① the back end of a ship or boat

② serious and often disapproving; expecting somet
you

3. My wife has never been a nurturing person even in he

① to have a feeling, an idea, a plan, etc. for a lo
encourage it to develop

② to care for and protect somebody while they are
developing

4. The females don't take care of the young.

Part 1 Daily Life | 일상생활

Part 2 Nature | 자연

Part **7** Education | 교육

부록

Part 1

Daily Life

[일상생활]

Family

|가족

01 accompany [əkʌ́mpəni] to go somewhere with them

vt. 동반하다, ~와 함께 가다
accompanying a. 수반하는, 동봉한

Most children were accompanied **by their families.**
대부분의 어린이들은 가족을 동반했다.

02 acquaintance [əkwéintəns] someone who you have met and know slightly

n. 지식, 면식, 아는 사람(사이)
acquaint vt. 익히 알게 하다, 알리다

I have no personal acquaintance **with your older brother.**
나는 너의 형과는 알면식도 없다.

03 adolescent [ædəlésnt] no longer children but who have not yet become adults

n. 청소년 a. 사춘기의, 미숙한
adolescence n. 사춘기 | adolesce vi. 사춘기에 이르다

The psychology of the adolescent **is complex.**
청소년의 심리는 복잡하다.

04 adult [ədʌ́lt, ǽdʌlt] a mature, fully developed person

n. 성인, 어른
adulthood n. 성인기

Young users can't be allowed to view adult **content on the Internet.**
청소년 사용자는 인터넷 성인물을 이용할 수 없다.

05 ancestor [ǽnsestər] the people from whom you are descended

n. 선조, 조상
ancestral a. 조상의 | ancestry n. (집합적) 조상, 선조, 가문, 문벌

The custom has come down from our ancestors since 1950.

그 풍습은 1950년대부터 우리 선조로부터 전해 내려온 것이다.

06 behave [bihéiv] to do things in a particular way

vi. 행동하다
behavior n. 행동, 행실 | well-behaved a. 행실이 단정한 | ill-behaved a. 버릇없는

The little children don't behave well.

어린이들은 예절 바르게 행동하지 않는다.

07 care [kέər] to feel something is important and be concerned about it

vi. 걱정하다, 염려하다, 돌보다
careful a. 조심성 있는, 꼼꼼한 | caring n. 상냥함, 돌보기, 간호
easycare a. 손질하기 쉬운

I have to take care of my mother today.

나는 오늘 어머니를 돌봐드려야 한다.

08 colonist [kάlənist] the people who start a colony

n. 식민지 사람, 이주민
colonize vt. 식민지로서 개척하다, 식민지를 만들다 | colony n. 식민지
colonizer n. 식민지 개척자, 이주해 온 유권자

Her land was distributed among her relatives and American colonists.

그녀의 땅은 친척들과 이주민들 사이에서 분배되었다.

09 dependent [dipéndənt] relying on something or someone for support

a. 의지하고 있는, 의존하는
depend vi. 의존하다, 의지하다, 믿다 I dependence n. 의지, 의존
dependable a. 의존할 수 있는

She is dependent on her parents for her living expenses.
그녀는 부모님에게서 생활비를 받고 있다.

10 depressed [diprést] sad and feel gloomy

a. 우울한, 슬픈
depress vt. 낙담시키다, 우울하게 하다 I depression n. 의기소침, 불경기, 불황
depressing a. 억압적인, 침울하게 만드는, 울적한

They were so depressed after their parents passed away.
부모님이 돌아가신 후 그들은 우울증에 빠졌다.

11 divorce [divɔ́:rs] the formal ending of a marriage by law

n. 이혼 v. 이혼시키다
divorced a. 이혼한, 분리된

Every third marriage ends up in divorce in Korea these days.
요새 한국에서 부부 세 쌍 중 한 쌍은 결국 이혼한다.

12 domestic [dəméstik] within one particular country

a. 가정의, 국내의
domesticate vt. 길들이다 I domestically ad. 가정적으로, 가사상, 국내에서

My father and I are going to meet at the domestic terminal.
아빠와 나는 국내선 터미널에서 만나기로 하였다.

13 **elder** [éldər] someone who is older than other

n. 연장자 a. 손위의, 연장의
eldest a. 가장 나이 많은

She is not quite so pretty as her elder **sister.**

그녀는 미모에 있어서 언니만 못하다.

14 **embrace** [imbréis, em-] to put your arms around someone and hold him tightly

vt. 껴안다, 포옹하다
embracement n. 포옹, 받아들임, 수락

My family needs to embrace **change in spite of their many problems.**

많은 어려움에도 불구하고 우리 가족은 모두 변화를 받아들여야 한다.

15 **emotion** [imóuʃən] a feeling such as happiness, love, fear, anger, or hatred

n. 감동, 감정
emotionless a. 무표정한, 무감동의 ㅣ emotional a. 감정적인
emotionality n. 감격성, 감동성

My father's voice was getting thick with emotion.

아버지의 목소리는 감정에 겨워 잠겨 있었다.

16 **enable** [inéibl, en-] to do a particular thing and to take the opportunity to do it

vt. ~에게 힘을 주다, 가능성을 주다
amenable a. 유순한, 순종하는, 고분고분한

These phones enable **mothers to see the location of their children.**

이 휴대폰을 통해 엄마는 아이들의 위치를 확인할 수 있다.

17 enthusiastic [inθúːziǽstik, en-] showing how much you like or enjoy it

a. 열심인, 열광적인
enthusiastically ad. 열광적으로 | unenthusiastic a. 냉담한, 열성이 없는

My husband was less than enthusiastic about my idea.
남편은 나의 생각에 전혀 열의를 보이지 않았다.

18 fond [fánd] feeling affection for something or someone

a. 애정 있는, 다정한
fondly ad. 다정하게 | fondness n. 애정, 애호 | fondle vt. 귀여워하다

I have fond memories of my grandparents from my childhood.
나는 어린 시절 조부모님에 대한 좋은 추억을 가지고 있다.

19 generation [dʒenəréiʃən] the people in a group or country who are of a similar age

n. 세대
generational a. 세대의 | regeneration n. 갱생, 개혁, 쇄신
degeneration n. 퇴보

A labor shortage will be inevitable due to the Baby Boom generation.
베이비붐 세대 때문에 노동력 부족이 불가피해진다.

20 grateful [gréitful] feeling thankful

a. 감사하고 있는
gratefully ad. 감사하여 | gratefulness n. 감사, 고맙게 여김
ungrateful a. 은혜를 모르는, 배은망덕한

I am grateful for your family's kindness.
나는 당신의 가족의 친절에 감사하게 생각하고 있다.

21 gracious [gréiʃəs] very well-mannered and pleasant

a. 호의적인, 친절한
graciously ad. 우아하게 l ungracious a. 불쾌한, 공손하지 않은

We received a gracious **and thankful e-mail from our children.**
우리는 아이들로부터 공손하고 감사해 하는 이메일을 받았다.

22 grim [grím] unpleasant, depressing, and difficult to accept

a. 엄격한, 냉혹한
grimly ad. 엄하게, 잔인하게 l grimy a. 때묻은, 때로 더러워진
grimness n. 잔인, 무서움, 엄격함

Her face went grim **because her son had broken her favorite vase.**
아들이 그녀의 아끼는 꽃병을 깨서, 그녀의 얼굴이 험악해졌다.

23 grow [gróu] to increase in size and change physically over a period of time

v. 성장하다, 자라다
growth n. 성장, 발달 l growing a. 성장하는 l grown a. 성장한

We want to grow **old together with you.**
우리는 너와 함께 늙어 가면 좋겠다.

24 heir [ɛ́ər] a person who has the legal right to receive someone's property, money or title when that person dies

n. 상속인, 후계자
heiress n. 여자 상속인 l heirless a. 상속인이 없는
heirship n. 상속, 상속인의 지위

My father acknowledged the child as his heir.
내 아버지는 그 아이를 상속자로 인정했다.

25 heritage [hérɪtidʒ] the history, traditions and qualities that a country or society has had for many years.

n. 유산, 상속, 재산

We have to teach our heritage to our children.

우리는 아이들에게 문화유산을 가르쳐야 한다.

26 humble [hʌmbl, ʌm-] having a low opinion of oneself

a. 천한, 겸손한 vi. 낮추다, 겸손해 하다

However humble it may be, there is no place like home.

아무리 누추할지라도 집 만한 곳은 없다.

27 infant [ínfənt] a baby or very young child

n. 유아, 젖먹이
infancy n. 유아기, 초창기

Parents have a responsibility for the actions of their infants.

부모는 유아의 행동에 대한 책임이 있다.

28 inherit [inhérit] to receive money or property from someone who has died

vt. 상속하다, 물려받다
inheritance n. 상속, 유산 | inheritor n. 상속인, 후계자
inheritable a. 상속권이 있는, 상속할 수 있는

He inherited his weak heart from his father.

그는 아버지로부터의 유전으로 심장이 약하다.

29 intimate [íntəmət] knowing someone or something very well

a. 친밀한, 정통한
intimately ad. 친밀히

There are intimate relations among our family members.

우리 가족은 관계가 친밀하다.

30 maternity [mətə́:rnəti] the state of being or becoming a mother

n. 모성애
maternal a. 어머니의

She just came back from maternity leave today.

그녀는 출산 휴가에서 오늘 막 돌아왔다.

31 mature [mətjúər, -tʃúər] fully developed and or grown

a. 성숙한, 심사숙고한
premature a. 너무 이른, 시기상조의 | immature a. 미숙한
maturity n. 성숙

Children our age aren't mature enough to experience those emotions.

우리 또래의 아이들은 그런 감정을 경험할 만큼 아직 성숙하진 못하다.

32 mutual [mjú:tʃuəl] experienced by each of two or more

a. 서로의, 공동의
mutually ad. 서로 | mutuality n. 상관, 상호 관계

My mother let us go over mutual areas of interest.

엄마는 우리의 공통 관심사를 살펴보게 했다.

33 **nurture** [nə́:rtʃər] to care for something while it is growing and developing

v. 양육하다, 기르다

Children have to be both influenced and nurtured **by their parents.**

아이들은 부모로부터 영향을 받으며 양육되어져야 한다.

34 **orphan** [ɔ́:rfən] a child whose parents are dead

n. 고아
orphanage n. 고아, 고아원 ∣ orphanhood n. 고아 신세

She adopted the orphan **and gave all of her property to him.**

그녀는 그 고아를 양자로 삼았고 전 재산을 다 주었다.

35 **overlook** [òuvəlúk] to see something wrong or bad but decide to ignore it

vt. 눈감아 주다, 바라보다
overlooker n. 반장, 감독자

My parents overlooked **my mistake.**

나의 부모님은 나의 잘못을 눈감아 주셨다.

36 **paternity** [pətə́:rnəti] the state or fact of being the father of a particular child

n. 부성애, 부권
paternal a. 아버지의

He denied a blood test confirming paternity.

그는 아버지임을 확인하는 혈액 검사를 부인했다.

37 peer [píər] the people who are the same age or the same status as you

n. 동료 v. 응시하다, 뚫어지게 보다

My little child used to be depressed due to peer pressure.

내 어린 자녀가 또래 집단에서 받는 압력 때문에 괴로워하곤 했다.

38 pregnant [prégnənt] having a baby or babies developing in her body

a. 임신한
pregnancy n. 임신

Most victims are pregnant women and children under thirteen.

희생자 대부분이 임신한 여자들과 15세 미만 어린이들이다.

39 protect [prətékt] to prevent someone from being harmed or damaged

vt. 보호하다, 막다
protection n. 보호 | protector n. 보호자

I will protect my family from anything.

나는 어떤 것으로부터든 나의 가족을 보호할 것이다.

40 relative [rélətiv] the members of your family

n. 친척 a. 상대적인
relatively ad. 상대적으로, 비교적으로 | correlative n. 상관물, 상호 관계
irrelative a. 부적당한, 관계가 없는

I have a distant relative who is a famous movie star.

나의 먼 친척 중에 유명한 영화배우가 있다.

41 resemble [rizémbəl] to be similar to each other

vt. ~와 닮다

The sisters resemble **each other in eating habits.**

그 자매는 식습관이 서로 닮았다.

42 scold [skóuld] to speak angrily because of doing something wrong

vt. 꾸짖다, 잔소리하다
scolding n. 꾸지람

I'm surprised that my father didn't scold **me.**

아버지가 나를 꾸중하지 않는 것에 놀랐다.

43 sensitive [sénsətiv] showing understanding and awareness of something

a. 민감한, 감수성이 강한
insensitive a. 둔감한 | hypersensitive a. 과민한, 과민증의
sensitivity n. 민감, 예민함

My parents tend to be sensitive **about my grades in school.**

부모님은 나의 성적에 매우 민감하신 편이다.

44 sibling [síbliŋ] brothers and sisters

n. 형제, 자매 a. 형제의

Don't blame your siblings **for what you experienced.**

당신이 겪은 일에 대해 다른 형제들을 비난하지 마라.

45 sincere [sinsíər] genuine or real

a. 성실한, 진실한
sincerely ad. 마음으로부터, 진정으로 ㅣ insincere a. 성의 없는, 성실치 못한

She may indeed not be rich, but she is sincere.
그녀는 부유하지 않을지는 몰라도 성실하다.

46 stern [stə́:rn] very severe

a. 엄격한, 단호한

My husband was brought up in a stern family.
남편은 엄격한 가정에서 자랐다.

47 stubborn [stʌ́bərn] very unwilling to change their mind

a. 완고한, 고집센
stubbornness n. 완고함 ㅣ stubbornly ad. 완고하게

I want to make up, but he's being stubborn.
나는 그와 화해하고 싶지만, 그는 고집을 부린다.

48 tender [téndər] gentle and delicate

a. 부드러운
tenderness n. 다정, 친절 ㅣ tenderly ad. 상냥하게
tenderize vt. 연하게 하다

Her tender words melted my heart and I forgave her.
난 그녀의 부드러운 말에 마음이 누그러서 그녀를 용서했다.

49 widow [wídou] a woman whose husband has died and hasn't married again

n. 미망인, 과부
widower n. 홀아비 l widowhood n. 과부 신세

She married a rich and kind man after 20 years as a widow.

20년 동안 과부로 지내다가, 부유하고 친절한 남자와 결혼했다.

50 wife [waif] a married woman

n. 아내

A lot of wives were widowed by the war.

전쟁으로 많은 부인들이 과부가 되었다.

Check up

A 다음 각 문장에서 강조한 단어의 의미가 본문에서 쓰인 것과 같은 것을 고르시오.

1. I think you are mature enough to do that.

   ① fully grown and developed

   ② ready to be paid in business

2. The stern look on her face was enough to send the students hurrying back.

   ① the back end of a ship or boat

   ② serious and often disapproving; expecting somebody to obey you

3. My wife has never been a nurturing person even in her childhood.

   ① to have a feeling, an idea, a plan, etc. for a long time and encourage it to develop

   ② to care for and protect somebody while they are growing and developing

4. The females don't take care of the young.

   ① the process of caring for somebody and providing what they need for their health or protection

   ② to make the effort to do something

5. Humble yourself, and you'll be lifted up by yourself.

① showing you don't think that you are as important as other people

② having a low rank or social position

B 알맞은 반대말끼리 연결하시오.

1. acquaintance ·   · tough

2. adult ·   · descendant

3. ancestor ·   · stranger

4. mutual ·   · non-reciprocal

5. tender ·   · juvenile

Lesson 2
Shelter
주거

01 accommodate [əkámədèit] to provide someone with a place to live or stay

vt. ~에 편의를 도모하다, 숙박시키다
accommodation n. 숙박설비, 편의 | accommodating a. 남의 말을 잘 듣는

Constructed of white granite, the building can accommodate 100 people.

하얀색 화강암으로 건축된 이 건물은 100명을 수용할 수 있다.

02 aisle [aíl] a long narrow gap that people can walk along it

n. 통로, 복도

You must not stand in the aisle.

통로에 서 있으면 안 된다.

03 antique [æntí:k] an old object which is valuable because of its beauty or rarity

n. 골동품
antiquity n. 낡음, 태고 | antiquated a. 고풍스러운, 노후한

Some people consider antiques to be priceless.

어떤 사람들은 골동품을 아주 귀중하게 여긴다.

04 appliance [əpláiəns] a device or machine in your home that you use to do a job

n. 기구, 장치, 설비
apply v. 적용되다, 신청하다 | application n. 사용, 신청, 적용, 지원

I'm looking for an appliance for mixing and grinding.

즙을 내고 섞는 가전제품을 찾고 있다.

05 architecture [ɑ́:rkətektʃər] the art of planning, designing, and constructing buildings

n. 건축술, 건축 양식
architect n. 건축가 | architectural a. 건축술의

The architecture is a beautiful combination of old and new.
그 건축물은 옛것과 새것이 아름답게 결합한 것이다.

06 avenue [ǽvənjùː] a street in a town or city

n. 가로수 길, 큰 거리

The street will be renamed Maru Avenue.
그 거리는 "마루" 길이라고 개칭될 예정이다.

07 block [blák] a group of buildings with streets on all side

n. 블록, 구역
blockade n. 봉쇄 | blocked a. 막힌, 폐색된
blocker n. 차단제, 블로커, 방해하는 사람

Go straight one block, then you'll find the bank on the left.
한 블록 직진해서 가면, 왼쪽에서 은행을 찾을 수 있을 것이다.

08 circular [sə́:rkjulər] shaped like a circle

a. 원형의, 순환의
circuit n. 순회, 회로 | circulate v. 순환하다, 돌다
circularity n. 원형, 순환성

This statue is made up of a variety of circular stone formations.
이 조각상은 다양한 원형의 석재 구조로 이루어져 있다.

09 comparison [kəmpǽrəsn] the process of comparing two or more people or things

n. 비교, 대조

compare v. 비교하다, 비유하다 | comparisonshop vt. 가격·품질을 비교하다

There is no comparison between this old building and that new building. 이 오래된 건물과 저 새 건물은 비교가 안 된다.

10 complex [kəmpléks, kámpleks] a collection of buildings with a common purpose

a. 복잡한, 어려운 n. 복합물

complexity n. 복잡성 | complexion n. 안색, 양상, 외관

The company started to supply the housing complex to the homeless. 그 회사는 집 없는 사람들에게 주택단지를 공급하기 시작했다.

11 construct [kənstrʌ́kt] to build or make a building, road, or machine

vt. 조립하다, 세우다, 구상하다, 건설하다

construction n. 건설 | constructive a. 건설적인, 구조적인
constructor n. 건설자, 조선 기사

The civil officer has a plan to construct a house and a bridge.
그 시의원은 집과 다리를 짓겠다는 계획을 가지고 있다.

12 conversion [kənvə́ːrʒən, -ʃən] the act or process of changing something

n. 변환, 전환

convert vt. 변하게 하다, 전환하다, 개종시키다

The government is set to approve the conversion of aisles into stairs.
정부는 복도를 계단으로 전환하는 것을 허용할 계획이다.

13 decorate [dékərèit] to make something attractive by adding things to it

vt. 꾸미다, 장식하다
decorated a. 훌륭하게 꾸민, 장식의 | redecorate vt. 다시 장식하다, 개장하다
decoration n. 장식, 훈장

The couple decorated a room with flowers and pictures.
그 부부는 꽃과 그림으로 방을 장식했다.

14 design [dizáin] to plan something and make a detailed drawing of it

vt. 디자인하다, 설계하다 n. 디자인, 도안
designer n. 설계자, 디자이너 | designate a. 지명된 v. 지명하다, 지정하다

This research helped us design our product to sell better.
이 조사는 우리 상품이 더 잘 팔리도록 고안하는 데 도움이 되었다.

15 destruct [distrʌ́kt] to destroy or to do damage itself

vt. 파괴하다, 자폭시키다
destruction n. 파괴 | destructive a. 유해한, 파괴적인

This building was designed to destruct upon enemy invasion.
이 건물은 적이 침입했을 때 자폭되도록 설계되었다.

16 displace [displéis] to move something out of its place, position, or role

vt. 바꾸어 놓다, 옮기다
displacement n. 이동, 바꾸어 놓기 | displaced a. 추방된, 유민의

Homes were destroyed and hundreds of people displaced.
일반 주택이 철거되고 수백 명의 사람들이 강제이주를 당했다.

17 district [dístrikt] a particular area of a town or country

n. 지역, 지구
redistrict vt. 재구획하다

Grapes are especially abundant in this district.
특히 이 지역에는 포도가 풍부하다.

18 furnish [fə́:rniʃ] to put furniture in a room or building

vt. 공급하다, 비치하다
furnishing n. 가구 I furnished a. 가구 딸린 I furnisher n. 공급자

This house is well furnished for a young man.
이 집은 젊은이를 위한 가구가 잘 갖추어져 있다.

19 garden [gá:rdn] a piece of land next to a house with flowers and vegetables

n. 정원, 뜰
gardener n. 원예사, 원예가 I gardening n. 원예, 정원 가꾸기

He has a house which has a garden overlooking the sea.
그는 바다가 내려다보이는 정원이 있는 집을 소유하고 있다.

20 gymnasium [dʒimnéiziəm] a building where people go to do physical exercise and get fit

n. 체육관
gym n. 체육관 I gymnastics n. 체조, 체육

We divided the gymnasium into two sections for running and soccer.
우리는 체육관을 육상과 축구를 위한 두 개의 구역으로 나누었다.

21 **handy** [hǽndi] useful or nearby and easy to get or reach

a. 편리한, 가까이 있는
handyman n. 무엇이든지 할 수 있는 사람 | **unhandy** a. 손재주가 없는

It's handy **to have a hospital and a pharmacy so close.**
병원과 약국이 매우 가까이 있어서 편리하다.

22 **household** [háushòuld] all the people in a family or group who live together

n. 가족, 세대
householder n. 가장, 세대주

She works, provides for her family and takes care of the household.
그녀는 일을 하고 가족을 부양하며 집안일을 한다.

23 **housing** [háuziŋ] the building in which people live

n. 주택, 주택 공급
house vt. 집을 주다 | **inhouse** a. 조직 내의, 회사 내의
house-to-house a. 호별의, 집집마다의

The shortage of housing **supply can lead to a rise in home prices.**
주택 공급 부족이 주택가격 상승으로 이어질 수 있다.

24 **improve** [imprúv] to get better

vt. 개선하다, 향상시키다
improving a. 개량하는, 유익한 | **improver** n. 개량하는 사람, 식품 첨가물
improvable a. 개량할 수 있는

Bringing in a foreign bank could help improve **the quality of life.**
외국 은행을 유치하는 것이 삶의 질을 향상시킬 수 있다.

25 **install** [instɔ́:l] to fix equipment or funiture into position so that it can be used

vt. 설치하다
installation n. 설치, 장치

Installing the home network system will be completed by 2010.

홈네트워크 시스템 설치가 2010년까지 완료될 것이다.

26 **interval** [íntərvəl] the period of time between two events or dates

n. 간격, 틈, 거리

The trees are planted on the street at intervals of seven feet.

도로에는 나무가 7피트 간격으로 심어져 있다.

27 **lease** [li:s] to be lent something for a period of time in return for money

vt. 빌리다, 임대하다 n. 임대, 리스
leasehold n. 임차권 a. 임차권이 있는 I leaseholder n. 임차인
leaseback n. 임대차 계약부 매각

The lease which we contracted runs for 5 years.

우리가 했던 그 임대차 계약은 5년 동안 유효하다.

28 **locate** [lóukeit] to put or build in a particular place

vt. 위치를 정하다, 찾아내다
local a. 공간의, 지방의 I location n. 위치 선정, 위치 I located a. 위치해 있는

We can't locate her even though we got her address.

주소는 알고 있음에도 그녀를 찾을 수가 없다.

29 lot [lάt, lɔ́t] a small area of land that belongs to a person or company

n. 한 구획의 토지, 부지, 땅

He'll sell his house and lot to anyone who passes the test.

그는 시험을 통과한 사람 누구에게든 가옥과 대지를 팔 것이다.

---

30 maintenance [méintənəns] the process of keeping something in good condition

n. 유지, 정비, 보수
maintain vt. 지속하다, 유지하다, 간수하다

When you have a problem, you can come to the Maintenance Department.

문제가 발생하면, 관리부로 연락하시오.

---

31 moderate [mάdərət] not extreme or neither large nor small in amount or degree

a. 알맞은, 보통의
moderation n. 알맞음, 온건 ㅣ moderately ad. 알맞게
immoderate a. 무절제한, 중용을 잃은

People with low or even moderate incomes must go to other places.

저소득층이나 심지어 중산층조차도 다른 곳으로 이동해야 한다.

---

32 neighbor [néibər] someone who lives near you

n. 이웃 (사람)
neighboring a. 이웃의, 근처의 ㅣ neighborhood n. 이웃, 인근, 주위환경

He took legal action against his neighbor for the noise between floors. 그는 층간 소음 때문에 이웃을 제소했다.

33　occupy [ákjupài] to use something such as a room, seat, or bed

vt. (방·건물을) 사용하다, 차지하다, 점령하다
occupation n. 직업, 점유 | occupier n. 토지 사용자, 임차인
occupied a. 사용 중인, 바쁜, 지배된, 점령된

The fact that the house is occupied **is a surprise to me.**

나는 그 집에 사람이 살고 있다는 것에 놀랐다.

34　outlet [áutlèt, -lit] a hole or pipe through which liquid or air can flow away

n. 배출구, 출구, 소매점, 코드 구멍
outlet mall n. 아울렛 몰 | a retail outlet n. 소매점
socket outlet n. 콘센트

The outlet **pipe is often a problem and that makes me mad.**

배출구가 자주 막혀서 골치 아프다.

35　own [óun] belonging to oneself or itself

a. 자기 자신의, 고유한
owner n. 소유자 | ownership n. 소유 | owned a. ~이 소유하는

He is too young to have his own **house.**

그는 자신만의 집을 소유하기에는 너무 어리다.

36　pave [péiv] to be covered with flat blocks of stone or concrete

vt. (길을) 포장하다
pavement n. 포장도로 | paved a. 포장된 | paving n. 포장, 포장 재료

Most residents are against the plan to pave **the road.**

거주자 대부분이 도로포장에 반대한다.

37 **pedestrian** [pədéstriən] a person walking in the street

n. 보행자, 도보자
pedestrianize vi. 도보 여행을 하다, 차량 통행을 금지하다

His cat was hit by a car on a pedestrian crossing yesterday.
그의 고양이가 어제 횡단보도에서 차에 치였다.

38 **remove** [rimúːv] to move something from a place or to take it away

vt. ~을 옮기다, 이동시키다
removal n. 이동 ㅣ removed a. 떨어진, 먼
removable a. 이동할 수 있는, 제거할 수 있는

She will remove to New York because of her business.
그녀는 사업 때문에 뉴욕으로 이사할 예정이다.

39 **rent** [rént] to regularly pay its owner a sum of money to be able to have it

vt. 빌리다, 임대하다 n. 지대, 임대료
rentable a. 임대할 수 있는 ㅣ rent-a-car n. 임대용 자동차
rental n. 임대료, 임차료 a. 임대의, 임대할 수 있는

I can barely pay the rent due to my debt.
빚 때문에 집세도 못 낼 지경이다.

40 **repair** [ripέər] to make something work properly

vt. 수리하다, 보수하다 n. 수리, 보수
repairer n. 수리공, 수리 도구 ㅣ repairable a. 수리할 수 있는

The road damaged by the heavy rain is under repair.
폭우로 부서진 도로가 보수 공사 중이다.

41 replace [ripléis] to put something back in its previous position

vt. 제자리에 놓다, ~에 대신하다, 대체하다
replacement n. 교체, 대체

Replace the camera when finished.

카메라를 다 사용한 후에는 제자리에 놓아라.

42 resident [rézədənt] the people who live in a house or area

n. 거주자, 주민 a. 거주하는, 고유의
residence n. 거주, 주거 ∣ reside vi. 거주하다, 존재하다
residentiary a. 거주하는

He is not a resident of this city.

그는 이 도시의 주민이 아니다.

43 settle [sétl] to become positioned or established

vt. 자리잡게 하다, 살게 하다, 정착시키다
settled a. 안정적인 ∣ settler n. 식민자 ∣ settlement n. 결산, 해결, 화해

One famous actor settled down and started a family.

한 유명한 배우가 정착하여 가정을 이루게 되었다.

44 slum [slʌ́m] an area of a city where living conditions are very bad

n. 빈민굴, 슬럼가
slummy a. 슬럼의, 빈민가의 ∣ slumdweller n. 슬럼 거주자

The plague is more common in the slums than in the downtown.

전염병은 도심보다 빈민가에서 더 흔하다.

45 stable [stéibl] firmly fixed

a. 안정된, 견실한
stability n. 안정 | unstable a. 불안정한

Recently, young couples now prefer to be married and in a stable situation.
최근에 젊은 커플들은 결혼해서 안정된 상황에 있기를 더 원한다.

46 suburb [sʌ́bəːrb] an area where people live that is outside of the city

n. 교외, 근교
suburban a. 교외의 | suburbia n. 교외 | suburbanite n. 교외 거주자

More and more young married couples have moved into the suburbs.
점점 더 많은 젊은 부부들이 교외로 이주한다.

47 tenant [ténənt] someone who pays rent for the place they live in or for land

n. 거주자, 소작인
tenantable a. 임차할 수 있는, 거주할 수 있는

The landlord sent his tenant a warning without any reminder.
집주인이 아무런 경고 없이 세입자에게 독촉장을 보냈다.

48 terrace [térəs] a flat area next to a building where people can sit

n. 테라스, 넓은 베란다

Most condos with a beautiful terrace were already reserved.
아름다운 테라스가 있는 대부분의 콘도들은 이미 예약되었다.

49 vacant [véikənt] not being used by anyone

a. 공허한, 비어 있는
vacancy n. 공허, 빈터 | vacate vi. 그만두고 물러나다, 집을 비우다

There are no vacant areas in my town.

우리 마을에는 빈 공터가 없다.

50 zigzag [zígzæg] bent from side to side altenately

a. 지그재그의, Z자형의 n. Z자형, 지그재그

You can reach home through the zigzagged road and
across the river.

너는 구불구불한 길을 지나고 강을 건너서 집에 닿을 수 있다.

A 우리말과 같은 뜻이 되도록 다음 철자로 시작되는 단어를 쓰시오.

1. It took a lot of time for us to get this room d_____.

   이 방을 꾸미는 데 많은 시간이 들었다.

2. We quarreled with our n_____ about the noise.

   우리는 소음 때문에 이웃과 말다툼을 했다.

3. My family far prefers living in the s_____ than in the urban.

   우리 가족은 도심보다 교외에서 사는 것을 더 좋아한다.

4. There are no v_____ houses in this town.

   이 마을에는 빈 집이 없다.

5. You have to pay in order to break your l_____ by tomorrow.

   임대 계약을 파기하기 위해서는 내일까지 돈을 지불해야 한다.

B 주어진 표현에 해당하는 단어를 보기에서 고르시오.

| handy | antique | displace | resident | accommodate |

1. _____ : house; take someone in; put somebody up

2. _____ : old; unfashionable; unstylish

3. _____ : move; go; travel; locomote

4. _____ : convenient; accessible; adroit

5. _____ : citizen; inhabitant; dweller; householder

C 우리말은 영어로, 영어는 우리말로 바꾸시오.

1. architecture   2. 비교, 대조

3. 파괴하다, 자폭시키다   4. furnish

5. improve   6. (길을) 포장하다

7. settle   8. 테라스, 넓은 베란다

9. 차지하다, 점령하다   10. rent

Lesson 3
Clothes
| 의류

01   alter [ɔ́:ltər]   to change

vt. 바꾸다, 변경하다
alteration n. 변경 | alternative n. 대안, 양자 택일 a. 대안이 되는, 대체의
alternate vi. 번갈아 일어나다 | alternation n. 교대

The designer altered **the old clothes into new ones by repairing them.** 디자이너는 수선을 통해 오래된 옷을 새것으로 바꾸었다.

02   appropriate [əpróuprièit]   suitable or acceptable for a particular situation

a. 적합한, 적절한
appropriation n. 충당 | inappropriate a. 부적당한, 부적절한

It's not appropriate **to attach too many decorations on the dress.** 드레스에 너무 많은 장식을 붙이는 것은 적절하지 않다.

03   attract [ətrǽkt]   to have features that cause someone to come to it

vt. 끌다, 끌어당기다
attractive a. 매력이 있는 | attraction n. 매력, 인기물
attractor n. 끌어당기는 것

Her leading fashion style is attracting **people's attention.**
그녀의 앞선 패션스타일이 사람들의 이목을 끌고 있다.

04   bleach [blíːtʃ]   to use a chemical to make something white or pale in color

vt. 희게 하다, 표백하다
bleacher n. 표백업자, 표백제 | bleached a. 표백한
bleaching a. 표백하는, 표백성의 n. 표백

Bleach **the jeans and then dry them in the sun.**
청바지를 표백한 다음 햇볕에 말려라.

05   brand [brǽnd]   the version is made by one particular manufacturer

n. 상표, 브랜드
branded a. 소인이 찍힌, 유명 상표의

In Korea, the national brand **clothes are now selling at a high price.** 한국에서 국산 브랜드 의류가 높은 가격에 판매되고 있다.

06   casual [kǽʒuəl]   relaxed and not very concerned about something

a. 격식을 차리지 않는, 가벼운
casually ad. 우연히

Some casual **apparel enjoyed strong sales in the summer.**
여름에는 몇몇 캐주얼 의류가 강한 매출을 누렸다.

07   charm [tʃáːrm]   the quality of being pleasant or attractive

n. 매력, 마력 v. 매혹하다
charming a. 매력 있는 ㅣ charmed a. 매혹된, 마법에 걸린
charmless a. 매력 없는, 재미 없는

I got a charm **bracelet as a lucky present from my best friend.**
친한 친구로부터 행운의 의미로 행운의 팔찌를 선물 받았다.

08   clothe [klóuð]   to provide someone with clothes to wear

vt. ~에게 옷을 주다(입히다)
clothes n. 옷, 의복 ㅣ cloth n. 직물 ㅣ clothing n. (집합적) 의류

She clothed **her children in the latest fashions.**
그녀는 아이들에게 최신 유행하는 옷을 입혔다.

09 comfortable [kʌ́mftəbl, -fərtə-] feeling physically relaxed

a. 기분 좋은, 편한
comfort vt. ~을 위로하다 | uncomfortable a. 불편한, 기분이 언짢은

My grandfather has perfectly comfortable shoes and a hat.
할아버지는 굉장히 편한 신발과 모자를 가지고 있다.

10 content [kəntént] fairly happy or satisfied

a. 만족하는 n. 내용, 목차
contentment n. 만족 | contented a. 만족한
discontent n. 불평, 불만

She isn't content with buying pretty clothes like other girls.
그녀는 다른 소녀들처럼 예쁜 옷을 사는 것에 만족하지 않는다.

11 coordinate [kouɔ́:rdənət, -nèit] of the same rank, type, etc.

v. 조정하다, 꾸미다, 코디하다 a. 동등한, 동격의
coordination n. 동등 | incoordiante a. 동격이 아닌, 동등하지 않은

It'll take time for the model to coordinate some jewelry with her dress.
모델이 드레스와 보석류를 코디하는 데는 시간이 걸릴 것이다.

12 cost [kɔ́:st, kɑ̀st] the amount of money that is needed in order to buy or make it

n. 가격, 원가, 비용
costly a. 값비싼 | costing n. 원가 계산

Fabric and cloth are not the only things rising in cost this year.
올해엔 섬유와 천의 가격만이 오른 것이 아니다.

13 **costume** [kástjuːm] the set of clothes they wear while someone is performing

n. 의상, 복장, 복식
costumed a. 복장을 한 ㅣ costumer n. 의상업자

Korean people are usually in national costume **on New Year's Day.**

한국인은 보통 설날에 민속 의상을 입는다.

14 **custom** [kʌ́stəm] an activity which is usual or traditional in a particular society

n. 관습, 풍습
customary a. 습관적인 ㅣ customer n. 고객, 단골 손님
customarily ad. 관례상, 습관적으로

The custom, **wearing the Han-bok, has come down from our ancestors.**

한복을 입는 풍습은 우리 조상들로부터 전해 내려온 것이다.

15 **dandy** [dǽndi] very fashionable or elegant

a. 멋 내는, 굉장한, 일류의

Follow my simple dandy **steps and you'll be cool like me.**

간단히 멋 내는 방법을 따라 해보라, 그러면 나처럼 멋있게 변할 것이다.

16 **detergent** [ditə́ːrdʒənt] a chemical substance which is used for washing clothes

n. 세제, 합성 세제

Is it OK to wash these pants with a synthetic detergent?

이 바지를 합성세제로 세탁해도 될까요?

17 discomfort [diskʌ́mfərt] a painful or uncomfortable feeling

n. 불쾌, 불안, 불편

This zipper can cause extreme discomfort as well as many scratches.

이 지퍼는 많은 긁힌 상처뿐만 아니라 극도의 불편함도 유발한다.

18 dye [dái] to change its color by soaking it in a special liquid

vt. 물들이다, 염색하다
dyed a. 물들인, 염색된 | dyeing n. 염색, 염색업 | dyer n. 염색업자, 염색소

Why don't you have your white plain T-shirt dyed?

하얀 티셔츠 염색하는 게 어때?

19 elegant [éligənt] pleasing and graceful in appearance or style

a. 기품 있는, 우아한
elegance n. 우아, 고상 | inelegant a. 세련되지 않은

Classic, elegant styles were still strong as shown by new designers.

신인 디자이너가 선보인 고전적이고 우아한 스타일은 여전히 강세를 보였다.

20 expensive [ikspénsiv] costing a lot of money

a. 값비싼, 돈이 드는
expense n. 지출, 비용, 경비 | expend vt. 들이다, 소비하다
inexpensive 비용이 많이 들지 않는

A famous actress always wears expensive clothes.

어떤 유명 여배우는 항상 비싼 옷만 입는다.

21　fabric [fǽbrik]　cloth or other material produced by weaving together

n. 직물, 천
fabrication n. 날조, 제작, 조작 | fabricate vt. 만들다, 규격대로 만들다
fabricant n. 제조자

She took the fabric and made pretty skirts with it.
그녀는 그 천으로 예쁜 스커트를 만들었다.

22　fancy [fǽnsi]　special, unusual, or elaborate due to lots of decoration

a. 의장에 공들인, 장식적인
fanciful a. 공상에 잠기는 | fancier n. 애호가, 매니아, 공상가

The pants have a fancy button.
그 바지에는 장식 단추가 달려 있다.

23　fasten [fǽsn, fáːsn]　to close it by means of buttons or a strap or other device

vt. 묶다, 죄다
fastener n. 잠그는 사람, 죄는 금속 기구, 지퍼 | unfasten vt. 풀다

Shoelaces must be fastened before you run.
달리기 전에 신발끈을 매야 한다.

24　firsthand [fə́ːrsthǽnd]　gained or learned directly, rather than from others

a. 직접의 ad. 직접

I made my design with firsthand materials by myself.
나는 직접 구입한 재료들로 디자인을 만든다.

25 fit [fít] to be the right size and shape to go onto a person's body

a. 꼭 맞는, 알맞은, 적당한 v. ~에 맞다, 적합하다
befit vi. 적합하다 ㅣ fitted a. 꼭 맞게 만들어진

The coat is a poor fit with fat people.

그 외투는 뚱뚱한 사람에게는 잘 맞지 않는다.

26 handmade [hǽndméid] made by someone using their hands or tools

a. 손으로 만든, 수제의, 수공의

Old handmade work is sold at higher price than new machined goods.

지금의 기계품보다 옛날의 수제품이 고가에 팔린다.

27 inner [ínər] towards or close to the centre of a place

a. 안의, 안쪽의, 내면의
innermost n. 가장 깊은 부분 a. 가장 안쪽의

Especially in Korea, the old prefer an inner pocket on pants.

특히 한국에서 노인들은 안주머니가 있는 바지를 좋아한다.

28 jewel [dʒúːəl] a precious stone used to decorate valuable things

n. 보석, 장신구
jewelry n. 보석류 ㅣ jeweled a. 보석을 박은, 보석으로 장식한
jeweler n. 보석 세공인, 보석 상인

Her gaze was fixed on the jewels on a swim suit.

그녀의 시선은 수영복에 있는 보석에 고정되었다.

29 laundry [lɔ́:ndri, lɑ́:n-]   clothes, sheets, etc. that need washing

n. 세탁물
laundryman n. 세탁업자, 세탁소 종업원

Your shirt is in the laundry basket, so you have to wear the green one.

너의 셔츠가 세탁 바구니에 있어서 녹색 셔츠를 입어야 한다.

---

30 length [leŋkθ]   the size or measurement of something from one end to the other side

n. 길이
lengthy a. 긴, 장황한 ǀ lengthen vt. 길게 하다

The length of the sleeve has to be shortened to an acceptable length.

소매를 적절한 길이로 줄여야 한다.

---

31 man-made [mæn-méid]   created or caused by people rather than naturally

a. 인공의, 인조의, 합성의
handmade a. 손으로 만든 ǀ ready-made a. 이미 만들어져 있는, 기성품의

Such a cloth, being man-made, is relatively easy to clean.

그런 인조 천은 상대적으로 세탁이 쉽다.

---

32 match [mǽtʃ]   to have a pleasing appearance when they are used together

v. 어울리다, 걸맞다, 조화시키다
matching a. 어울리는, 조화된 ǀ mismatch v. 짝을 잘못 짓다
matchless a. 비길 데 없는

She wants to match these shoes with a similar bag.

그녀는 이 신발을 비슷한 가방과 짝을 맞추고 싶어한다.

33   **material** [mətíəriəl] a substance that things can be made from

n. 재료, 옷감, 자료
materially ad. 실질적으로, 물질적으로

Athletic wear is more flexible and made of more absorbent material.

운동복은 더 유연하고 더 흡수력이 좋은 소재로 만들어졌다.

---

34   **sew** [sóu] to pass thread through something with a needle

v. 꿰매다, 바느질하다
sewing n. 재봉 | sewer n. 바느질하는 사람, 재봉사

You can sew by hand or by machine.

너는 손이나 재봉틀로 꿰맬 수 있다.

---

35   **shrink** [ʃrínk] to become or make something smaller in size or amount

vi. 오그라들다, 수축되다, 줄어들다
shrinking a. 움츠리는, 겁내는 | shrinkage n. 수축, 축소, 감소량
shrinkable a. 줄어들기 쉬운, 수축되는

Be careful, it'll shrink if you wash with hot water.

주의해라, 뜨거운 물로 세탁하면 줄어들 것이다.

---

36   **shorts** [ʃɔ́ːrts] trousers with very short legs

n. 짧은 반바지, 남자용 팬티

It's impolite to go to work in shorts.

반바지 차림으로 회사에 가는 것은 예의 바르지 못하다.

37 splendid [spléndid] very good, beautiful, impressive, and extremely well-made

a. 빛나는, 화려한, 멋진
splendor n. 훌륭함, 빛남

The show was perfect, with beautiful models and splendid costumes.

그 쇼는 아름다운 모델들과 화려한 의상으로 완벽했다.

38 stain [stéin] a mark on something that is difficult to remove

n. 얼룩 vt. 더럽히다 vi. 더러워지다
stainless a. 때 끼지 않은 | stained a. 얼룩진 | stainability n. 염색성

This fruit stain won't wash out.

이 과일 얼룩은 빨아도 지워지지 않는다.

39 stitch [stitʃ] the short pieces of thread

n. 한 바늘, 한 땀
stitching n. 바느질, 꿰매기 | backstitch n. 박음질
topstitch vi. 장식 스티치를 넣다

You'll be taught a knit stitch today.

오늘 겉뜨기를 배우게 될 것이다.

40 suit [súːt] a to be acceptable, suitable or convenient for a particular person

vt. ~에 적합하다, 잘 어울리다 n. (의복) 한 벌
suited a. 적당한, 적합한 | suitable a. 적당한, 적절한
suitability n. 적합함, 적당함

Do these glasses suit you?

이 안경은 당신에게 잘 맞습니까?

41 **synthetic** [sinθétik] made from chemicals or artificial substances

a. 종합의, 합성의, 인조의
synthetically ad. 종합적으로, 종합하여 I synthetics n. 합성 화학
semisynthetic a. 반합성의

Good synthetic detergent washes out dirt and stains very
well.

좋은 합성 세제는 때와 얼룩이 잘 빠진다.

42 **tailor** [téilər] a person whose job is to make men's clothes

n. 재봉사, 재단사
tailoring n. 양복점 경영, 재단업 I tailorable a. 옷으로 만들 수 있는
tailor-made a. 양장점에서 지은, 몸에 꼭 맞는

The tailor measured the bride for the wedding dress.

재단사는 웨딩드레스를 만들기 위하여 신부의 치수를 쟀다.

43 **textile** [tékstail, -til] any type of cloth made by weaving or knitting

n. 직물, 옷감

He worked in the textile factory in his youth.

그는 어렸을 때 섬유공장에서 일했다.

44 **tidy** [táidi] neat and arranged in an organized way

a. 말쑥한, 단정한
untidy a. 단정치 못한

My mom always keeps our house tidy.

엄마는 항상 집을 말끔히 정돈하신다.

45 tight [táit] fitting closely to body and sometimes uncomfortable

a. 몸에 꼭 맞는, 빈틈 없는
tighten vt. 죄다 ｜ tightly ad. 단단히 ｜ tightness n. 견고, 긴장

Tight pants made her decide to lose her weight.

꼭 끼는 바지가 그녀로 하여금 살을 뺄 결심을 하게 만들었다.

46 trousers [tráuzərz] pants

n. 바지
trouser n. 바지의 한쪽 ｜ trousering n. 바지감

His trousers are worn out at the bottom.

그의 바지 밑단이 다 닳았다.

47 unique [ju:ní:k, ju-] being the only one of its kind

a. 유일한, 독특한

Most students buy the school uniform because of its unique design.

학생들 대부분이 독특한 디자인으로 인해 교복을 구입하고 있다.

48 unsuitable [ʌ̀nsú:təbl] not right or appropriate for a particular person

a. 부적당한, 어울리지 않는

Your clothes are unsuitable for the meeting with our customers.

당신의 옷차림은 우리 고객을 만나는 데는 어울리지 않는다.

49 vogue [vóug] a fashion

n. 유행

voguish a. 유행의, 맵시 있는 ㅣ voguey a. 유행하는

Short skirts are all the vogue **even if it's winter.**

겨울이라도 짧은 치마가 대유행이다.

50 widen [wáidn] to become wider

vt. ~을 넓히다

wide a. 폭이 넓은, 넓은 ㅣ width n. 폭, 너비, 가로

widening n. 넓히는 것, 확대

It has to be widened **three times more than your size.**

그것은 네 사이즈의 3배만큼 넓혀야 한다.

Check up

A 괄호 안의 단어 중 문맥상 적절한 것을 고르시오.

1. It is not (misappropriate / appropriate) to tip a taxi driver in foreign country.

2. We changed back into (casualty / casual) wear.

3. It is his (custom / customs) to go to church on Sundays.

4. Short pants are the (vague / vogue).

5. I have to (tidy / tiny) up my room with my younger brother.

B 보기에서 알맞은 단어를 골라 관용어를 완성하시오.

| stitch | charm | length | attract | shrink |
| match | alter | fasten | tight | brand |

1. an _____ ego : 제2의 자아, 둘도 없는 친한 친구

2. opposites _____ : 극과 극은 통한다

3. put a _____ on : (동물) ~에게 낙인을 찍다

4. a _____ made in heaven : 천생연분

5. wear a _____ : 부적을 몸에 지니다

6. _____ oneself on : ~을 귀찮게 굴다

7. _____ back from a person : ~을 피하다, 꺼리다, 겁내다

8. sleep _____ : 푹 자다

9. at full _____ : 큰 대자로, 자세히

C 빈 칸에 들어갈 단어를 보기에서 골라 적절한 형태로 변형하여
넣으시오.

| widen coordinate cost fit sew |

1. The pants _____ at that point.

2. The _____ of distribution between makers and customers is
high.

3. This shade _____ with a wide range of other colors.

4. My mom _____ pieces of cloth together to make my
handkerchief.

5. The dress doesn't _____ you, so you need to repair it.

Lesson 4
Something to eat
| 음식

01 absorb [æbsɔ́:*rb*, -zɔ́:*rb*] to take in a liquid, gas or other substance from the surface

vt. ~을 흡수하다, 열중시키다
absorption n. 흡수 I absorptive a. 흡수하는, 흡수성의
absorbed a. 열중한, 흡수된

The materials will be absorbed into the blood.
그 물질들은 혈액 속으로 흡수될 것이다.

02 appetite [ǽpətait] physical desire for food

n. 식욕
appitizer n. 식욕을 돋우는 것

She has never experienced a loss of appetite in her life.
그녀는 일생 동안 식욕을 잃어본 적이 없다.

03 barn [bá:*rn*] a large farm building for storing grain or keeping animals in

n. 헛간
barnyard n. 헛간 앞마당

My barns are filled with grain.
우리 헛간은 곡식으로 가득 차 있다.

04 beverage [bévəridʒ] any type of drink except water

n. 마실 것, 음료

The Lounge on the top floor offers light snacks and beverages.
건물 맨 윗층 라운지에서는 가벼운 간식과 음료를 제공한다.

05　bitter [bíter]　very serious and unpleasant

a. 쓴, 쓰라린, 지독한
bitterly ad. 쓰게 | **bitterness** n. 씀, 쓴 맛, 신랄함

You can give children a candy to chase the bitter taste.

쓴 맛을 없애기 위해 아이들에게 사탕을 줘도 된다.

06　blend [blénd]　to mix two or more substances together

v. 섞다, 섞이다　n. 혼합, 혼합물
blended a. 혼합한 | **blending** n. 혼합, 융합

Oil and water will not blend.

기름과 물은 섞이지 않는다.

07　cafeteria [kæfətíəriə]　a restaurant where you choose and pay for your meal

n. 카페테리아, 구내식당

We have breakfast at a self-service cafeteria.

우리는 카페테리아에서 아침을 먹는다.

08　caffeine [kæfíːn]　a drug that makes you feel more active

n. 카페인
caffeinated a. 카페인을 함유한 | **decaffeinated** a. 카페인을 제거한[줄인]

Modern people drink too much caffeine.

현대인들은 카페인을 너무 많이 마신다.

09 **calorie** [kǽləri] a unit for measuring how much energy food will produce

n. 칼로리

These days, the growing obesity issue is caused by a high-calorie diet.

요즈음, 고칼로리 식품으로 인해 비만문제 증가가 야기되고 있다.

10 **canned** [kǽnd] of food preserved in a can

a. 통조림한, 통조림의
can n. 깡통, 금속제 용기 v. 통조림으로 만들다

Every store sells canned food and vegetables.

모든 가게에서는 통조림과 야채를 판다.

11 **capacity** [kəpǽsəti] the number of things or people that a container can hold

n. 용량, 수용력, 용적, 능력
capacious a. 널찍한 | incapacity n. 무능, 무자격
overcapacity n. 설비 과잉, 과잉 생산 능력

The box was filled to capacity with oranges.

상자는 오렌지로 가득 찼다.

12 **chef** [ʃéf] a professional cook, especially the most senior cook in a restaurant

n. 요리사, 주방장

The owner of this restaurant once used to work as a chef.

이 식당의 사장은 한때 요리사로 일한 적이 있다.

13 **contain** [kəntéin] to have something inside it or as part of it

vt. ~을 담고 있다, 포함하다
container n. 그릇, 용기 ｜ containerized a. 컨테이너에 담긴

Green tea and coffee contain **some caffeine.**

녹차와 커피는 카페인이 일부 포함되어 있다.

14 **cooker** [kúkər] a large piece of equipment for cooking food

n. 요리 도구
cookery n. 요리법

All I needed was not an expensive cooker **but a basic one.**

내가 필요한 모든 것은 비싼 것이 아니라 기본적인 요리 도구였다.

15 **dairy** [dέəri] a place where milk is kept and where cheeses are made

n. 낙농장, 유제품 회사 a. 유제품의, 낙농의
dairying n. 낙농업 ｜ dairyman n. 우유 장수, 낙농장 일꾼 ｜ dairyland n. 낙농 지대

Everyone knows that dairy **products are good for your health.**

유제품이 건강에 좋다는 사실은 모두 알고 있다.

16 **delivery** [dilívəri] the act of taking goods to the people they have been sent to

n. 배달, 인도
deliver vt. 배달하다, 넘겨 주다 ｜ deliveryman n. 상품 배달원

The average wait for the delivery **of food is about thirty minutes.** 평균 음식 배달시간은 30분이다.

17 devour [diváuər] to eat all of something quickly because of huger

vt. ~을 게걸스레 먹다
devouring a. 게걸스레 먹는

He devoured anything that he wanted in a moment.

그는 순식간에 그가 원하는 것은 무엇이든 먹어치웠다.

18 diet [dáiət] the food that you eat and drink regularly

n. 일상의 음식물, 규정식
dietary a. 음식물의, 규정식의

Children must have a balanced diet and exercise regularly.

아이들은 편식을 하지 않아야 하고 운동을 규칙적으로 해야 한다.

19 dine [dáin] to eat dinner

vi. ~와 식사를 하다, 정찬을 먹다
dinner n. 정찬, 식사 ┃ dining n. 식사 ┃ diner n. 식사하는 사람, 작은 식당

My family dines out four times a month.

우리 가족은 한 달에 네 번 외식을 한다.

20 dish [díʃ] a flat shallow container for cooking food in or serving it from

n. 큰 접시, 식기류, 요리, 음식
dishwasher n. 식기 세척기 ┃ dishcloth n. (접시 닦는) 행주

Kimchi is a traditional Korean side dish which is popular with foreigners.

김치는 외국인들에게도 인기가 있는 한국의 전통 반찬이다.

21 edible [édəbl]   suitable to be eaten

a. 먹을 수 있는
edibility n. 식용에 알맞음 | inedible a. 먹을 수 없는, 식용에 적합지 않은

My cousin likes to have an edible snail and an edible frog.
나의 사촌은 식용 달팽이와 식용 개구리를 즐겨 먹는다.

22 essential [isénʃəl, es-]   completely necessary, extremely important

a. 필수의, 절대 필요한 n. 필수 사항
essence n. 본질, 정수 | essentially ad. 본질적으로
essential a. 필수적인, 극히 중요한

You have to pay to economize on essentials in wartime.
전시에는 생필품을 아껴야 할 필요가 있다.

23 handful [hǽndfùl]   the amount of something that can be held in one hand

n. 한 움큼, 줌

Even a handful of rice is helpful to the poor.
한 줌의 쌀도 가난한 사람들에게는 도움이 된다.

24 kettle [kétl]   a container with a lid, handle and a spout, for boiling water

n. 주전자, 솥
teakettle n. 차관, 찻주전자

The kettle was steaming, which makes people feel warm in the winter.
주전자에서 김이 나면 겨울철에 사람들은 따뜻함을 느끼게 된다.

25 **leftover** [léftouvər]   food that has not been eaten at the end of a meal

n. 나머지, 찌꺼기 a. 나머지의

My mother usually eats leftovers.

엄마는 보통 남은 음식을 드신다.

26 **malnutrition** [mæ̀lnjuːtríʃən]   a poor condition of health caused by a lack of food

n. 영양부족, 영양실조
undernutrition n. 영양부족, 영양 결핍

Poor children under fifteen suffer from chronic malnutrition.

15세 이하의 가난한 아이들은 만성 영양부족을 겪고 있다.

27 **moderate** [mάdərət]   neither very good nor very bad

a. 절제 있는, 알맞은
moderation n. 알맞음, 온건 I moderately ad. 알맞게
immoderate a. 무절제한, 중용을 잃은

He has to be moderate in drinking and smoking.

그는 음주와 흡연에서 절도 있게 행동해야 한다.

28 **mutton** [mʌ́tn]   meat from a fully grown sheep

n. 양고기

She intends to serve a mutton cutlet to people.

그녀는 사람들에게 양고기 갈비를 대접할 계획이다.

29 nourish [nɔ́ːriʃ, nʌr-] to give a person or animal the food that is necessary for life

vt. 영양분을 공급하다
nourishment n. 육성, 영양분 ㅣ nourishing a. 자양이 되는, 자양분이 많은
undernourish vt. 영양실조가 되게 하다

The cream contains Vitamin A to nourish the skin.
그 크림은 피부에 영양분을 공급해 줄 비타민 A를 함유하고 있다.

30 nutrition [njuːtríʃən] the process by which living things receive the food

n. 영양물 섭취, 영양물

Good nutrition is good for health.
충분한 영양 섭취는 건강에 좋다.

31 odorless [óudərlis] scentless or inodorous

a. 무취의
odor n. 냄새, 악취

The food which has been stored in a refrigerator is odorless.
냉장고에 보관된 음식은 냄새가 없다.

32 ounce [áuns] a unit for measuring weight, 1/16 of a pound

n. 온스

A 7 ounce cappuccino costs 4,500 won.
7온스들이 카푸치노는 4,500원이다.

33 **portion** [pɔ́ːrʃən] one part of something larger

n. 일부, 몫 v. 분할하다
proportion n. 균형, 비례, 조화 I apportion vt. 배분하다, 할당하다
disproportion n. 불균형

This dish can be ordered by a double portion.

이 음식은 2인분씩 주문할 수 있다.

34 **protein** [próutiːin, -tiin] a natural substance found in meat, eggs, fish etc.

n. 단백질

When women are pregnant, they need to have more protein.

여성들이 임신했을 땐 단백질을 더 많이 섭취해야 한다.

35 **quality** [kwάləti] the standard of something when it is compared to other things

n. 품질, 우수함, 고급, 특성
qualification n. 자격, 조건 I qualify vt. ~에게 자격을 주다

The quality **of milk is declining.**

우유의 질이 점차 떨어지고 있다.

36 **quantify** [kwάntəfai] to describe or express something as an amount or a number

vt. ~의 양을 정하다, 수량화하다
quantity n. 양

The risks to health are impossile to quantify.

건강에 대한 위험은 수량화가 불가능하다.

37 **rare** [rέər] no found very often

a. 드문, 희귀한, 설익은
rarely ad. 드물게, 좀처럼 ~하지 않는

It's rare to see snow in October.
10월에 눈을 보는 것은 드문 일이다.

38 **recipe** [résəpi] a set of instructions that tells you how to cook something

n. 조리법

She is writing a recipe book and is planning to publish it.
그녀는 요리책을 집필해서 출판할 계획이다.

39 **ripe** [ráip] fully grown and ready to be eaten

a. 익은, 원숙한
ripen v. 익다, 숙성하다, 숙성시키다

Ripe apples fell off the tree standing in front of my house.
집 앞에 있는 나무에서 잘 익은 사과가 떨어졌다.

40 **rosy** [róuzi] pink and pleasant in appearance

a. 장밋빛의, 희망적인

A hen usually lays four rosy eggs.
암탉은 보통 4개의 붉은 달걀을 낳는다.

41 **rotten** [rátn] decayed and cannot be eaten

a. 썩은, 타락한
rot v. 썩다, 부패하다 n. 부식, 부패

The fish is rotten **and smelling bad even in the refrigerator.**

생선이 심지어 냉장고 속에서 썩어서 악취가 난다.

42 **sauce** [sɔːs] a thick liquid that is eaten with food to add flavor to it

n. 소스
saucepan n. 냄비

Served with a creamy mushroom sauce, **it's a fantastic.**

크림 버섯 소스와 함께 먹으면 정말 맛있다.

43 **spicy** [spáisi] having a strong taste

a. 양념을 넣은, 향긋한
spice n. 양념, 항신료, 묘미 l spicery n. (집합적) 양념류, 항신료

You've to stay away from anything too spicy.

너무 매운 것은 먹으면 안 된다.

44 **squeeze** [skwíːz] to get liquid out of something by pressing or twisting in hard

vt. ~을 압착하다, 짜다, 압박하다 n. 짜기, 압박
squeezer n. 압착기

Squeeze **the water out of the cabbage.**

양배추의 물을 짜내시오.

45 stale [stéil] no longer fresh

a. 싱싱하지 못한, 김빠진
stalemate n. 교착 상태, 수가 막힘

This is stale **beer in new bottles.**

이것은 새 병에 담긴 김빠진 맥주이다.

46 staple [stéipl] an important food, product, ingredient, etc.

n. 요소, 주성분, 원료, 재료

Electronic products are the staple **of our company.**

가전제품은 우리 회사의 주요 상품이다.

47 starve [stáːrv] to suffer or die because you don't have enough food to eat

v. 굶어 죽다, 굶주리다
starved a. 굶주린, 허기진

Still many people are starving **all over the world.**

아직도 전 세계의 많은 사람들이 굶어 죽어가고 있다.

48 stir [stə́ːr] to move a liquid or substance around, using a spoon

vt. ~을 휘젓다, 움직이다, 자극하다
stirring a. 감동시키는

Stir **vinegar into salad oil and then pour it on the main dish.**

샐러드 오일에 식초를 넣어서 저은 후, 그것을 주요리에 넣어라.

49 suitable [súːtəbl] right or appropriate for a particular purpose or occasion

a. 적당한

unsuitable a. 부적당한, 어울리지 않는 ㅣ suitably ad. 적당하게

The white wine is suitable **for the fish food.**

화이트 와인은 생선 요리에 적당하다.

50 thirst [θə́ːrst] the feeling of needing or wanting a drink

n. 갈증, 갈망

thirsty a. 목마른, 갈망하는 ㅣ thirstily ad. 목말라서, 목마르게

I had a terrible thirst **after the marathon.**

마라톤 경기 후에 목이 몹시 말랐다.

Check up

A 다음 내용이 설명하고 있는 단어를 〈보기〉에서 고르시오.

| a. bitter | b. calorie | c. devour | d. odorless | e. rotten |

1. that has decayed and cannot be eaten or used
2. to eat all of something quickly, especially because you are very hungry
3. having a strong, unpleasant taste; not sweet
4. a unit for measuring how much energy food will produce
5. be scentless

B 단어와 한글 뜻을 알맞게 짝지으시오.

1. appetite ·   · 단백질

2. caffeine ·   · 먹을 수 있는

3. chef ·   · 식욕

4. edible ·   · 카페인

5. protein ·   · 요리사

C 의미상 가장 알맞은 단어를 보기에서 골라 쓰시오.

| thirst | stir | ripe | nutrition | kettle |

1. _____ the materials to mix well.

2. I have a _____ for winning.

3. The _____ on the stove is steaming.

4. Over dieting caused her to have insufficient _____ .

5. The watermelon is not quite _____ .

D 영영풀이에 알맞은 단어를 고르시오.

1. completely necessary (essential / inessential)

2. the amount of something can be held in a hand (handful / much)

3. not done, seen, happening, etc. very often (common / rare)

4. to mix two or more substances together (split / blend)

5. it has that thing inside it or as part of it (contain / sustain)

Lesson 5
Fitness

| 건강

01 **abnormal** [æbnɔ́ːrməl] different from what is usual or expected

a. 비정상의
abnormality n. 이상, 변칙 | abnormally ad. 비정상적으로

The doctor said that there's no abnormal bleeding.

비정상적인 출혈은 보이지 않는다고 의사가 말했다.

02 **alcohol** [ǽlkəhɔːl, -hál] drinks such as beer, wine, etc.

n. 알코올, 알코올 음료, 술
alcoholic a. 알코올성의

It's illegal to sell alcohol and cigarettes to children.

아이들에게 술과 담배를 판매하는 것은 불법이다.

03 **bacteria** [bæktíəriə] the simplest and smallest forms of life

n. 박테리아
bacterial a. 박테리아의, 세균의

People are trying to find antibiotics acting on the unknown bacteria.

알려지지 않은 박테리아에 효능이 있는 항생제를 발견하기 위해 노력 중이다.

04 **bleed** [blíːd] to lose blood, especially from a wound or an injury

vi. 피가 나다, 출혈하다
blood n. 피, 혈기

My finger is bleeding.

내 손가락에서 피가 나.

05 blind [bláind] unable to see

a. 눈이 먼, 맹목적인
blindness n. 맹목 | blindly ad. 맹목적으로
blinding a. 눈을 멀게 하는, 현혹시키는

If you sit too close to the TV set, you may go blind.
TV에 너무 가까이 앉으면 눈이 나빠져서 앞을 못 볼 수도 있다.

06 breath [bréθ] the air that you take into your lungs and send out again

n. 숨, 호흡
breathe v. 숨을 쉬다, 호흡하다

I feel dizzy and get easily short of breath.
현기증이 나고 자주 숨이 차다.

07 cancer [kǽnsər] a serious disease in which growths of cells

n. 암
cancerate vi. 암에 걸리다 | canceration n. 발암, 암화

Smoking can increase the risk of cancer especially in pregnant women.
흡연은 특히 임산부들에게 암 발병률을 높일 수 있다.

08 chin [tʃín] the part of the face below the mouth and above the neck

n. 아래턱

Keep your chin up to your chest and take deep breath in.
턱을 가슴 쪽으로 당기고 심호흡을 크게 하세요.

09 chest [tʃést] the top part of the front of the body

n. 가슴

He felt some sharp pain in his chest and went to the doctor.

그는 가슴에 강렬한 통증을 느껴 병원에 갔다.

---

10 choke [tʃóuk] to be unable to breathe

vt. 질식시키다 vi. 숨이 막히다

People were choked with smoke caused by the fire.

사람들은 화재로 인한 연기에 숨이 막혔다.

---

11 common [kámən] happening often

a. 공통의, 보통의, 평범한, 사회 일반의
commonly ad. 대개, 보통, 일반적으로 I uncommon a. 보기 드문, 보통이 아닌

The doctor said that it is a very common disease.

그건 꽤 흔한 질병이라고 의사가 말했다.

---

12 condition [kəndíʃən] the state that something is in

n. 상태, 건강 상태, 상황
conditional a. 조건부의 I conditioned a. 조건부의, (어떤) 상태에 있는, 조절된

He has a heart condition so he can't run fast like others.

그는 심장병이 있어서 남들처럼 빨리 달릴 수 없다.

13 **disease** [dizíːz] an illness affecting humans, animals or plants

n. 병, 질환
diseased a. 병에 걸린, 병을 앓고 있는

I want to live in a world without disease.

나는 질병 없는 세상에서 살기를 원한다.

14 **disturb** [distəːrb] to interrupt somebody or to feel uneasy

vt. ~을 방해하다, ~에게 폐를 끼치다 vi. 어지럽히다, 방해하다
disturbed a. 매우 불안해하는 ㅣ disturbance n. 방해, 혼란

Do not disturb me!

방해하지 마세요!

15 **dizzy** [dízi] feeling as if everything is spinning around you

a. 현기증 나는, 어지러운
dizzily ad. 현기증 나게 하는, 어지럽게 하는 ㅣ dizziness n. 현기증

I'm feeling a little dizzy so I had to sit down for a while.

좀 어지러워서 잠깐 앉아 있어야 했다.

16 **drown** [dráun] to die because you have been underwater too long

v. 물에 빠져 죽다, 익사하다, (액체에) 잠기게 하다
drowned a. 물에 빠져 죽은, 몰두한 ㅣ drowning a. 익사하는, 이해할 수 없는

Many people drowned in the sea because the boat capsized.

배가 뒤집혀 많은 사람들이 바다에서 익사했다.

17 energetic [ènərdʒétik] having or needing a lot of energy and enthusiasm

a. 정력적인, 활기에 찬
energetically ad. 활동적으로, 원기 왕성하게 ǀ energy n. 힘, 정력, 활력

You don't seem as energetic **as usual due to hot weather.**
더운 날씨 탓인지 평상시 만큼 활기찬 것 같지 않다.

18 epidemic [èpədémik] a large number of cases of a particular disease

n. 전염병, 급속한 확산 a. 유행성의
epidemical a. 유행성의, 전염병의 ǀ epidemically ad. 전염되어, 급속히 확산되어

The epidemic **is spreading very fast to the neighboring countries.**
전염병이 급속히 인접 국가들로 퍼져 나가고 있다.

19 extreme [ikstríːm] very high in degree

a. 극도의, 극심한
extremely ad. 극도로, 극히

The heat in desert is extreme**.**
사막의 더위는 극심하다.

20 faint [féint] feeling weak because you are very ill, tired or hungry

a. 어지러운, 희미한, 어렴풋한 vi. 졸도하다
faintness n. 기절, 졸도 ǀ faintly ad. 희미하게

We felt faint **from lack of air at the top of the mountain.**
우리는 산의 정상에서 산소부족으로 인한 현기증을 느꼈다.

21 feeble [fíːbl] very weak

a. 연약한
feebleness n. 약함, 미약 I enfeeble vt. 약화시키다

She helps sick and feeble children by herself.
그녀는 스스로 아프고 연약한 아이들을 도와준다.

22 harmless [háːrmlis] unable or unlikely to cause damage or harm

a. 해롭지 않은
harmlessly ad. 해롭지 않게 I harm vt. 해치다 n. 해, 피해

The students were taught that ozone is harmless to people.
학생들은 오존이 인간에게 해롭지 않다고 배웠다.

23 lame [léim] (of people or animals) unable to walk well

a. 절름발이의, 다리를 저는
lamely ad. 절룩거리며, 불완전하게, 불안하게

The disabled with lame feet are disqualified from active work.
다리를 저는 장애인들은 활동적인 일을 하지 못한다.

24 lap [lǽp] the top part of your legs that forms a flat surface

n. 무릎

The little boy sat on his mother's lap.
어린 아들이 엄마의 무릎 위에 앉아 있다.

25 **liver** [lívər] a large organ in the body that cleans the blood

n. 간

These symptoms are associated with liver disease.
이러한 증상은 간 질환에 나타난다.

26 **medieval** [mi:díí:vəl, med-] connected with the Middle Ages

a. 중세의, 고풍의, 구식의
medievally ad. 중세풍으로

Your surgery style looks medieval which is fairly strange to others.
당신의 수술방법은 다른 이들에게는 이상해 보일 정도로 구식이다.

27 **moan** [móun] to make a long deep sound

vi. 신음하다, 탄식하다 n. 신음
moanful a. 신음 소리를 내는, 구슬픈 | moanfully ad. 구슬프게

She moaned that she had a terrible headache which has no cure.
그녀는 치료법이 없는 극심한 두통 때문에 아프다고 신음했다.

28 **motionless** [móuʃənlis] not moving

a. 움직이지 않는, 가만히 있는
motion n. 운동, 움직임, 동작

Stand motionless and don't touch your wound.
움직이지 말고 상처에 손을 대지 말아라.

29 pain [péin] the unpleasant feelings that you have in your body

n. 아픔, 고통 v. 괴롭히다
painfully ad. 아프도록, 고통스럽게 | painless a. 아픔이 없는, 힘이 안 드는, 쉬운
painkiller n. 진통제

He experienced constant pain as a result of his injury.

그는 부상으로 만성 통증을 느꼈다.

30 hygiene [háidʒiːn] the practice of keeping yourself clean to prevent illness

n. 위생(학)

They have no sense of hygiene so they need to be educated.

그들은 위생 관념이 없어서 교육 받을 필요가 있다.

31 pale [péil] (of a person, their face, etc.) having skin that is almost white

a. 창백한, 엷은
palely ad. 창백하게 | paleness n. 창백함

The doctor pointed out that her face turned pale with something.

의사는 무엇인가에 창백해지는 그녀의 얼굴을 가리켰다.

32 pill [píl] a small flat round piece of medicine that you swallow

n. 환약, 알약
pilular a. 알약(모양)의

Take a sleeping pill, and you'll have a deep sleep tonight.

수면제를 복용해라, 그러면 오늘 밤엔 깊은 잠을 잘 수 있을 것이다.

33 **prohibit** [prouhíbit, prə-] to stop something from being done

vt. ~을 금하다, ~하지 못하게 하다
prohibition n. 금지 | prohibitive a. 금지하는, 엄두도 못 낼 정도로 비싼

The sale of this drug is prohibited by law especially to children.

특히 아이들에게 이 약의 판매를 금하고 있다.

34 **recover** [rikʌ́vər] to get well again after being ill, hurt etc.

vt. 되찾다, 회복하다
recoverable a. 회복 가능한, 되찾을 수 있는 | recovery n. 되찾기, 회복

He recovered from an unknown illness by chance.

그는 우연히 불치병이 나았다.

35 **remedy** [rémədi] a way of dealing with or improving an unpleasantness

n. 치료, 해결책 v. 개선하다
remediable a. 치료할 수 있는, 구제할 수 있는

He'll give money to anyone who finds a sure remedy for the illness.

그는 그 병의 확실한 치료법을 찾는 자에게 돈을 줄 것이다.

36 **rest** [rést] free time without working

n. 휴식
restful a. 편안한, 평온한, 고요한 | resting a. 휴식하고 있는, 휴면하고 있는

As time goes by, rest gets necessary for modern people.

시간이 갈수록 휴식은 현대인에게 있어 점점 더 필수적인 것이 되어간다.

37 **rib** [ríb] twelve pairs of curved bones that surround your chest

n. 늑골, 갈비(뼈)

My rib **was cracked by the accident at the ski camp.**
스키 캠프에서의 사고로 갈비뼈에 금이 갔다.

38 **sensible** [sénsəbl] able to make good judgements based on reason

a. 분별 있는, 느낄 수 있는
sense n. 감각, 의식 | sensibility n. 감각, 감수성

He still isn't sensible **even though his mother cared for him.**
엄마의 돌봄에도 불구하고 그는 여전히 의식이 없다.

39 **sharp** [ʃá:rp] having a fine edge or point, especially of something

a. 날카로운, 가파른
sharpen vt. 예리하게 하다 | sharpness n. 예리함

You have to be careful not to be hurt by the sharp
instruments.
날카로운 도구에 의해 다치지 않게 조심해야 한다.

40 **shortage** [ʃɔ́:rtidʒ] a situation when something is not enough

n. 부족, 결핍, 결함
short a. 짧은, 키가 작은 | shorten vt. 짧게 하다

By developing the medical skill, job shortage **is increasing.**
의학 기술이 발달함에 따라, 일자리 부족이 증가하고 있다.

41 sickness [síknis] illness

n. 병, 메스꺼움
sick a. 병의, 병든 ｜ sicken v. 병나다, 역겹게 만들다

I always have motion sickness whenever I ride a bus.
나는 버스를 탈 때마다 늘 멀미를 한다.

42 spiritual [spíritʃuəl] connected with the human spirit, rather than the body

a. 정신의
spiritually ad. 정신적으로 ｜ spirit n. 정신, 태도, 영혼, 마음

We have to care about our spiritual and physical condition.
우리는 항상 정신적인 상태와 육체적인 상태에 신경 써야 한다.

43 thermometer [θərmámətər] an instrument used for measuring the temperature

n. 온도계

A thermometer shows a temperature.
온도계는 온도를 나타낸다.

44 twist [twíst] to bend or turn something into a particular shape

v. 꼬다, 비틀어 돌리다
twisted a. 꼬인, 취한 ｜ twisty a. 꾸불꾸불한, 정직하지 않은
twister n. 꼬는 사람, 비트는 사람

After you stretch, twist your arms and waist.
스트레칭을 한 후에, 팔과 허리를 비틀어라.

45 **vigor** [vígər] a state that is very active, determined or full of energy

n. 정력, 활기
vigorous a. 정력적인, 원기 왕성한

My father told me to choose a man who has vigor **and strong body.**
아버지께서는 활기차고 신체가 건강한 남자를 선택하라고 말씀하셨다.

46 **vital** [váitl] necessary or essential in order for something to succeed

a. 생명의, 극히 중대한, 필수의
vitality n. 생명력, 활기 l vitalize vt. 생명을 주다, 활력을 복돋아 주다
vitally ad. 치명적으로

It's vital **to take a first aid kit with me when we go camping.**
캠핑갈 때 구급상자를 챙기는 것은 중요하다.

47 **vomit** [vámit] to bring food from the stomach back out through the mouth

v. 토하다
vomiting n. 구토, 토하기

The baby vomited **all he had eaten because of a high fever.**
아기는 고열 때문에 먹은 것을 다 토해냈다.

48 **waist** [wéist] the area around the middle of the body

n. 허리

She became paralyzed from the waist **down due to the car accident.**
자동차 사고로 그녀는 하반신이 마비되었다.

49   weaken [wíːkən]   to make someone less strong or powerful

vt. ~을 약화시키다 vi. 약해지다
weak a. 약한, 불충분한 ㅣ weakened a. 약해진

A damaged immune system extremely weakens a person.
손상된 면역체계는 극도로 사람을 약하게 만든다.

50   wound [wúːnd]   an injury to a part of the body

n. 상처, 부상
wounded a. 부상한

Take care to prevent the wound from getting infected.
상처가 감염되지 않도록 주의하시오.

Check up

A 다음 빈 칸에 가장 알맞은 것을 고르시오.

1. She almost died because the doctor could not stop the _____.

   a. alcohol   b. bleeding   c. common   d. liver   e. chest

2. The best way to _____ from a serious illness is to sleep and eat well.

   a. abnormal   b. blind   c. feeble   d. remedy   e. recover

3. She couldn't breathe due to the _____ of oxygen at the top of the mountain.

   a. shortage   b. rib   c. waist   d. sickness   e. wound

4. This _____ will relieve your backaches.

   a. faint   b. pill   c. moan   d. drown   e. lap

5. First of all, the immune system is _____ for our health.

   a. weaken   b. sensible   c. medieval   d. vital   e. breath

B 다음 단어의 반의어를 고르시오.

1. abnormal behavior

   a. rogue   b. common   c. deviant   d. non-standard

2. as blind as a bat

   a. unseeing   b. sightless   c. sighted   d. irrational

3. be faint from lack of air

   a. distinct   b. weak   c. ill   d. perceptible

4. as harmless as a fly

   a. innocent   b. innocuous   c. harmful   d. benefit

5. as sharp as a needle

   a. terse   b. curt   c. clipped   d. dull

Lesson 6
Interests & Exercises
| 취미와 운동

01 **adjourn** [ədʒə́:rn] to stop a meeting or an official process for a period of time

vt. ~을 연기하다, 휴회하다

The football match was adjourned due to the heavy rain.

폭우로 축구 경기가 연기되었다.

02 **advantage** [ədvǽntidʒ] a thing that helps you to be better or more successful

n. 유리, 유리한 점
advantaged a. 유리한, 혜택받은 ｜ advantageous a. 유리한, 이로운

The host will have an advantage of a home field.

개최국은 홈구장의 이점을 갖게 될 것이다.

03 **aerobics** [ɛəróubiks] physical exercises intended to make your body stronger

n. 에어로빅, 에어로빅 체조

Regular aerobics makes you healthy, especially middle-aged women.

규칙적인 에어로빅은 특히 중년 여성들을 건강하게 해준다.

04 **awesome** [ɔ́:səm] very impressive or very difficult and perhaps rather frightening

a. 무시무시한, 굉장한, 아주 멋진
awe n. 외경심, 경외감

The play of our national team was awesome in the Olympics.

올림픽에서 우리나라 국가대표팀의 경기는 굉장했다.

05 applaud [əplɔ́:d] to show your approval of someone by clapping your hands

v. 박수치다, 갈채를 보내다

applause n. 박수(갈채)

The spectators applauded **the march of the prize winners.**

관중들이 수상자들의 행진에 박수갈채를 보냈다.

06 archery [ɑ́:rtʃəri] the art of or sport of shooting arrows with a bow

n. 궁술, 활쏘기

archer n. 궁수, 활 쏘는 사람

They are masters of archery.

그들은 양궁의 명수이다.

07 arrow [ǽrou] a thin stick with a sharp point at one end, which is shot from a bow

n. 화살, 화살표

bow n. 활

The sprinter was just as fast as an arrow.

그 단거리 선수는 마치 화살처럼 빨랐다.

08 cheat [tʃí:t] to trick somebody or make them believe something is not true

v. ~을 속이다, 부정행위를 하다

cheater n. 사기꾼, 협잡꾼

If you cheat **in an exam, you will be punished.**

시험에서 부정행위를 하면, 벌을 받게 될거다.

09 **climbing** [kláimiŋ] the sport or activity of climbing rocks or mountains

n. 등산, 기어오름 a. 기어오르는, 등산하는
climb v. 오르다, 올라가다 ㅣ climber n. 등산가

He likes mountain climbing and it is his only hobby.

그는 등산을 좋아하고 그건 그의 유일한 취미이다.

10 **coach** [kóutʃ] a person who trains a person or team in sport

n. 코치 v. 코치하다, 지도하다

He is the new coach of our team.

그는 우리 팀의 새 코치이다.

11 **collect** [kəlékt] to bring things together from different people or places

vt. ~을 모으다, 징수하다
collected a. 모은, 수집한 ㅣ collective a. 집합적인, 집단적인
collection n. 수집, 수집물

The boy has been interested in collecting rare stamps since he was seven.

그 소년은 7살 때부터 희귀한 우표를 모으는 데 관심이 있었다.

12 **court** [kɔ́ːrt] an area in which you play a game such as tennis, basketball, or squash

n. (테니스 등의) 코트, 경기장, 법정

Tennis is usually played on clay courts, but some tournaments are played on grass.

테니스는 보통 클레이 코트에서 진행되지만 일부 토너먼트에서는 잔디 위에서 경기가 치러지기도 한다.

13 **clay** [kléi] a type of heavy, sticky earth that becomes hard when it is baked

n. 점토

The children made pots out of different colors of clay.

아이들은 다양한 색깔의 점토로 항아리를 만들었다.

14 **craft** [krǽft, krɑ́ːft] an activity involving a special skill at making things with your hands

n. 기능, 공예
craftman n.공예사, 숙련공 I craftwork n. 공예품

My child won the craft competition.

공예 대회에서 우리 아이가 우승했다.

15 **dice** [dáis] a small cube with a different number of spots on each of its sides

n. 주사위

With one roll of the dice, he won $100.

그 남자는 주사위를 한 번 굴려서 100달러를 땄다.

16 **excel** [iksél] to be very good at doing something

vi. 능가하다, 탁월하다
excellence n. 우수 I excellent a. 우수한

Students at Ivy League schools excel in studying and sports as well.

아이비리그 학교 학생들은 공부뿐만 아니라 운동 역시 잘한다.

17   face [féis] the front part of the head between the forehead and the chin

n. 얼굴, 표면 vt. 향하다, 직면하다
facial a. 얼굴의 I facing n. 직면, 면함 I faceless a. 익명의, 얼굴이 없는

He looks pale and thin in the face.

그는 얼굴이 창백하고 말라 보인다.

18   fair [fέər] acceptable and appropriate in a particular situation

a. 공정한, 공평한
fairly ad. 꽤, 공정히 I fairness n. 공정성, 공평함
unfair a. 부당한, 부정한, 불공평한

I thought the decision was very fair.

그 결정은 매우 공정했다고 생각했다.

19   fan [fǽn] a person who admires someone or enjoys watching very much

n. 팬
fanatic n. 광신자, 광적인 사람 I fanatical a. 열광적인

Basketball fans **crowded into the stadium to watch
Michael Jordan play.**

마이클 조던의 플레이를 보기 위해 농구팬들이 경기장으로 모여들었다.

20   fencing [fénsiŋ] the sport of fighting with long thin swords

n. 펜싱
fencer n. 검객, 검술가

The school has fencing **as its extra curricular activity.**

그 학교에서는 과외활동으로 펜싱을 할 수 있다.

21 field [fíːld] an area of land in the country used for growing crops

n. 들판, 벌판, 분야
on-field a. 경기장의, 경기장에서의 | **midfield** n. 미드필드
He swept the fields and got a lot of money.
그는 모든 경기를 휩쓸었고 많은 돈을 벌었다.

22 foul [fául] to do something to another player against the rules of the game

v. 반칙을 하다 n. 반칙, 파울
foulness n. 불결, 악랄, 불결한 것

He shouldn't have committed a foul against the other player.
그녀는 상대 선수에게 파울을 범하지 말았어야 했다.

23 fury [fjúəri] extreme anger that often includes violent behavior

n. 격노
furious a. 노하여 펄펄 뛰는 | **furiously** ad. 미친듯이 노하여

The land was full of hatred and fury.
그 땅은 증오와 분노로 가득 찼다.

24 glider [gláidər] a light aircraft that flies without an engine

n. 글라이더
hang glider n. 행글라이더, 행글라이딩을 하는 사람
glide vi. 활주하다, 미끄러지다

You must follow the safety instructions before you take
flight in your glider.
글라이더를 타기 전에 안전수칙을 반드시 따라야 한다.

25 grip [gríp] to hold something tightly

vt. ~을 꽉 잡다 n. 잡음, 손잡이

The lifter covered his hand with flour and gripped **the barbell.**

역도 선수는 손에 밀가루를 묻히고 역기를 잡았다.

---

26 hinder [híndər] to make it difficult for somebody to do something

vt. ~을 방해하다, 막다

The heavy rain hindered **our play, so we had to postpone it.**

폭우도 경기를 못하게 되어 미루어야 했다.

---

27 knit [nít] to make clothes, etc. from wool or cotton thread

vt. ~을 뜨다, 짜다
knitted a. 짠, 뜬, 메리야스의 I knitting n. 뜨개질, 편물, 니트

She is so good at knitting **that it looks machine-made.**

그녀는 뜨개질에 능숙해서 기계로 짠 것처럼 보인다.

---

28 obstacle [ábstəkl] a situation, an event, etc. that makes it difficult for you to do

n. 장애

Show jumping is one of the obstacle **races for horse riding.**

장애물 뛰어넘기는 승마에서 장애물 경주 중 하나이다.

29 **official** [əfíʃəl]　relating or belonging to an office or position of authority.

a. 공식의
officialdom　n. 공무원, 관리, 관료주의 ∣ officialism　n. 형식주의, 관료주의
officially　ad. 공무상

He holds the official record for fastest man in the world.
그는 세상에서 가장 빠른 사나이라는 공식기록을 갖고 있다.

30 **opening** [óupəniŋ]　a hole or empty space through which thing or people can pass

n. 열기, 트인 구멍, 개막식

Many people gathered together to celebrate the opening
of the gym.
체육관 개장을 축하하기 위해 많은 사람들이 모였다.

31 **opponent** [əpóunənt]　a person who is playing or fighting against

n. 상대, 적수　a. 적대하는
opponency　n. 반대하는 일, 저항

He defeated his opponent by the second round with a
knockout.　그는 두 번째 라운드에서 상대 선수를 녹아웃시켰다.

32 **outdoor** [áutdɔːr]　used, happening or located outside rather than in a building

a. 집 밖의
outdoors　ad. 문 밖에서, 옥외에서

Tennis and soccer are typical outdoor sports that I enjoy
on weekends.
테니스와 축구는 내가 주말마다 즐기는 대표적인 야외 스포츠이다.

33 indoor [índɔːr] located, done or used inside a building

a. 실내의
indoors ad. 실내에서, 실내로

The indoor facility will have a swimming pool, a wellness center and a place for other leisure activities.

그 실내 시설에는 수영장과 건강관리 센터, 다른 레저 활동을 위한 장소들이 들어설 것이다.

34 inferior [infíəriər] not good or not as good as someone else

a. 하위의, 열등한
inferiority n. 하위, 열등 ǀ inferior court n. 하급 법원
inferior planet n. 내행성

She felt she was inferior to her sister.

그녀는 언니보다 열등하다고 느꼈다.

35 interval [íntərvəl] a period of time between two events

n. 간격, 틈

The proper interval should be kept among players.

선수들 사이에 적당한 거리를 유지해야 한다.

36 lapse [læps] a small mistake, especially one that is caused by forgetting it

n. 착오, 실수, 시간의 경과
lapsed a. 지나간, 없어진, 폐지된

A temporary lapse in judgement, that's nothing at all.

판정에서의 일시적 오류일 뿐, 아무것도 아니다.

37 martial arts [mά:ɾʃəl ά:rts] military arts

n. 무술
martial artist n. 격투기 선수, 무술가

In Korean the martial arts Taekwondo, one wears a blue helmet and chest protector, the other red.

대한민국 무술인 태권도에서, 한 선수는 파란색 헬멧과 가슴보호대를 착용하고, 상대방 선수는 빨간색 헬멧을 착용한다.

38 pace [peis] the speed at which somebody walks, runs or moves

n. 걸음걸이, 걷는 속도
paced a. 걸음이 ~인

Working out at too intense of a pace increases your chances of injury. 너무 격렬하게 운동하면 부상의 위험이 커진다.

39 rejoice [ridʒɔ́is] to express great happiness about something

v. ~을 기쁘게 하다, 기뻐하다
rejoicing n. 기쁨

We rejoiced that North Korea and South Korea would be together. 남북한이 함께 하게 되어 우리는 기뻤다.

40 relax [rilǽks] to rest while you are doing something enjoyable

vt. ~을 늦추다 vi. 풀리다, 나른해지다
relaxation n. 풀림, 이완 ㅣ relaxed a. 느슨한, 관대한

Just try to relax and find your center with your arms stretched. 긴장을 풀고 양팔을 벌리며 중심을 찾아라.

41 **repose** [ripóuz] a state of rest, sleep or feeling calm

n. 휴식 vt. 눕히다 vi. 쉬다
reposeful a. 평온한, 조용한, 침착한

The famous star players' repose was on a bed of roses
after retiring.
유명 스타 선수들은 은퇴한 후 호화롭게 살고 있다.

42 **rival** [ráivəl] a person, company, or thing that competes with another in sport

n. 경쟁자
rivalrous a. 경쟁의 | rivalry n. 경쟁

She kept ahead of her rivals and built up a commanding
lead.
그녀는 경쟁자들을 앞서서 압도적으로 우세했다.

43 **routine** [ru:tí:n] the normal order and way in which you regularly do things

n. 판에 박힌 일 a. 일상의, 정기적인

Listening to the music is a distraction from my daily routine.
음악감상은 틀에 박힌 일상생활에서 기분 전환되는 것이다.

44 **score** [skɔ́:r] the number of points, goals, etc. scored by each player or team

n. 득점, 점수
scorer n. 점수 기록원, 득점자 | scoreboard n. 득점판

Ronaldo scored numerous goals through his career.
로날도는 선수 생활 내내 수많은 골을 넣었다.

45 self-confidence [sélfkánfədəns] reliance on one's own abilities

n. 자신(감)

Outside activities help promote self-confidence **and a positive attitude.**

야외활동은 자신감과 긍정적 태도를 심어준다.

46 stately [stéitli] impressive in size, appearance or manner

a. 위풍당당한

We welcomed stately **players who won the three gold medals.**

3개의 금메달을 딴 위풍당당한 선수들을 환영했다.

47 superior [su:píəriər, su-] better in quality than someone else

a. 뛰어난, 우수한, 상급의
superiorly ad. 우세하게, 위에, 상부에 | superiority n. 우월
superior court n. 상급 법원, 고등 법원

My hobbies now are superior **to those I had as a boy.**

어릴 적보다 지금의 나의 취미들이 더 우수하다.

48 track [trǽk] ground with a special surface for people to have races on

n. 경주로, 트랙, 지나간 자취, 철도 선로
tracker n. 추적자 | trackman n. 육상 경기 선수
racetrack n. 경주 트랙, 경주로 | race track n. 경마장

The racetrack **is about 1km long and made of red clay.**

그 경주 트랙은 약 1km 길이의 붉은 점토로 만들어져 있다.

49 weight [wéit] the heaviness of something

n. 무게, 부담
weigh vi. 무게를 달다, 심사숙고하다 | weighted a. 무거워진, 무거운 짐을 실은
weightless a. 무게가 없는, 중력이 없는

She's determined to lose weight **to win the beauty contest.**
그녀는 미인대회에서 우승하기 위하여 살을 빼기로 결심했다.

50 wrestling [réslin] a sport in which two people fight by holding each other

n. 레슬링
wrestle v. 맞붙어 싸우다 | wrestler n. 레슬링 선수

There are many kinds of attack skills in wrestling.
레슬링에는 다양한 종류의 공격 기술이 있다.

Check up

A 다음과 뜻이 가장 가까운 것을 고르시오.

1. It was an advantage to have that team as our opponent in the second round.

   a. penalty   b. disadvantage   c. benefit   d. power   e. mastery

2. He tried to excel in studying to get the degree.

   a. surpass   b. exceed   c. except   d. expect   e. evolve

3. He also felt inferior compared to other men due to his lower education.

   a. superior   b. poor   c. noticeable   d. famous   e. fast

4. I am tired of my daily routine and the same exercise.

   a. soft   b. tight   c. late   d. bright   e. ordinary

B 다음 뜻을 모두 포함하는 단어를 보기에서 고르시오.

face | field | fair | awesome

1. _____

a. very impressive or very difficult and perhaps rather frightening

b. very good, enjoyable, etc.

2. _____

a. an area of land in the country used for growing crops or keeping animals in

b. a particular subject or activity that somebody works in or is interested in

3. _____

a. acceptable and appropriate in a particular situation

b. quite large in number, size or amount

4. _____

a. the front part of the head between the forehead and the chin

b. to be opposite somebody; to be looking or pointing in a particular direction

Lesson 7
Journey

| 여행

01 **abroad** [əbrɔ́ːd] in or to a foreign country

ad. 국외로, 해외로, 널리

The student planned to study abroad to learn English better.

그 학생은 영어를 좀 더 잘 배우기 위해 유학을 계획하였다.

02 **adventure** [ədvéntʃər] an unusual, exciting or dangerous experience, journey

n. 모험, 희한한 사건
adventurous a. 모험을 좋아하는, 모험적인 ㅣ adventurer n. 모험가

It was an adventure to visit that place and it required tremendous courage.

그 곳을 방문하는 것은 모험이었고 많은 용기가 필요했다.

03 **aero** [ɛ́ərou] of or relating to aircraft or aeronautics

a. 항공(기)의, 항공학의
aerospace n. 항공 우주 ㅣ aeroplane n. 비행기

The sports car had a very sleek and aero design.

그 스포츠카는 매우 매끄럽고 항공학적인 디자인이다.

04 **afford** [əfɔ́ːrd] to have enough money or time to be able to buy or to do something

vt. ~할 여유가 있다
affordable a. 줄 수 있는, 알맞은

We can not afford to stay in a more expensive hotel.

우리는 더 비싼 호텔에 묵을 여유가 없다.

05 arrange [əréindʒ] to plan or organize something in advance

vt. 가지런히 하다, 배열하다

arrangement n. 정돈, 배열 | arrangeable a. 가지런히 할 수 있는

We have arranged long journey for a two weeks.

2주 동안 장기 여행 준비를 해오고 있다.

06 beware [biwɛ́ər] to be careful (used only in infinitives and orders)

vt. ~을 조심하다

Beware what you do and what you eat wherever you go.

어디를 가든 행동하는 것과 먹는 것을 조심해라.

07 brunch [brʌ́ntʃ] a meal that you eat in the late morning

n. 늦은 아침 식사, 아침 겸 점심

This hotel provides brunch for tourists.

이 호텔은 여행객들을 위해 늦은 아침식사를 제공한다.

08 confident [kɑ́nfədent] feeling sure about your own ability to do things

a. 확신하는, 자신만만한

confidence n. 신임, 자신 | confide vi. 신임하다 vt. 털어놓다

confidential a. 비밀의, 신임이 두터운, 속내를 터놓는

I'm confident that you'll have a great experience on your trip.

이번 여행에서 네가 멋진 경험을 하게 되리라고 확신한다.

09 **confirm** [kənfɔ́ːrm] to state or show that something is definitely true or correct

vt. ~을 확인하다, 승인하다
confirmation n. 확정, 확인 | disconfirm vt. 확인하지 않다
reconfirm vt. 재확인하다

You have to confirm your reservation before you leave home.
집을 나서기 전에 예약을 확인해야 한다.

10 **connect** [kənékt] to join together two or more things

vt. ~을 연결하다, 관련시키다
connector n. 연결하는 것, 연결기, 커넥터
connected a. 연속된, 일관된, 관계가 있는 | connection n. 연결, 접속, 관계

This KTX train connects with another at Busan.
이 고속열차는 부산에서 다른 열차와 연결된다.

11 **contact** [kántækt] the act of communicating with somebody, especially regularly

n. 접촉, 교제
contactable a. 연락 가능한

This virus is spread by physical contact.
이 바이러스는 신체적 접촉에 의해 전파된다.

12 **customs** [kʌ́stəm] taxes paid on imports

n. 관세

You must pay customs on imported goods.
수입품에 대해서 관세를 내야만 한다.

13 delightful [diláitfəl] very pleasant

a. 매우 기쁜
delight n. 기쁨 vt. 매우 기쁘게 하다

It was delightful that we could stay in Vietnam one more night.

베트남에서 하룻밤 더 묵을 수 있어서 매우 기뻤다.

14 delay [diléi] to make something late

vt. ~을 늦추다, 미루다 n. 지연
delayed a. 지연된

You must delay your vacation until next week.

당신은 휴가를 다음 주까지 연기해야 합니다.

15 disappoint [dìsəpɔ́int] to make somebody feel sad

vt. ~을 실망시키다
disappointment n. 실망 ǀ disappointed a. 실망한
disappointing a. 실망스러운

She was disappointed that the flight was postponed.

비행기가 연착되어서 그녀는 실망했다.

16 dormitory [dɔ́ːrmətɔːri] a room for several people to sleep in, especially in a school

n. 기숙사

I'll meet my son who stays at a dormitory for foreign students.

외국 유학생 기숙사에서 머물고 있는 아들을 만날 예정이다.

17 **eager** [í:gər] very interested and excited by something that is going to happen

a. 열망하는, 간절히 하고 싶어하는
eagerly ad. 열망하여 ǀ eagerness n. 열의

She is eager to be alone even in other countries.

그녀는 심지어 타국에서도 혼자 있고 싶어한다.

18 **enthusiasm** [inθú:ziæzm, en-] a strong feeling of excitement

n. 열광, 열의, 열정
enthusiastic a. 열렬한 ǀ enthusiastically ad. 열광적으로

The young have enthusiasm for travel.

젊은이들은 여행에 대한 열정이 있다.

19 **guest** [gest] a person that you have invited to your house

n. 손님
houseguest n. 손님, 유숙객 ǀ guesthouse n. 숙소, 여관, 영빈관

You have to treat him as a guest of distinction.

그를 귀빈으로 대접해야 한다.

20 **hospitality** [hὰspətǽləti] friendly and generous behavior towards guests

n. 환대
hospitable a. 대접이 좋은, 손님 접대를 잘 하는 ǀ inhospitality n. 냉대, 푸대접

They showed hospitality to us so we were happy to stay there.

그들이 우리를 환대해 주어서 그곳에서 행복하게 머물렀다.

21 **inn** [ín] a pub, usually in the country and often one where people can stay

n. 여인숙

We'll stay at a country inn due to having no money.

우리는 돈이 없어서 시골 여인숙에서 머물 예정이다.

22 **intend** [inténd] to have a plan, result or purpose in your mind when you do it

vt. ~할 작정이다, 의도하다, (~하려고) 생각하다
intention n. 의향, 의도 ǀ intent a. 집중된, 열심인

After I get the message from you, I intend to go there.

너의 연락을 받고 나서 그곳에 갈 생각이다.

23 **invite** [inváit] to ask somebody to come to a social event

vt. ~을 초청하다
invitation n. 초대, 초대장 ǀ inviting a. 초대하는, 유혹적인, 마음을 끄는

My boss was invited to the conference in Spain next month.

나의 상사가 다음달 스페인에서 열리는 회의에 초대되었다.

24 **jet lag** [dʒét læg] the feeling of being tired and confused after a long plane journey

n. 시차로 인한 피로

To avoid jet lag, adjust your schedule to your new local time.

시차로 인한 피로를 피하기 위해, 새 현지 시간에 맞춰 스케줄을 조정하세요.

25 **journey** [dʒə́ːrni] an act of traveling from one place to another

n. 여행

They were on a journey to South Africa.

그들은 남아프리카공화국을 여행 중에 있었다.

26 **luggage** [lʌ́gidʒ] bags, cases, etc. that contain somebody' s clothes and things

n. 수화물

They charge an extra fee for overweight luggage.

초과 중량 수화물에 대해서는 추가 요금을 부과하고 있다.

27 **map** [mǽp] a drawing or plan of the earth' s surface or part of it

n. 지도

This mark on the map represents the tower you are looking for.

지도상에 있는 이 표시가 당신이 찾고 있는 타워를 나타내고 있다.

28 **marvel** [máːrvəl] a wonderful and surprising person or thing

n. 놀라운 일
marvelous a. 놀라운, 믿기 어려운

It was a marvel that she recovered from that incurable disease.

그녀가 그 불치병에서 회복되었다는 것은 놀라운 일이었다.

29 memory [méməri] your ability to remember things

n. 기억, 기억력, 추억
memorial n. 기념물 | memorize vt. 암기하다, 기억하다

The date of the camp slipped my memory.

캠프 날짜를 잊어버렸다.

30 overseas [ouvərsíːz] coming from, existing in, or happening in a foreign country

a. 해외의 ad. 해외로
go overseas 외국에 가다

This visit would be his third overseas trip.

이번 방문은 그의 세 번째 외국방문이 된다.

31 pack [pǽk] to put clothes, etc. into a bag in preparation for a trip

vt. 꾸리다, 채워 넣다
package n. 짐, 소포, 꾸러미 | packet n. 봉지, 봉투, 한 묶음
packed a. 채워진, 가득 찬

Pack the clothes in order not to crease them.

옷이 구겨지지 않도록 싸라.

32 pass [pǽs, pàːs] to move past or to the other side of something

vt. ~을 지나가다, 추월하다, 통과하다
passenger n. 승객 | passing a. 통행하는 | password n. 암호

She can pass the border between two countries with her passport.

그녀는 여권으로 두 나라의 국경을 통과할 수 있다.

33 passport [pǽspɔ:rt, pá:s-] an official document that identifies you as a citizen of a country

n. 여권
passport control 출국 수속, 출입국 관리

For the other countries, you have to check if you need passport or visa.

다른 나라 여행시 여권이나 비자가 필요한지 알아봐야 한다.

34 plan [plǽn] something that you intend to do or achieve

n. 계획 v. 계획하다
planning n. 계획, 입안 | planned a. 계획된, 조직적인

Their plan to visit Venezuela has been canceled because of the hyperinflation.

극심한 인플레이션으로 인해 베네수엘라를 방문하려던 그들의 계획은 취소되었다.

35 postpone [poustpóun] to arrange for an event, etc. to take place at a later time or date

vt. ~을 연기하다, 미루다

Their vacation was postponed due to the company's situation.

회사 사정으로 인해 그들의 휴가가 연기되었다.

36 reserve [rizə́:rv] to ask for a seat, table, room, etc. to be available for you

vt. ~을 남겨두다, 예약해두다
reserved a. 내성적인 | reservation n. 예약 | preserve vt. 보존하다, 보호하다

I reserved the hotel room as you told me to do.

말씀하신 대로 호텔방을 예약했습니다.

37 reasonable [ríːzənəbl] fair, practical and sensible

a. 너무 비싸지 않은, 도리에 맞는, 온당한
unreasonable a. 부당한, 비이성적인, 터무니없는
reasonably ad. 사리에 맞게

The price of riding a taxi isn't reasonable **especially to the foreigners.**

특히 외국인들에게 택시 요금은 터무니없다.

38 reluctant [rilʌ́ktənt] hesitating before doing something

a. 마음 내키지 않는, 꺼려하는
reluctance n. 싫음, 주저함

She is reluctant **to take a picture with us.**

그녀는 우리와 함께 사진 찍는 것을 꺼려한다.

39 resort [rizɔ́ːrt] a place where a lot of people go on holiday

n. 행락지, 휴양지

We'll go to the ski resort **with friends next month.**

우리는 다음 달에 친구들과 스키장에 갈 것이다.

40 currency [kə́ːrənsi, kʌ́r-] the system of money that a country uses

n. 통화, 유통, 지폐
current a. 지금의, 현행의

I have to exchange foreign currency **to buy some souvenirs.**

기념품을 사기 위해 환전해야 한다.

41 **sight** [sáit] the ability to see

n. 시각, 봄, 시력
sighting n. 관찰, 목격 | **sightseeing** n. 관광 | **sightseer** n. 관광객

People were attracted by a beautiful sight.

사람들이 아름다운 광경에 매료되었다.

42 **scenery** [síːnəri] the natural features of an area

n. 풍경, 배경
scene n. 현장, 장면, 풍경 | **scenic** a. 경치가 좋은

This historical site is also famous for its beautiful scenery.

이 유적지는 아름다운 경치로도 유명하다.

43 **souvenir** [sùːvəníər] a thing that you buy and keep to remind yourself of a place

n. 기념품
souvenir shop 기념품 가게

Many souvenir shops and change booths are located downtown.

많은 기념품 가게와 환전소가 시내에 위치해 있다.

44 **stranger** [stréindʒər] a person that you do not know

n. 낯선 사람, 생소한 사람
strange a. 이상한, 모르는 | **strangely** ad. 이상하게

I'm a stranger to this place and I don't know where to go.

나는 여기 지리에 어두워서 어디로 가야 할지 모르겠다.

45 **tour** [túər] a visit round a particular area

n. 관광 여행
tourist n. 관광객 I tourism n. 관광객, 관광 여행
touristic a. 여행의, 여행자의

He has just returned from his tour of China.
그는 중국 여행을 마치고 방금 돌아왔다.

---

46 **transit** [trǽnsit, -zit] the process of being moved or carried from one place to another

n. 통과, 통행, 횡단, 운송, 운반
transition n. 변천 I transitional a. 변천하는, 과도적인, 과도기의
transitory a. 일시적인, 잠시 동안의

I lost my luggage in transit from America to Korea.
나는 미국에서 한국으로 이동 중에 짐을 잃어버렸다.

---

47 **vehicle** [víːikl, víːhi-] a thing that is used for transporting people or goods

n. 탈것, 차
vehicle licence 자동차 검사증

Can I see your vehicle registration?
자동차 등록증 좀 보여 주실래요?

---

48 **visa** [víːzə] a stamp or mark put in your passport by officials of a foreign country

n. 사증, 비자
entry visa 입국 사증 I exit visa 출국 사증

She is required to apply for a visa for the United States.
그녀는 미국 방문을 위해 비자를 신청해야 한다.

49 **voyage** [vɔ́iidʒ] a long journey, especially by sea or in space

n. 항해
voyager n. 항해자

I started on my voyage **two weeks ago.**
나는 2주 전부터 항해를 시작했다.

50 **willing** [wíliŋ] not objecting to doing something

a. 기꺼이 ~하는
willingness n. 자진해서 하는 것 ǀ willingly ad. 자진해서
unwilling a. 꺼리는, 마음이 내키지 않는

I am willing **to stay in a temple while in Korea.**
한국에 있는 동안 절에서 머물 의향이 있습니다.

Check up

A 주어진 단어의 동의어나 반의어를 보기에서 골라 쓰시오.

> disarrange | unpack | rational | enthusiastic | negate
> view | diffident | plan | cruise | unwilling

1. confident ≠

2. eager =

3. pack ≠

4. intend =

5. willing ≠

6. sight =

7. arrange ≠

8. voyage =

9. confirm ≠

10. reasonable =

B 다음 단어와 같은 의미로 쓰인 것을 보기에서 찾으시오.

1. I stay in contact with friends.

2. The bomb exploded on contact with the earth.

3. They got a pass to town.

4. Could you pass along my thanks?

5. She is abroad.

6. Your answer is all abroad.

7. You are breaking an old custom.

8. You have to be checked at the customs.

a. a contact lens

b. Has she been in contact?

c. Pass on step by step.

d. Pass me the sugar.

e. The rumor about one sexy star has become abroad.

f. I got the e-mail from abroad.

g. Let's preserve our traditional customs.

h. The customs office will open next month.

Part 2

Nature

[자연]

Lesson 1
Nature
|자연

01 **adapt** [ədǽpt] to make something suitable for a new situation or purpose

v. (환경, 목적 등에) 적응시키다

adaptation n. (환경, 목적 등에의) 적응, 적합 | adopt vt. 채택하다

She has the ability to adapt **to new circumstances.**

그녀는 새로운 상황에 적응하는 능력이 있다.

02 **appear** [əpíər] to become visible

v. 나타나다, 등장하다

appearance n. 출현, 등장, 외모

A Korean hostage in Iraq appeared **on TV.**

이라크에 있는 한국인 인질의 모습이 **TV**에 공개되었다.

03 **balance** [bǽləns] the ability to remain steady and staple

n. 균형, 조화 v. 균형을 유지하다

balanced a. 균형이 잡힌

The whole environmental balance **is getting better.**

전체적인 환경의 균형이 점점 나아지고 있다.

04 **blossom** [blásəm] a flower or a mass of flowers

n. 꽃 v. 꽃이 피다

The scent of blossoms **made me fall in love with him.**

꽃향기로 나는 그와 사랑에 빠지게 되었다.

05 chaos [kéiɑs] a state of complete confusion and lack of order

n. 혼돈, (성서) 천지 창조 이전의 혼돈
cosmos n. (질서 정연한) 세계, 우주, 조화

The destruction of the Amazon could lead to climatic chaos.
아마존이 파괴되면 기후상의 혼돈이 올 수도 있다.

06 conserve [kənsə́:rv] to keep something from being damaged

v. 보존하다, 보호하다
conservation n. (자연, 자원의) 보호, 보존, 유지

We should take steps to conserve the environment.
우리는 환경을 보존하기 위한 조치를 취해야 한다.

07 create [kri:éit] to make something new or original

v. 창조하다, 만들다
creature n. (신의) 창조물, 생물 | creation n. 창조, 창작
creative a. 창조적인, 독창적인 | creativity n. 창조력, 독창력

The 50 million-year-old fossilized remains of a creature
are found in China.
5천만 년 된 동물의 화석이 중국에서 발견되었다.

08 crisis [kráisis] a situation in which something or someone is affected by one or more very serious problems

n. 위기, 결정적 단계, 중대 국면

The world environmental communities are warning the
present crisis to the human beings.
세계 환경 단체들은 인류에게 현재 위기를 경고하고 있다.

09 daybreak [déibrèik] the time in the morning when light first appears

n. 새벽
daylight n. 낮, 주간

The rising sun in Dong-hae at daybreak is fantastic
enough to fascinate people who are visiting there.
동해의 새벽 일출은 그곳을 찾은 사람들을 매료시키기에 충분히 환상적이다.

10 decay [dikéi] to rot or go bad

v. 썩다, (번영이나 건강이) 쇠퇴하다 n. 부패, 쇠퇴

It takes too much time for plastic bags to decay naturally.
비닐 봉지는 자연적으로 썩는 데 너무 많은 시간이 걸린다.

11 depend [dipénd] to rely on someone or something

v. 의존하다, 의지하다
dependent a. 의존하는, 종속되어 있는 | dependence n. 의존, 종속

Human beings are originally dependent on one another.
인간들은 본래 서로에게 의지하는 존재이다.

12 disappear [dìsəpíər] to stop being visible

v. 사라지다, 보이지 않게 되다
disappearance n. 없어짐, 행방불명

The surface of the Earth is gradually disappearing below
the horizon.
지구의 지면이 점차 수평선 아래로 가라앉고 있다.

13 **distinct** [distíŋkt] clearly different or of a different kind

a. 뚜렷한, 별개의
distinctive a. 구별할 수 있는, 독특한 | distinction n. 구별, (구별되는) 특색
distinguish v. 구별하다

The short glossy hair is the most distinct feature of the cats.

짧고 윤기 있는 털이 그 고양이의 가장 뚜렷한 특징이다.

14 **drastic** [drǽstik] having a strong or extreme effect

a. 급격한, 철저한
drastically ad. 급격히, 철저히

People will be affected by a drastic change of the climate.

기후의 급격한 변화는 사람들에게 영향을 미칠 것이다.

15 **eclipse** [iklíps] a time when all parts of the sun or moon become dark

n. (일식, 월식의) 식, 퇴색

There is a saying, "An eclipse of the moon makes people raise their original nature."

"월식이 사람들의 본성을 일깨워준다." 라는 속설이 있다.

16 **element** [éləmənt] an important basic part of something

n. 요소, 성분, 원리
elemental a. 요소의

Each creature is the element of the whole nature.

각각의 생명체는 모든 자연의 근원이다.

17 emerge [imə́:rdʒ] to appear or come out of something

v. 출현하다, 발생하다
emergence n. 출현, 발생 ǀ emergent a. 나타나는

We has waited for the sun to emerge from the horizon.
우리는 수평선에서 태양이 나타나기를 기다렸다.

18 eventual [ivéntʃuəl] happening in the end

a. 결과의, 최종적인
eventually ad. 마침내, 결국

Our eventual aim is to let the environment revive.
우리의 최종적인 목적은 환경을 되살리는 것이다.

19 evolve [iválv] to develop gradually or naturally

v. 진화하다, 발전하다
evolution n. 진화 ǀ evolutive a. 진화의, 진화의 경향이 있는

The Christian church claims that the human beings
haven't evolved from the anthropoid.
기독교는 인류가 유인원으로부터 진화하지 않았다고 주장한다.

20 explore [iksplɔ́:r] to travel through a place to find out more about it

v. 탐험하다, (미지의 지역을) 탐사하다
exploration n. 탐험, 답사 ǀ explorer n. 탐험가

The Koreans who had succeeded to explore the Antarctic
made us feel proud.
남극 탐험에 성공한 한국인들은 우리에게 긍지를 심어주었다.

21 extinction [ikstíŋkʃn] the death of all its remaining living members

n. (종족, 생물 등의) 멸종
extinct a. (종족, 생물 등이) 멸종한, 절멸한

The teachers in the school must inform the students that
the species of the fish are in danger of extinction.

학교에서 교사들은 학생들에게 멸종 위기에 처한 어종들에 대해 알려야 한다.

22 fascinate [fǽsənèit] to attract and interest someone very strongly

v. 매혹하다
fascinating a. 매혹적인 | fascinated a. 매료된

The sunset over the beach fascinated my eyes.

해변의 일몰이 나를 사로잡았다.

23 flourish [flə́:riʃ] to grow and develop strongly

v. 번창하다, (초목이) 우거지다
flourishing a. 번창하는, 우거진

The trees that we planted ten years ago have flourished
for 10 years.

10년 전에 심었던 나무들이 그동안 우거져 있었다.

24 fossil [fάsəl] the remains of a prehistoric animal or plant preserved in rock

n. 화석

We get to know about the age from fossils that have been
in that place.

우리는 그곳에 있던 화석들로부터 그 시대를 알 수 있게 된다.

25 indistinct [ìndistíŋkt] not distinct; not clear

a. 불분명한, 분명하지 않은

distinct a. 뚜렷한, 다른, 별개의

There are a lot of remains of which ages are indistinct yet.

아직까지도 시대가 불분명한 유적들이 많이 있다.

26 inevitable [inévətəbl] impossible to avoid or prevent

a. 피할 수 없는, 필연적인

inevitably ad. 불가피하게, 필연적으로

Unless people on this planet think more about the Earth, the exhaustion of resources will be inevitable.

모든 사람들이 지구를 아끼지 않는다면 자원 고갈은 피할 수 없을 것이다.

27 jeopardy [dʒépərdi] a danger or risk

n. 위험

jeopardize v. 위태롭게 하다

The planet where we live is in jeopardy.

우리가 사는 이곳, 지구는 위험에 처해 있다.

28 landscape [lǽndskèip] an area of land that is beautiful to look at

n. (한눈에 바라보이는) 경치, 조망

townscape n. 도시 조경

We can see the landscape of the mountain when the sky is clear.

하늘이 맑은 날에는 그 산의 경치를 볼 수 있다.

29 **magnificent** [mægnífəsnt] extremely good, beautiful, or impressive

a. 장대한, 훌륭한
magnificence n. 장대함, 훌륭함 | magnify v. 확대하다

The view from the top of the mountain was more magnificent than I expected.
산 정상에서 본 풍경은 내가 생각했던 것 이상으로 장대했다.

30 **meadow** [médou] a field where has grass and flowers growing

n. 목초지, 초원

The cows that are running on the meadow have a very high quality meat.
초원에서 뛰노는 소들은 육질이 매우 좋다.

31 **oxygen** [áksidʒən] a colorless gas that exists in large quantities in the air

n. 산소

The Earth is the only planet that contains oxygen in the air.
지구는 공기 중에 산소를 포함하는 유일한 행성이다.

32 **paw** [pɔ́:] the foot of an animal that has claws or nails

n. (개, 고양이 등의 갈고리 발톱이 있는) 발

A role of paws for animals and human beings is almost the same, for we are also animals.
인간도 동물이기 때문에, 동물과 인간의 발의 역할은 거의 비슷하다.

33 **predator** [prédətər] an animal that kills and eats other animals

n. 육식동물
herbivore n. 초식동물

A grampus is the most dreadful predator in the ocean.
범고래는 바다에서 가장 무시무시한 육식동물이다.

34 **prey** [préi] an animal that is caught and eaten by another animal

n. (특히 육식동물의) 먹이, 희생 v. 잡아먹다, 빼앗다

A plant becomes food for herbivores, and then the herbivores become prey for predators.
식물은 초식동물의 먹이가 되고, 초식동물은 다시 육식동물의 먹이가 된다.

35 **ranch** [rǽntʃ] a large farm used for raising animals, especially, cattle, horses, or sheep

n. 대목장, (특정 동물, 과실의) 농장, 사육장 v. 목장을 경영하다, 목장에서 일하다

The ranch that I have been to was providing plentiful grass for cows.
내가 방문했던 그 목장은 소들을 위한 풍부한 풀들을 제공하고 있었다.

36 **remain** [riméin] to continue unchanged

v. 남다, 잔존하다, 살아남다
remaining a. 남아 있는

A mosquito is the live fossil that is remaining now from the primitive age.
모기는 원시시대부터 지금까지 남아 있는 살아 있는 화석이다.

37 scenery [síːnəri] the natural features of an area

n. (한 지방 전체의) 풍경, 경치
scene n. (사건이 일어난) 장소, 장면

The scenery is beautiful beyond all description.

경치가 형용할 수 없을 만큼 아름답다.

38 source [sɔ́ːrs] the place from which something comes

n. 원천, 근원, 공급원

Dr. Wilkins insists that we have to find another source of energy as soon as possible.

윌킨스 박사는 가능한 빠른 시간 내에 또 다른 에너지원을 찾아야 한다고 주장한다.

39 species [spíːʃiːz, -siːz] a group of animals or plants that are similar in some way

n. 종류, (생물의) 종

Many species of trees are created by hybridizing.

여러 종의 나무가 교배에 의해 만들어졌다.

40 sprout [spráut] a new shoot in a plant

n. 새싹 vt. (싹을) 나게 하다

The sprout from a tree shows people the future of this wasteland.

나무의 새싹이 이 메마른 땅의 미래를 보여준다.

41 submerge [səbmə́:rdʒ] to go under water

v. 물 속에 가라앉히다, 침몰하다

This heavy rain submerged all the roads in the city.
이번 폭우가 도시의 모든 도로를 침수시켰다.

42 suffer [sʌ́fər] to experience something very unpleasant or painful

v. 경험하다, 고통을 받다
sufferer n. 고통 받는 사람, 재해를 입은 사람 | suffering n. 수난, 노고

The pollution of environment is making all the creatures of the Earth suffer.
환경오염이 지구상의 모든 생물체에 고통을 주고 있다.

43 support [səpɔ́:rt] to provide necessary things in order to live

v. 부양하다, 지지하다, 후원하다, 지탱하다, 유지하다
supporting a. 지지하는, 후원하는 | supporter n. 지지자, 후원자

Recycling resouces is the way to support the life of the Earth.
자원 재활용은 지구의 수명을 유지하는 방법이다.

44 surface [sə́:rfis] the top layer or outside of something

n. 표면, 수면, 외관

The surface of the Earth is becoming higher and higher.
지구의 해수면이 점점 더 높아지고 있다.

45 **surrounding** [səráundiŋ] all the circumstance, people, things, and events around them that influence their life

n. 주변(의 상황), 처지, 환경, 주위
surround vt. 둘러싸다, 에워싸다

A chameleon changes the color of its body to its surroundings.

카멜레온은 주변에 따라 몸의 색을 바꾼다.

46 **vivid** [vívid] bright and clear

a. 생생한, (빛, 색 등이) 선명한
vividly ad. 생생하게

An astronomical telescope gives us the vivid feature of the surface of the Moon.

천체망원경은 우리에게 달표면의 생생한 모습을 보여준다.

47 **voyage** [vɔ́iidʒ] a long journey on a ship or in a spacecraft

n. 항해, 항행, (배, 비행기 등에 의한 비교적 긴) 여행 v. 항해하다, 바다를 건너다, 여행하다

A salmon has an instinct that it has to endure a long voyage.

연어는 긴 항해를 견뎌야 한다는 본능이 있다.

48 **vulnerable** [vʌ́lnərəbl] weak or easy to hurt

a. 상처받기 쉬운, 공격받기 쉬운, 취약한
vulnerability n. 상처받기 쉬움, 취약성

Slow runners in Savanna are very vulnerable to predators such as lions.

사바나에서는 발이 느린 동물들은 사자와 같은 육식동물에게 매우 취약하다.

49   wither [wíðər] to become weaker and smaller, and then disappear

vi. (식물이) 시들다 vt. 시들게 하다

Too much sunlight can also make plants wither.
과도한 햇빛도 식물을 시들게 할 수 있다.

50   wreck [rék] to completely destroy or ruin it

v. 난파하다, 파멸하다, 망치다 n. 난파, 조난, 파괴

In the middle of the Pacific, a wrecked **cruiser that disappeared 2 years ago was discovered this morning.**
태평양 한가운데에서 2년 전에 사라진 난파선이 오늘 아침에 발견되었다.

Check up

A 다음 내용이 설명하고 있는 단어를 〈보기〉에서 골라 그 기호를 쓰시오.

> a. adapt   b. appear   c. balance   d. blossom   e. chaos

1. a flower or a mass of flowers, especially on a fruit tree or bush

2. a state of complete confusion and lack of order

3. to change something in order to make it suitable for a new use or situation

4. a situation in which different things exist in equal, correct or good amounts

5. to give the impression of being or doing something

B 단어와 한글 뜻을 알맞게 짝지으시오.

1. conserve ·   · 새벽

2. create ·   · 창조하다, 만들다

3. crisis ·   · 위기, 결정적 단계

4. daybreak ·   · 썩다, 쇠퇴하다

5. decay ·   · 보존하다, 보호하다

C 의미상 가장 알맞은 단어를 보기에서 골라 쓰시오.

| depend | disappear | distinct | drastic | eclipse |

1. We observed a solar _____ last year.

2. We _____ upon the internet for foreign news.

3. He posits that the spirit and the soul are _____ .

4. Chances are you won't like so _____ a change.

5. People said she would appear and _____ .

D 영영풀이에 알맞은 단어를 고르시오.

1. no longer in existence
   (extinct / extant)

2. that cannot be seen, heard or remembered clearly
   (distinct / indistinct)

3. that you cannot avoid or prevent (evitable / inevitable)

4. to continue to be something (change / remain)

5. a place, person or thing that you get something from
   (source / sink)

Lesson 2

Weather & Geography

| 날씨와 지리 |

01   **altitude** [ǽltətjùːd]   the height of a place or thing above sea level

n. (산, 천체 등의) 높이, 고도

As she got to the altitude of 1,000 meters, she felt dizzy.
그녀는 1,000미터 고지에 올랐을 때 어지러움을 느꼈다.

02   **annual** [ǽnjuəl]   happening once a year

a. 1년의, 해마다의 n. 연보
annually ad. 매년, 해마다

The report of the climate of the year is showing the annual increase of temperature.
연간 기후 보고서는 기온이 매년 상승하고 있음을 보여준다.

03   **Antarctic** [æntáːrktik]   the area around the South Pole

n. 남극(권) a. 남극의
Antarctica n. 남극 대륙

The surface of Antarctic became higher because of a rise in temperature.
기온 상승으로 남극 해수면이 점점 상승했다.

04   **Arctic** [áːrktik, áːrtik]   the area around the North Pole

n. 북극(권) a. 북극의

The explorers went to the Arctic Ocean so that they could find potential resources.
잠재적인 자원을 찾기 위해 탐험가들은 북극해로 갔다.

05 atlas [ǽtləs] a book of maps

n. 지도책

You need the up-to-date atlas, it's too old.

넌 최신 지도책이 필요하다, 그것은 너무 오래되었어.

06 blast [blǽst, blɑ́:st] a big explosion, especially one caused by a bomb

n. (한 줄기의) 센 바람, 돌풍, 폭발, 폭풍 v. 폭파[폭발]하다, 폭발시키다

An electric leakage burst a lot of light bulbs by a strong blast.

돌풍으로 인한 누전으로 많은 전구들이 폭발했다.

07 breeze [brí:z] a gentle wind

n. 산들바람, 미풍, 연풍 v. 산들산들 불다, (필기 시험 등을) 수월하게 해치우다
breezy a. 산들바람의, 바람이 잘 통하는 상쾌한

I could do well in this exam thanks to the breeze.

산들바람 덕에 시험을 잘 볼 수 있었다.

08 Celsius [sélsiəs, -ʃi-] a system for measuring temperature in which water freezes at 0 and boils at 100

n. 셀시우스가 발명한 온도 측정법 (섭씨) a. 섭씨의

The thermometer indicated 39.7 degrees Celsius.

온도계가 섭씨 39.7도를 가리키고 있었다.

09 **chilly** [tʃíli] unpleasantly cold

a. (날씨 등이) 차가운, 으스스한, 냉담한
chill n. 냉기, 쌀쌀함, 한기 | chilling a. 차가운, 냉담한

In spite of the chilly weather, I went to the hospital to see my grandmother.
차가운 날씨에도 불구하고, 나는 할머니를 보기 위해 병원에 갔다.

10 **climate** [kláimit, -mət] the normal weather in a particular area

n. 기후
climatic a. 기후의

The planet was endangered because of the extreme climate change.
급격한 기후 변화로 그 행성은 위험에 처해 있다.

11 **continent** [kántənənt] one of the main areas of land in the world

n. 대륙
continental a. 대륙의

Australia is the smallest continent and the big country itself.
오스트레일리아는 가장 작은 대륙이고, 그 자체가 커다란 나라이다.

12 **crust** [krʌst] the thick outside surface of the Earth

n. (지구의) 지각, 딱딱한 외피

We live in the building built on the crust.
우리는 지각 위에 지어진 건물에서 살고 있다.

13 current [kə́:rənt, kʌ́r-] a flow of water or air

n. 해류, 기류, 전류 a. 현재의, 통용되는
currently ad. 지금, 일반적으로

We can divide a current with a difference of its temperature.
온도의 차이로 해류를 구분할 수 있다.

14 drought [dráut] a long period without any rain

n. 가뭄
droughty a. 가뭄의, 모자라는

It hasn't dried up as badly as the drought last spring.
지난 봄 가뭄 때처럼 심하게 가물지는 않았다.

15 earthquake [ə́:rθkwèik] a violent movement of part of the Earth's surface

n. 지진, (사회적, 정치적) 대변동

An investigation committee has been sent there to measure the extent of the damage by this earthquake.
이번 지진으로 인한 피해의 정도를 측정하기 위해 조사단이 파견되었다.

16 equator [ikwéitər] an imaginary line around the middle of the Earth halfway between the North and South Poles

n. 적도
equatorial a. 적도에 가까운 ㅣ equation n. 방정식, 동일시

It is terribly hot near the equator.
적도 부근은 굉장히 덥다.

17 erode [iróud] to wear something away

vt. 침식하다, 부식시키다 vi. 부식되다
erosion n. 부식, (자연의 힘에 의한 토지 등의) 침식

An acid solution is powerful enough to erode everything.

산성용액은 모든 것을 부식시킬 수 있는 힘이 있다.

---

18 erupt [irʌ́pt] to burst out

vi. (화산 등이) 폭발하다, (감정 등을) 분출하다
eruption n. (화산 등의) 폭발

The volcano is possible to erupt again.

그 화산은 다시 폭발할 가능성이 있다.

---

19 extreme [ikstríːm] very great in degree and intensity

a. (성질, 상태 등이) 심한, 극도의, 극단적인
extremely ad. 대단히, 심하게, 몹시

They had no choice but to take such an extreme action.

그들은 그러한 극단적인 행동을 할 수밖에 없었다.

---

20 Fahrenheit [fǽrənhait] a system for measuring temperature in which water freezes at 32° and boils at 212°

n. 패런하이트가 발명한 온도 측정법 (화씨) a. (온도계의) 화씨의

The system of Fahrenheit is not used in Korea .

한국에서는 화씨온도를 쓰지 않는다.

21 **flood** [flʌd] a large amount of water covering an area

n. 홍수, (사람, 사물의) 쇄도 v. 범람시키다, 물속에 잠기게 하다
flooded a. 범람한, 물에 잠긴

Noah made his ark and then he stayed there during a period of the flood.
노아는 방주를 지어 홍수 기간 동안 그곳에 있었다.

22 **freeze** [fríːz] to turn into ice or become covered with ice

v. 얼다, 냉동시키다
frozen a. 얼음이 언, (식품이) 냉동의 | freezing a. 얼음이 어는 듯한, 몹시 추운

When thermometer is below zero, water will freeze.
온도계가 0° 이하로 내려가면 물이 언다.

23 **frost** [frɔ́ːst, fráːst] powdery ice that covers the ground in freezing weather

n. 서리, (서리가 맺는) 추위 v. 서리가 내리다

The farmers worried about their crops because of the last night's frost.
농부들은 지난밤 서리 때문에 농작물을 걱정했다.

24 **geography** [dʒiáɡrəfi] the study of the countries of the world and its climate, people, etc.

n. 지리학, 지리, 지형
geographical a. 지리(학)적인

Geography is her favorite subject.
그녀가 가장 좋아하는 과목은 지리학이다.

25 geology [dʒiɑ́lədʒi] the study of the Earth's crust and its layers

n. 지질학, (어느 지역의) 지질

A geologic formation survey is used to know more about Geology.

지질학에 대해 더 많이 알기 위해 지층 답사가 사용된다.

---

26 glacier [gléiʃər] a very large mass of ice that moves very slowly

n. 빙하

glacial a. 빙하의, (태도 등이) 냉담한 ∣ glaciate vt. 얼리다

As we went farther and farther, the graceful figure of the glacier kept being seen.

우리가 점점 더 멀어지면서 빙하의 멋진 모습이 계속 보였다.

---

27 harsh [hɑ́:rʃ] cruel or severe

a. 가혹한, 호된

harshly ad. 가혹하게, 호되게 ∣ harshen v. 거칠게 만들다

All the people in this country got a harsh lesson with this situation.

이 나라 국민들 모두는 이번 사태로 호된 교훈을 얻었다.

---

28 hemisphere [hémisfiər] one half of the earth

n. (지구 전체의) 반구

There are much more people in the North hemisphere than the South.

남반구보다는 북반구에 훨씬 더 많은 사람이 산다.

29 horizon [həráizn] the line where the sky appears to meet the land or sea

n. 지평선, 수평선
horizontal a. 가로의

The horizon that I saw today would ring in my heart for a long time.
오늘 본 지평선은 오랫동안 내 기억에 남을 것 같다.

30 humid [hjú:mid] damp, moist

a. (불쾌할 정도로) 습한
humidify v. 축축하게 하다 l humidity n. 습기, 습도

I have sometimes thought that I would get out of this humid room.
난 가끔 이 습한 방에서 나갈 생각을 한다.

31 indicate [índikèit] to be a sign or symbol of something

v. ~의 표시이다, 나타내다
indicator n. (신호의) 표시기 l indication n. 표시, 징후

I'm sorry that I couldn't recognize it as quickly as possible when it was indicated.
그 사건의 징후가 나타났을 때 빨리 파악하지 못한 것이 아쉽다.

32 liquid [líkwid] a substance such as water or oil that can flow

n. 액체 a. 액체의, 물 같은

Some liquid that had a fragrant odor was given to me.
향이 있는 액체가 내게 주어졌다.

33 **melt** [mélt] to turn something into liquid by heating it

v. (열로) 녹다, 녹이다
melting a. 녹는, (감정 등을) 누그러지게 하는

The shining sunlight is melting the snow that covered the street.

눈부신 햇살이 길을 덮었던 눈을 녹이고 있다.

34 **mild** [máild] gentle, not harsh or severe

a. (태도, 말 등이) 상냥한, (기후 등이) 온화한
mildness n. (태도, 말 등이) 상냥함, (기후 등이) 온화함

This country must be blessed to be mild like this.

이 나라는 이처럼 기후가 온화한 것을 보니 축복받았음에 틀림없다.

35 **moist** [mɔ́ist] slightly wet

a. 촉촉한, 습한
moisten v. 적시다 I moisture n. 습기, 수분

The constant rain made the land moist.

계속되는 비가 땅을 촉촉하게 만들었다.

36 **moonlight** [múːnlàit] the light that comes from the moon at night

n. 달빛, 월광 a. 달빛의, 야간의

A bird was preparing to fly up to the sky from the lake in the moonlight.

새 한 마리가 달빛에 물든 호수에서 날기 위해 준비 중이었다.

37 peninsula [pənínsjulə] a piece of land that is almost completely surrounded by water

n. 반도
peninsular a. 반도의

Any peninsula can only become a very important military spot.

어떤 반도라도 군사적 요충지가 될 수 밖에 없다.

38 phenomenon [fənámɪnən, -nən] a remarkable event or fact

n. 현상
phenomenal a. 자연현상의, 인지할 수 있는

They have to try hard to improve this phenomenon.

그들은 이 현상을 증명하기 위해 많은 노력이 필요하다.

39 pour [pɔ́ːr] to make a liquid flow out of a container; to rain heavily

v. 붓다, (비가) 내리퍼붓다

The nasty sky has been pouring rains for 3 hours.

얄미운 하늘은 3시간째 비를 퍼붓고 있다.

40 rainfall [réinfɔːl] the amount of rain that falls in a particular area

n. 강우량
rainy a. 비 오는 | raindrop n. 빗방울

Jang Young-Sil made the device for measuring rainfall in Korea for the first time.

장영실은 한국에서 처음으로 강우량을 측정하는 장치를 만들었다.

41 **solid** [sálid] hard or firm, with a fixed shape, not a liquid or a gas

a. 고체의 n. 고체
solidify v. 고체로 만들다

Water becomes solid in 0 degree of Celsius.
물은 섭씨 0도에서 고체가 된다.

42 **temperature** [témpərətʃər, -tʃúər] a measurement of how cold and hot a place is

n. 온도, 기온, 체온
temperate a. 절도 있는, (기후가) 온화한

The inside of the car kept rising in temperature.
차 내부 온도가 계속해서 올라갔다.

43 **tempest** [témpist] a very violent storm

n. 폭풍우, 폭설, 대소동   v. 몹시 사나워지게 하다, 소란을 일으키다

This harsh tempest killed 255 people in this area.
이번 강한 폭풍우로 이 지역에서 255명이 사망했다.

44 **thermometer** [θərmámətər] an instrument for measuring temperature

n. 온도계

This thermometer is very accurate without error.
이 온도계는 오차 없이 매우 정확하다.

45 tide [táid] the regular rising and falling of the sea

n. 조수(밀물과 썰물), 조수의 간만
tidal a. 조수의, (비유적) 주기적인

In this town, the mayor is trying to construct a powerhouse using the tide.

이 마을 시장은 조수 간만의 차를 이용하는 발전소를 건설하려 하고 있다.

46 tropic [trápik] the hottest part of the Earth

n. (the ~s) 열대지방
tropical a. 열대 (지방)의

Those fruits are imported from the tropics.

저 과일들은 열대 지방에서 수입한 것들이다.

47 typical [típikəl] being a characteristic or representitive example

a. 전형적인, 대표적인
typically ad. 전형적으로 I type n. 유형, 타입

An environmental pollution is a typical **problem of a developed country.**

환경오염은 선진국의 전형적인 고민거리이다.

48 vertical [və́ːrtikəl] going directly upwards

a. 수직의 n. 수직선
vertically ad. 수직으로

She always confuses a vertical **with a horizon.**

그녀는 항상 수직선과 수평선을 혼동한다.

49 **weather** [wéðər] the condition of the atmosphere at a particular time or place

n. 날씨 v. 비바람에 맞다, 풍화하다

You have to watch the weather **forecast in England.**

영국에서는 꼭 일기예보를 봐야 한다.

50 **zone** [zóun] a special distinct area

n. (특정) 지대, 지역

People must not build any building in a greenbelt zone.

그린벨트 지역에서는 어떤 건물도 지을 수 없다.

Check up

A 다음 각 문장에서 쓰인 의미를 고르시오.

1. The annual salaries which the manager opened to the public are not exact.

   a. happening or done once every year
   b. a book, especially one for children, that is published once a year, with the same title each time, but different contents

2. The scientist was killed in the blast.

   a. a sudden strong movement of air
   b. an explosion or a powerful movement of air caused by an explosion

3. Then, cut the crust off the bread.

   a. the hard outer surface of bread
   b. a hard layer of surface, especially above or around something

4. Current gum prices range between 500 won and 2,000 won.

   a. happening now; of the present time
   b. being used by or accepted by most people

5. It is expected that Waikite may one day erupt again.

  a. to start happening suddenly and violently break out

  b. the burning rocks, etc. are thrown out from the volcano.

B 알맞은 반대말끼리 연결하시오.

1. freeze •

2. harsh •

3. vertical •

4. typical •

5. indicate •

  • fine

  • contraindicate

  • boil

  • horizontal

  • atypical

Lesson 3

Environment & Contamination

| 환경과 오염

01 **accumulate** [əkjúːmjuleit] to collect or be gathered over a period of time

v. (장기간에 걸쳐 조금씩) 모으다, 축적하다, 모이다, 축적되다
accumulation n. 축적, 누적, 축적물
accumulative a. 축적하는, 누적적인, 적립식의

I seem to have accumulated a lot of books.
내가 책을 많이 모은 것 같다.

02 **aerial** [éəriəl] inhabiting, occurring in, or done in the air

a. 공기의, 대기의, (식물) 기생의

The captain tells the passengers that the aerial current affects the flight.
기장은 기류가 비행에 영향을 준다고 승객들에게 말한다.

03 **ashore** [əʃɔ́ːr] from the sea onto the shore; on the beach

ad. 물가에, 해변에, 육상에

The boy threw the letter in a bottle because he thought it would be taken ashore across the sea.
그 소년은 편지가 든 병이 바다를 건너 육지에 닿을 것이라 믿고 그것을 던졌다.

04 **atmospheric** [æ̀tməsférik, -sfíər-] related to the earth's atmosphere

a. 대기의, 공기의
atmosphere n. 대기, 공기, 분위기

The atmospheric pressure becomes lower with higher altitude.
고도가 높아질수록 기압은 낮아진다.

05 **avail** [əvéil] to be helpful or useful to someone

v. 이롭게 하다, 쓸모가 있다, 도움이 되다 n. 이익, 유용성, 효용
available a. 쓸모 있는, 도움이 되는, 이용 가능한

The action doesn't avail me at all.

그 행동은 나에게 아무런 도움이 되지 않는다.

06 **cricket** [kríkit] a small jumping insect that produces short, loud sounds by rubbing its wings together

n. 귀뚜라미

The chirping sound of a cricket means a rich harvest of that year.

귀뚜라미 우는 소리는 그 해의 풍년을 의미한다.

07 **damp** [dǽmp] slightly wet

a. 축축한, 습기 찬 n. 습기, 물기, 안개
dampen vt. 축축하게 하다

People feel angry easily in summer because the weather is hot and damp.

여름에는 덥고 습한 날씨 때문에 쉽게 짜증이 난다.

08 **decay** [dikéi] to be gradually destroyed by a natural process

v. 부식하다, 삭다, 썩다, 부패시키다 n. 부식, 쇠퇴, (방사성 물질의) 자연 붕괴

Keeping food in a fridge in summer prevents them from decaying.

여름에는 음식을 냉장 보관하는 것이 부패하는 것을 막아준다.

09 **descent** [disént] a movement from a higher to a lower level or position

n. 하강, 강하, 출신, 혈통, 몰락
descend v. 내려가다, 계통을 잇다, 전해지다

The crops were frozen by the sudden descent of the temperature.

갑작스런 기온 하강으로 농작물이 얼어버렸다.

10 **destruct** [distʌ́kt] to cause destruction; ruin, destroy

v. 파괴하다
destructive a. 파괴적인 | destruction n. 파괴

This project around the rivers may destruct an ecosystem.

강에 대한 이번 계획은 생태계를 파괴할 수도 있다.

11 **diary** [dáiəri] a book which has a separate space for each day of the year

n. 일기, 일지

All managers have to keep a daily diary.

모든 관리자들은 일지를 써야만 한다.

12 **disgusting** [disgʌ́stiŋ] criticizing it because it is extremely unpleasant

a. 메스꺼운, 역겨운
disgust n. 혐오감, 역겨움 v. 역겹게 하다

The sanitary landfill in that town was disgusting to smell.

그 마을의 쓰레기 매립장은 냄새가 역겨웠다.

13 **drench** [drént∫] to make something completely wet

v. 흠뻑 물에 적시다, 액체에 담그다 n. 흠뻑 젖음, 호우, 폭우
drencher n. 호수, 폭우

The dog was drenched with rain.

그 개는 비에 흠뻑 젖었다.

14 **dusty** [dʌ́sti] covered with earth or sand, usually because it has not rained for a long time

a. 먼지투성이의, 먼지가 많은, 생기 없는
dust n. 먼지, 흙먼지, 소란 v. (가루 따위를) 뿌리다

The strong wind made my car dusty.

강한 바람이 내 차를 먼지투성이로 만들었다.

15 **echo** [ékou] a sound which is caused by a noise being reflected off a surface like a wall

n. 메아리, 반향, 자취, 흔적 v. 울리다, 울려 퍼지다

Echoes that people make can be felt like a weapon to animals.

사람들의 메아리는 동물들에게는 무기로 느껴질 수 있다.

16 **extract** [ikstrǽkt, eks-] to obtain it from something else, for example by using industrial or chemical processes

v. 뽑다, 뽑아내다, 추출하다, 끌어내다 n. 추출물
extractive a. 추출할 수 있는 | extracted a. 추출한

The cosmetics extracted from this plant will be good for your skin and the environment.

이 식물에서 추출한 화장품은 피부와 환경에 좋을 것이다.

17 **flock** [flák] a group of things, especially animals

n. (양, 새 등의) 떼, 무리 v. 떼를 짓다, 모이다

A flock of birds that is flying together suggests that the season is changing.

무리 지어 날아가는 새 떼는 계절이 바뀌고 있음을 암시한다.

18 **grove** [gróuv] a group of trees that are close together

n. 작은 숲, 과수원

Almost all the apples in the grove fell down due to this heavy rain.

이번 폭우로 그 과수원의 사과 대부분이 떨어졌다.

19 **hedge** [hédʒ] a row of bushes or small trees, usually along the edge of a garden, field, or road

n. 산울타리, 울타리, 경계, 장벽 v. 에워싸다, (남의 자유 등을) 제한하다, 한정하다

The driver rushed to the hedge because he couldn't see at all due to rain.

그 운전사는 비 때문에 전혀 볼 수 없어서 울타리로 돌진했다.

20 **hillside** [hílsaid] the sloping side of a hill

n. 산허리, 구릉의 중턱

I feel sorry that the hillside of the mountain is getting bold.

산자락이 민둥산이 되고 있는 것이 안타깝다.

21 **investigation** [invèstəgéiʃən] an official examination of the facts about situation, crime, etc.

n. 조사, 수사, 연구, 연구 논문
investigate v. 조사하다, 수사하다, 연구하다 | investigator n. 조사관

The investigation about the river of that area is underway now.
그 지역의 강에 대한 조사가 지금 진행 중이다.

22 **lighthouse** [láithàus] a tower containing a powerful flashing lamp that is built on the coast or on a small island

n. 등대

It was too foggy to see the lighthouse.
등대가 보이지 않을 만큼 안개가 심했다.

23 **lumber** [lʌ́mbər] large pieces of wood that have been roughly cut up

n. 재목, 톱으로 켠 나무, 판재 v. (재목을) 벌채하다, 제재하다

The house built with lumber products harmonizes with the environment.
목재로 만든 집은 환경과 조화를 이룬다.

24 **maple** [méipl] a tree with five-pointed leaves which turn bright red or gold in autumn

n. 단풍나무, 단풍나무 재목, 담갈색

Many maples may live in a wet place.
단풍나무는 습기가 있는 곳에 많을 것이다.

25   marsh [má:rʃ]   a wet, muddy area of land

n. 늪, 습지(대)

The rain-fog in the marsh looks like a painting.

그 습지대의 물안개는 그림 같다.

26   mist [míst]   a large number of tiny drops of water in the air, which make it difficult to see very far

n. 안개, 가랑비, 이슬비   v. 안개로 덮다, 희미하게 하다, 안개가 끼다
misty a. 안개가 짙은, 안개 자욱한, 희미한

When the rain stopped, the place would be covered with
a mist.

비가 멈추면 그곳은 안개로 덮이곤 했다.

27   moor [múər]   an area of open and usually high land with poor soil

n. 황무지, 황야, 습지
moorish a. 황야의, 황야에 자라는

A writer says the crops that can make a moor fertile may
be beans.

어떤 작가는 황무지를 비옥하게 할 수 있는 작물이 콩이라고 말한다.

28   moss [mɔ́:s, más]   a very small soft green plant which grows on damp soil, or on wood or stone

n. 이끼 v. 이끼로 덮다

Mosses cannot live in a dry land.

이끼는 건조한 곳에서는 살 수 없다.

29 mound [máund] a large rounded pile

n. (고대 성의 폐허, 묘 등의) 흙무더기, 고문, 제방, 방죽 v. ~에 둑을 쌓다, 쌓아올리다

Mounds prevent the river from flowing over.

제방은 강이 넘치는 것을 막아준다.

30 mountainous [máuntənəs] having a lot of mountains

a. 산이 많은, 산지의, 거대한
mountain n. 산, 산악, 산지

Guerilla rains come frequently in the mountainous area.

산악지역에는 게릴라성 호우가 자주 온다.

31 noise [nɔ́iz] a loud or unpleasant sound

n. (특히 불쾌하고 비음악적인) 소리, 소음, 잡음 v. 소문 내다, 소리를 내다
noisy a. 시끄러운, 소음의

There are many ways to keep away the noise pollution.

소음공해를 막기 위한 방법은 여러 가지가 있다.

32 orchard [ɔ́ːrtʃərd] an area of land on which fruit trees are grown

n. 과수원, (과수원의) 과수

Farmers worry about the harmful insects that strike their orchards.

농부들은 그들의 과수원을 공격하는 해충들에 대해 고민하고 있다.

33 paradise [pǽrədàis, -daiz] a wonderful place where people go after they die, if they led good lives

n. 천국, 극락, 지상 낙원, 유원지

They felt like they were in paradise after breathing the fresh air.
그들은 신선한 공기를 마신 후 천국에 있는 기분이 들었다.

---

34 parallel [pǽrəlèl, -ləl] an imaginary line round the earth that is parallel to the equator

n. 위도선, 위선, 평행선 a. 평행의, 병렬의, 나란한 v. ~와 유사하다, ~와 평행하다

In the standard parallel, an accurate length appears.
표준위선에서는 정확한 길이가 투영된다.

---

35 pollution [pəlúːʃən] the process of polluting water, air, or land, especially with poisonous chemicals

n. 오염, 공해, 더러움
pollute v. 더럽히다, 오염시키다, 모독하다

They are trying hard to minimize environmental pollution.
그들은 환경오염을 최소화하려고 애쓰고 있다.

---

36 raindrop [réindrɑ̀p] a single drop of rain

n. 빗방울, 낙숫물

A rainbow in the evening means that there are plenty of raindrops in the east.
저녁 무지개는 동쪽에 빗방울이 많다는 뜻이다.

37	rake [réik]	a garden tool consisting of a row of metal or wooden teeth attached to a long handle

n. 갈퀴, 고무래, (고무래 모양의) 부지깽이 vt. 갈퀴질하다, 꼼꼼하게 찾다

Raking fallen leaves can prevent a fire.

낙엽을 긁어내는 것은 화재를 예방할 수 있다.

38	smog [smǽg, smɔ́:g]	a mixture of fog and smoke which occurs in some busy industrial cities

n. 스모그, 연무 v. 스모그로 덮다

So far we aren't damaged from smog in Korea.

우리나라는 아직까지 스모그에 피해를 입지는 않는다.

39	smoking [smóukiŋ]	the act or habit of smoking cigarettes, cigars, or a pipe

n. 흡연, 그을림, 연기가 남 a. 그을리는, 담배 피우는

As you know, smoking is very harmful for teenagers.

모두가 아는 것처럼, 흡연은 청소년들에게 매우 해롭다.

40	spray [spréi]	a lot of small drops of water which are being thrown into the air

n. 스프레이액, 분무기, 향수, 물안개 v. 물보라를 날리다, 소독액을 뿌리다, 물을 뿌리다

The sprays that many fashionable people use destroy an ozone layer.

패션에 관심 있는 많은 사람들이 사용하는 스프레이는 오존층을 파괴한다.

41 stain [stéin] to make things dirty, or make destoryed; to be colored or marked

v. 더럽히다, 훼손하다, 녹슬다 n. 얼룩, 때, 오점, 착색

Climbers who love mountains can stain them as they throw wastes away.

산을 좋아하는 등산객들은 쓰레기를 버림으로써 산을 훼손할 수도 있다.

42 sulfur [sʌ́lfər] a yellow chemical which has a strong smell

n. (유)황 a. 유황의, 유황빛의

Many laboratories are studying about using sulfur as fuel.

많은 연구소에서 연료로 유황을 이용하는 것에 대해 연구하고 있다.

43 swamp [swámp] an area of very wet land with wild plants growing on it

n. 늪, 습지 v. 늪에 빠지게 하다, 침수시키다

Studies about the swamp are progressing favorably.

습지에 관한 연구가 순조롭게 진행 중이다.

44 vapor [véipər] a mass of very small drops of liquid in the air

n. 증기, 수증기 v. 증발하다

The company found a way to create an electricity with vapor.

그 회사는 수증기를 이용하여 전기를 생성하는 방법을 발견했다.

45 vast [væst, vá:st] extremely large

a. 광대한, 광막한, (수, 양, 금액이) 막대한

It was like a waterdrop in a vast desert.

그것은 광대한 사막의 물 한 방울과 같았다.

46 ventilation [vèntəléiʃən] the state that allows fresh air to get into it

n. 통풍, 공기의 유통, 환기
ventilate vt. 환기하다

In summer, you had better focus on ventilation rather than air cooling.

여름에는 냉방보다는 통풍에 중점을 두는 것이 더 좋다.

47 westward [wéstwərd] towards the west

a. 서쪽으로 향하는, 서쪽의, 서부의
eastward a. 동쪽으로

We are driving in a westward direction.

우리는 서쪽으로 운전해 가고 있다.

48 wilderness [wíldərnəs] a desert or other area of natural land which is not used by people

n. 황무지, 황야, 미개지, 자연 보호 구역

Building structures are forbidden in the wilderness.

자연 보호 구역 내에서는 건축물 설립이 금지된다.

49 **windmill** [wíndmìl] a mechanical device operated by wind-driven sails

n. 풍차, 풍력 발전소 v. (풍차처럼) 회전시키다

Let's inspect carefully the principal of energy using the windmill.

풍차를 이용한 에너지의 원리를 살펴봅시다.

50 **woodland** [wúdlənd] land with a lot of trees

n. 삼림지, 삼림 지대

Lumbering is mostly performed in woodlands.

벌목은 거의 삼림 지대에서 행해진다.

Check up

A 우리말과 같은 뜻이 되도록 빈 칸에 주어진 철자로 시작되는 단어를 쓰시오.

1. The a＿＿＿＿＿＿ points may be redeemed at any time.

   누적된 포인트는 언제든지 사용이 가능하다.

2. The airplane did a＿＿＿＿＿ tricks such as flying upside-down.

   그 비행기는 거꾸로 비행하는 것과 같은 공중곡예를 선보였다.

3. They tried to persuade her to reverse his decision but to no a＿＿＿＿＿＿.

   그들은 그녀의 마음을 바꿔보려 설득했지만 아무런 소용도 없었다.

4. The low pressure from China clashed with the d＿＿＿＿＿ air from the south.

   중국에서 발생한 저기압이 남쪽에서 유입된 습윤한 공기와 만났다.

5. The bodies are d＿＿＿＿＿ and it's getting difficult to identify them.

   시신이 부패하면서 신원 확인이 더욱 어려워지고 있다.

B 주어진 표현에 해당하는 단어를 보기에서 고르시오.

| echo | marsh | disgusting | investigation | dusty |

1. _____ : foul, revolting, repulsive, offensive, gross

2. _____ : dirty, grubby, unclean, unswept

3. _____ : ring, ring out, reverberate, resound, resonate

4. _____ : survey, poll, enquiry, case, probe, inquest, check

5. _____ : swamp, wetland, bog

C 우리말은 영어로, 영어는 우리말로 바꾸시오.

1. mist

2. 평행선, 위도선, 위선

3. 파괴하다

4. pollution

5. mound

6. 더럽히다, 훼손하다, 녹슬다

7. 소리, 소음, 잡음

8. vapor

9. orchard

10. 황무지, 황야

Part 3

Science

[과학]

Lesson 1
Technology
| 기술

01 acceptable [əkséptəbl] agreed or approved of by most people in society

a. 받아들일 수 있는, 만족스러운, 마음에 드는
acceptance n. 수락, 승인, 수용 | accept v. 수락하다, 받아들이다

The development of this system will yield an acceptable result.

이 시스템의 개발이 만족스러운 결과를 낳을 것이다.

02 amend [əménd] to change something in order to improve it or make it more accurate

v. (행실 등을) 고치다, 개선하다, 수정하다
amendable a. 수정할 수 있는

The government amended the system of sharing information.

정부는 정보공유 시스템을 개선하였다.

03 artistic [ɑːrtístik] good at drawing or painting, or arranging things in a beautiful way

a. 정교한, 예술적인

The paintings show the artistic skills of the ancients.

그 그림들은 고대의 정교한 기술을 보여준다.

04 automatic [ɔːtəmǽtik] performing a task without needing to be constantly operated by a person

a. (기계, 장치 등이) 자동의, 자동식의, 기계적인
automation n. 자동화

An automatic fire extinguisher will be recalled because it is very inferior.

자동식 소화기가 매우 불량이라 리콜될 수도 있다.

05 **bind** [báind] to tie rope, string, tape, or other material around

v. 묶다, 포박하다, 매다, 둘러 감다

In a packaging company, the skill of binding goods is the most important.

포장회사에서는 제품을 묶는 기술이 가장 중요하다.

06 **binocular** [bənákjulər, bai-] an instrument, like two small telescopes fixed together, that makes objects that are far away seem nearer you look through it

n. 쌍안경, 쌍안 망원[현미]경

The binocular was very interesting, so I looked around through it.

망원경이 매우 흥미로워서 난 그것으로 주변을 둘러봤다.

07 **bronze** [branz] a yellowish-brown metal which is a mixture of copper and tin

n. 청동, 청동제품

A long time ago people made bronze mirrors.

옛날에는 사람들이 청동을 거울로 만들었다.

08 **cling** [klíŋ] to hold onto someone or something tightly

v. 달라붙다, 응집하다, 매달리다

These days the portal sites cling to a lot of information.

요즘에는 포털 사이트들이 많은 정보를 응집하고 있다.

09 **coffin** [kɔ́:fin, kǽf-] a box in which a dead body is buried or cremated

n. 관, 널, (옛 목판 인쇄기의) 판의 나무틀 v. 관에 넣다, 납관하다

They have a technique of putting meals in coffins.

그들은 통에 음식물을 넣는 기술을 보유하고 있다.

10 **commence** [kəméns] to begin or to start something

v. 개시하다, 시작하다, 착수하다

We finished the work a week after it had been commenced thanks to you.

우리는 여러분 덕분에 그 작업을 시작한 지 일주일 만에 완료했다.

11 **construction** [kənstrʌ́kʃən] the building of things such as houses, factories, roads, and bridges

n. 건설, 구조, 건물
construct v. 건설하다, 구성하다

The safety of the construction laborers is a matter of the highest priority.

건설 인부들의 안전이 최우선 사항이다.

12 **cooler** [kúːlər] a container for keeping things cool, especially drinks

n. 냉각기, 공기 조정 장치, 냉방 장치

A notebook cooler is a support that cools down temperature inside of the notebook.

노트북 냉각기는 노트북 내부의 온도를 낮춰 주는 보조품이다.

13 cork [cɔ́:rk]   a soft, light substance which forms the bark of a type of Mediterranean tree

n. 코르크, 코르크 마개

I relished the fume on the cork stained with wine.

나는 와인이 묻어 있는 코르크의 향을 음미했다.

14 crooked [krúkid]   being bent or twisted

a. 구부러진, 굴곡된, 기형의

Your nose may look crooked.

네 코는 휘어져 보인다.

15 ditch [dítʃ]   a long narrow channel cut into the ground at the side of a road or field

n. (보통 밭 등 관개용) 수로, 배수구   v. 도랑을 치다

No one knows the importance of the ditch before it is choked.

아무도 배수관이 막히기 전에는 그 중요성을 모른다.

16 enable [inéibl, en-]   to give someone permission or the right to do something

v. 허락[허용, 허가]하다

Developing the IT industry enables a comfortable life.

IT산업의 발전은 편안한 삶을 가능하게 한다.

17 equip [ikwíp] to give someone the tools or equipment that are needed

v. (~에게 필요한 것을) 갖추어 주다, 장비하다
equipment n. 장비, 용품

Our factory is equipped with modern conveniences.
우리 공장은 현대적 설비를 갖추고 있다.

18 evolution [èvəlúːʃən, ìːvə-] a process of gradual development in a particular situation or over a period of time

n. 진화, 발전, 발달
evolve v. 서서히 발전하다, 점진적으로 변화하다
evolutional a. 발전하는, 진화적인

The CEO has thought that the workers are the motive power of the evolution.
사장은 직원들이 발전의 원동력이라고 생각해 왔다.

19 exceed [iksíːd] to be greater or larger than that amount or number

v. (수, 양, 정도를) 넘다, 초과하다, 능가하다
excess n. 초과, 초과량, 과잉 | excessive a. 과도의, 지나친, 과대한

We exceeded the targeted level of the second quarter.
우리는 2사분기의 목표량을 초과했다.

20 exquisite [ikskwízit, ékskwizit] extremely beautiful or pleasant, especially in a delicate way

a. 정교한, 섬세한

The painters needed an exquisite touch to make the fantastic colors.
화가들은 환상적인 색을 만들기 위해 정교한 터치가 필요했다.

21 **handy** [hǽndi] skillful at using a particular tool; useful in a particular situation

a. 손재주 있는, 솜씨 좋은, 편리한
handily ad. 솜씨 있게, 편리하게, 수월하게

No one in the factory is as handy with the equipment as him.
공장에서 그만큼 그 장비를 잘 다루는 사람은 없다.

22 **hardware** [hɑ́ːrdwɛər] tools and equipment that are used in the home and garden

n. 철물, 금속 기구류

Keep the hardware away from water.
그 금속 기구는 물로부터 멀리 보관하시오.

23 **improvement** [imprúːvmənt] the process of improving

n. 개량, 개선, 향상
improve v. 개선하다, 증진하다, 나아지다

The production line brought the improvement in quality.
그 생산 라인이 품질의 향상을 가져왔다.

24 **invention** [invénʃən] the act of inventing something that has never been made or used before

n. 발명, 고안, 발명품
invent v. 발명하다, 창안하다 ㅣ inventive a. 발명의, 독창적인

Necessity is the mother of invention.
필요는 발명의 어머니이다.

25 microscope [máikrəskòup] a scientific instrument that produces a magnified image of small objects

n. 현미경

The invention of the microscope lets us know about 'Nano'.

현미경의 발명으로 '나노'에 대해 알게 되었다.

---

26 motionless [móuʃənlis] not moving at all

a. 움직이지 않는, 부동의, 정지한
motion n. 운동, 이동, 운행

Though he tried to avail the device, it was still motionless.

그는 그 장비를 이용하려고 했지만 움직이지 않았다.

---

27 pave [péiv] to cover with flat blocks of stone or concrete, so that it is suitable for walking or driving on

v. (길을) 포장하다, 덮다, 준비하다
pavement n. 포장, (도로) 포장

There are few paved roads leading to the base station.

기지국으로 가는 길에는 포장된 도로가 없다.

---

28 precaution [prikɔ́:ʃən] an action that is intended to prevent something dangerous or unpleasant from happening

n. 조심, 예방 조치, 사전 대책
caution n. 조심, 신중 vt. ~에게 경고하다

As a safety precaution, all the workers have to be educated.

안전 조치로서 모든 직원들은 교육을 받아야 한다.

29 prevail [privéil] to gain influence or be accepted, often after a struggle or argument

v. 보급되다, 유행하다, 효과를 나타내다, 우세하다
prevalent a. 일반적으로 행하여지는, 널리 퍼진

Now using a mobile phone prevails.
이제 휴대폰 사용은 보편화되어 있다.

30 progressive [prəgrésiv] advanced in outlook

a. (제도, 주의, 방침, 정책 등이) 진보적인, 혁신적인
progress n. 전진, 진보, 향상, 증가, 증대 vi. 전진하다, 진보하다

Only progressive companies will survive.
오직 혁신적인 회사만이 살아남을 것이다.

31 qualify [kwáləfai] to have the right to do something or have it

v. 면허[인가]를 받다, 자격을 얻다
qualification n. 자격 부여, 면허, 자격 증명서 ǀ disqualify vt. 자격을 박탈하다

The person who is qualified for this job will lead the team.
이 작업에 자격이 있는 사람이 그 팀을 맡을 것이다.

32 reconstruct [rìːkənstʌ́kt] to build something that has been destroyed or badly damaged, and to make it work again

v. 개조하다, 복구하다, 재건하다
construct vt. 건설하다

Many CEOs decided to reconstruct their companies.
많은 경영자들이 회사를 개조하기로 마음 먹었다.

33 **rust** [rʌ́st] to become covered in rust and often lose its strength

v. (금속 등이) 녹슬다, 부식하다, 못쓰게 되다 n. (금속의) 녹
rusty a. 녹슨

The rusted machines should be replaced with new ones.

녹이 슨 기계들은 새것으로 교체되어야 한다.

34 **screw** [skrú:] to twist something to fix it in place

v. 나사로 죄다, 고정시키다, 비틀다 n. 나사, 나사못, 볼트

A loosened screw caused the big problem.

느슨해진 나사 하나가 큰 문제를 초래한다.

35 **shipping** [ʃípiŋ] the transport of cargo as a business, especially on ships

n. (집합적) 선박, 적하, 선적
ship v. 수송하다, 실어나르다 n. 배, 선박

I couldn't contact the shipping business company.

나는 그 선박회사와 연락할 수 없었다.

36 **spiral** [spáiərəl] a shape which winds round and round, with each curve above or outside the previous one

n. 나선형, 소용돌이, 나선 용수철

We are putting our blood into the spiral that you ordered.

우리는 당신이 주문한 용수철 제품에 심혈을 기울이고 있다.

37 sophisticated [səfístəkèitid] clever and complicated in the way that it works or is presented

a. 세련된, 정교한, 복잡한

They're much more sophisticated **and much better than that.**

그것들은 저것보다 훨씬 더 정교하고 좋다.

38 split [splít] to divide something into two or more parts

v. 분열[분리]시키다, (이익, 비용 등을) 나누다, 분배하다 n. 분열, 파편, 조각, 균열

We can't use this wood because it splits **easily.**

이 나무는 잘 쪼개져서 우리는 사용할 수 없다.

39 steamer [stí:mər] a ship or a machine that has an engine powered by steam

n. 증기 기관, 증기로 움직이는 것, 기선
steam n. 김, 증기, 수증기 v. 증기를 내뿜다

The invention of the steamer **increased industrial output.**

증기의 발명으로 공업 생산량이 증가했다.

40 substance [sʌ́bstəns] a solid, powder, liquid, or gas with particular properties

n. 물질, 재질, 재료
substantial a. 물질의, 물질적인, 본질적인, 많은
substantiate v. 실체[구체]화하다, 구현시키다

Explosive substances **should be kept away from sparks.**

폭발 물질은 스파크로부터 떨어져서 보관되어야 한다.

41 **technologic** [tèknəláːdʒik] relating to or associated with technology

a. 과학 기술의, (생산) 기술 혁신으로 인한
technology n. 과학 기술

Developing countries can grow very successfully with technologic innovation.

개발도상국들은 기술 혁신으로 성공할 수 있다.

42 **telegraph** [téligræf, -gràːf] a system of sending messages using radio or electrical signals

n. 전신, 전보 v. 전보를 치다

Please send me the bill by telegraph.

전신으로 어음을 보내주세요.

43 **thrive** [θraiv] to become, and continue to be, successful, strong, healthy, etc.

v. 번영하다, 무성해지다
thriving a. 번화한, 무성한, 번성하는

Our company continues to thrive these days.

요즘 우리 회사는 날로 번성하고 있다.

44 **thorough** [θə́ːrou, θʌrə] including every possible detail

a. 철저한, 완전한, 충분히 숙달된
thoroughly ad. 완전히, 철저히

The company succeeded in a thorough reform.

그 회사는 완전한 개혁에 성공했다.

45   **toil** [tɔil]   to work very hard doing unpleasant or tiring tasks

v. 힘써 일하다, 수고하다, 고생하다 n. 노고, 수고, 노역

After the mass dismissal, workers toiled hard to survive.
집단 해고 후, 근로자들은 살아남기 위해 열심히 일했다.

46   **transform** [trænsfɔ́ːrm]   to change or convert something into something else

v. 변형시키다, (성질, 기능, 용도 등을) 바꾸다

A scientist found out how to transform electricity into mechanical energy.
한 과학자가 전기를 기계 에너지로 바꾸는 방법을 알아냈다.

47   **veteran** [vétərən]   someone who has been involved in a particular activity for a long time

n. 노련가, 경험 많은 대가, 노병 a. 노련한, 많은 경험을 쌓은

Our department needs a veteran like you.
우리 부서는 당신과 같은 베테랑이 필요하다.

48   **weave** [wiːv]   to make cloth or a carpet by crossing threads over and under each other using a frame or machine called a loom

v. 천을 짜다, 조립하다

People are forgetful that mothers wove cloth out of thread for their family.
사람들은 어머니들이 가족을 위해서 실로 천을 짰던 것을 잊고 있다.

49 whirl [*hwə́:rl*] to move around or turn around very quickly

v. 빙글빙글 돌리다, 소용돌이치게 하다 n. 회전
whirlpool n. 소용돌이

The electric power can be gathered as the pinwheel
whirls in the breeze.

바람개비가 바람에 돌면서 전기를 모을 수 있다.

---

50 wireless [wáiərlis] using radio waves rather than electricity without any wires

a. 무선의, 무선 전신[전화]의
wire n. 철사, 전선 v. 전보를 치다, 전송하다

Today we can make a call to our friends using a wireless
microphone.

오늘날 우리는 무선 마이크를 이용해 친구와 통화를 할 수 있다.

Check up

A 문맥상 적절한 것을 고르시오.

1. She wanted to (amend/worsen) for the damage that she had caused.

2. My mother wants to buy an (autograph/automatic) machine for cleaning.

3. You should (bind/bounce) a blue string to a white box.

4. They are (clip/cling) to old customs despite living in modern society.

5. It's not legal, reselling a (coffin/coffee).

B 알맞은 단어를 골라 관용어를 완성하시오.

| pave | screw | handy | cork | ditch | commence |
| equip | split | construction | microscope | | |

1. be driven to the last _____ : 궁지에 몰리다

2. put ~ under the _____ : (사람, 사물을) 자세히 조사하다

3. be _____ with gold : 성공하기 쉽다

4. a _____ loose : 느슨해진 나사, 고장, 결함

5. _____ firing! : 사격 개시!

6. come in _____ : 여러모로 편리하다, 곧 쓸 수 있다

7. _____ hairs : 사소한 것에 지나치게 신경을 쓰다

8. _____ oneself : 준비하다, 채비하다

9. blow one's _____ : 울화통을 터뜨리다

10. put a _____ on : ~을 해석하다

C 빈 칸에 들어갈 단어를 보기에서 골라 알맞은 형태로 넣으시오.
  (변형가능)

| transform | toil | weave | wireless | telegraph |

1. We'll learn about sending a message by _____.

2. My mother used to _____ a sweater for us.

3. It's possible to _____ cars into robots in the movie.

4. You have gotten mental stress as well as physical _____.

5. They gave information about the war by _____.

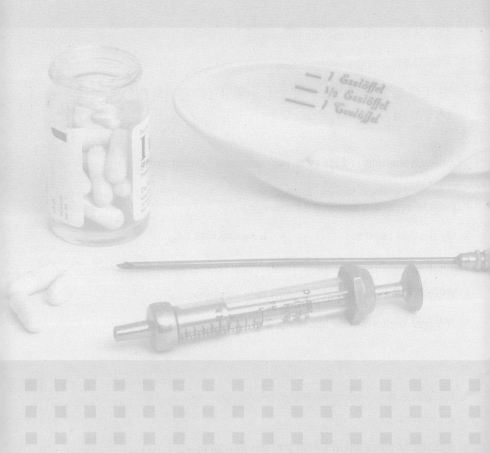

Lesson 2
Medical Science
| 의학

01 **abuse** [əbjúːs] the use of something in a way that is wrong or harmful

n. 남용, 오용, 악용 v.남용하다, 학대하다

She had a long history of drug abuse.

그녀는 오랜 약물 남용 병력이 있다.

02 **acute** [əkjúːt] very serious or severe

a. 격렬한, 예리한, 심각한

Suddenly I felt acute pains in my stomach.

갑자기 배에서 심한 고통을 느꼈다.

03 **adverse** [ǽdvəːrs] negative and unpleasant; not likely to produce a good result

a. 거스르는, 반대의
adversiry n. 불운, 불행, 역경

This drug is known to have adverse side effects.

이 약물은 좋지 않은 부작용이 있는 것으로 알려져 있다.

04 **allergic** [əlɔ́ːrdʒik] suffering from an allergy

a. 알레르기의, 알레르기가 있는
allergy n. 과민증, 알레르기

I am allergic to cats.

나는 고양이 알레르기가 있다.

05 artificial [ɑ̀:rtəfíʃəl] created by people; not happening naturally

a. 인공적인, 인공의 n. 인공물
artificially ad. 인위적으로, 부자연스럽게

He has an artificial **leg on his left.**
그는 왼쪽 다리에 의족을 하고 있다.

06 bloody [blʌ́di] covered in a lot of blood

a. 피투성이의, 유혈의, 혈액을 함유한

A man had bloody **nose continuously, so he went to the hospital.**
한 남자가 계속해서 코피가 나서 병원에 왔다.

07 cause [kɔ́:z] the thing or person that makes an event, usually a bad event happen

n. 원인, 원인이 되는 사람[것] v. ~의 원인이 되다, 야기하다

Till now scientist has found the root cause **of the common cold.**
지금까지 어떤 과학자도 감기의 근본적인 원인을 찾지 못했다.

08 cell [sél] the smallest part of an animal or plant that is able to function independently

n. 세포, (조직 내의) 공동부 v. ~와 한방을 쓰다

The disease originates from lack of white blood cells.
그 질병은 백혈구의 부족으로 생기는 병이다.

09 **clone** [kloun] an animal or a plant produced by scientists from one cell of another animal or plant, so that they ar exactly the same

n. 복제품, 클론, 복제(생물)

We are not trying to create clones.

우리는 복제품을 만들려고 하지 않는다.

10 **chronic** [kránik] lasting for a long time; difficult to cure or get rid of

a. 장기간에 걸친, 만성적인
chronicle n. 기록, 연대기 ㅣ chronicity n. 만성

Chronic **stress can lead to heart attack.**

만성적인 스트레스는 심장 발작을 유발할 수 있다.

11 **combination** [kàmbənéiʃən] a mixture of things

n. 결합, 접합, 결합된 것
combinational a. 결합된, 조합이 된

The combination **of smoking and drinking must cause the disease.**

흡연과 음주를 병행하면 병을 얻을 것이다.

12 **conscious** [kánʃəs] aware of something; noticing something

a. 의식하고 있는, 지각이 있는
unconscious a. 모르는, 의식[정신]을 잃은

She was only half conscious **because of high fever.**

그녀는 고열로 정신이 혼미해졌다.

13 **continue** [kəntínju:] to keep doing something and do not stop

v. 계속되다, 연속되다, 연장되다
continuous a. 계속되는, 지속되는

The emergency surgery continued **again.**

(중단되었던) 그 응급수술은 다시 계속되었다.

14 **depend** [dipénd] to rely on something or someone

v. (원조 등에) 의존하다, (형편이나 상황에) 좌우되다
dependent a. 의지하는, ~에 따른

Regaining your health depends **on your family's care.**

당신의 건강 회복 여부는 가족의 돌봄에 달렸다.

15 **DNA** an acid in the chromosomes in the center of the cells of living things

n. 디옥시리보 핵산 (유전 정보를 가진 세포핵, 염색체 기초물질)

Many reports tell that each person's pattern of DNA **is unique.**

DNA패턴이 개인마다 다르다는 많은 보고가 있다.

16 **dose** [dóus] a measured amount of medicine or a drug which is intended to be taken at one time

n. (약의) 1회 복용량, 한첩 v. (약을) ~에게 복용시키다, 투약하다, 약을 먹다

Never take a large dose **of any medicine.**

어떤 약이든 많이 섭취하지 마시오.

17 **feeble** [fí:bl] physically or mentally weak

a. (신체적으로) 약한, 연약한, (지능이) 낮은, 저능의
enfeeble vt. 약화시키다 | feebly ad. 약하게, 힘없이, 희미하게

Feeble **old people can be hurt easily.**

허약한 노인들은 쉽게 다칠 수 있다.

18 **fiber** [fáibər] a thread like substance or structure as a muscle cell or fine root

n. (신경, 근육 따위의) 섬유질[조직]

When a muscular fiber **is hurt, protein can replace it.**

근육의 섬유질 조직이 손상되면 단백질이 그것을 보충할 수 있다.

19 **gene** [dʒí:n] the part of a cell which controls a particular quality in a living thing that passed on its parents

n. 유전자, 유전인자

Maybe gene **manipulation makes a new creature with only dominant** genes.

유전자 조작으로 우성인자만을 가진 생물이 탄생할지 모른다.

20 **heal** [hí:l] to cure someone who is sick; to make someone feel happy again

v. 고치다, 낫게 하다

It should heal **about 3 weeks.**

그것은 3주면 나을 것이다.

21 **hospitalization** [hὰspitəlizéiʃən] a period of placing in a hospital as a patient

n. 입원, 입원 기간
hospitalize v. 입원시키다

In spite of his opposition, he couldn't avoid hospitalization.
그의 반항에도 불구하고, 입원은 피할 수 없었다.

22 **insomnia** [insάmniə] a symptom to make it difficult to sleep

n. (특히 만성적인) 불면, 불면증

A cup of warm milk can treat insomnia.
따뜻한 우유 한잔이 불면증을 고칠 수 있다.

23 **inspection** [inspékʃən] an act of viewing closely and critically

n. (면밀한) 조사, 검사, (서류 따위의) 열람
inspect v. 면밀하게 살피다, 점검[검사]하다 I inspector n. 검사관, 검열관

All of the workers have to undergo a medical inspection.
모든 직원들은 건강 진단을 받아야 한다.

24 **insurance** [inʃúərəns] an arrangement with a company in which you pay them regular amount of money and they agree to pay the costs

n. 보험, 보험료
insure v. 보험에 들다, 보증하다

She doesn't worry about the medical fee because she has health insurance.
그녀는 건강 보험에 가입되어 있기 때문에 병원비에 대해 걱정하지 않는다.

25 **lung** [lʌŋ] the two organs inside your chest which fill with air when you breathe in

n. 폐, 허파, 인공폐[호흡장치]

A common cold grew to be inflammation of the lungs.
감기가 발전해 폐렴이 되었다.

26 **medication** [mèdəkéiʃən] medicine that is used to treat and cure illness

n. 약물 치료[처리], 투약, 의약, 약물
medicated a. 의약용의

The patient is on medication.
그 환자는 약물 치료를 받고 있다.

27 **medicine** [médəsin] the treatment of illness and injures by doctors and nurses

n. 의학, 의술, (외과, 산과와 구별하여) 내과 의학, 약
medicinal a. 약의, 건강에 좋은

Every doctor has a license to practice medicine.
모든 의사는 의사 개업 면허를 소유하고 있다.

28 **nerve** [nə́:rv] a part inside human's body which look like thread and carry messages between the brain and other parts of the body

n. 신경, 신경 섬유, 치신경, 신경 과민
nerval a. 신경의 ｜ nervous a. 불안해하는, 신경이 과민한

The visual nerve was so tired that the doctor recommended a sound sleep.
시신경이 매우 지쳐 있어서 그 의사는 숙면할 것을 권했다.

29 painful [péinfəl] causing you a lot of physical pain

a. (상처, 몸의 국소가) 아픈, (수술, 병 따위가) 아픔을 수반하는
pain n. 아픔, 고통 vt. 괴롭히다

Every patient asks if the operation is painful.

모든 환자는 수술이 아픈지 물어본다.

30 pale [péil] looking lighter or whiter than usual, usually because someone is ill, frightened or shocked

a. (얼굴이) 창백한, 핏기 없는

She looked pale **and got absentminded when she got here.**

그녀가 이곳에 왔을 땐 창백해 보였고 넋을 잃고 있었다.

31 paralyze [pǽrəlàiz] to make someone lose the ability to move part or all of body

v. 마비시키다, 쓸모 없게 만들다
paralysis n. 마비, 무력 ｜ paralytic a. 무력한

The effect of the drug on our body is to paralyze **the nerves.**

그 약의 효과는 신경을 마비시키는 것이다.

32 pill [píl] a small solid piece of medicine that you swallow whole

n. 알약, 환약

On the envelope, it shows when you should take these pills.

봉투에는 언제 이 알약을 복용해야 하는지 적혀 있다.

33 prescription [priskrípʃən] the piece of paper on which your doctor writes an order for medicine

n. (의사가 약사에게 써 주는) 처방, 처방약
prescribe v. 처방하다, 처방전을 쓰다

The doctor examined the patient, and wrote a prescription.

그 의사는 환자를 진찰한 뒤 처방전을 써주었다.

---

34 recover [rikʌ́vər] to become well again from an illness or an injury

v. (건강, 의식 등을) 회복하다, 회복시키다
recovery n. 회복

He has to be in hospital until he recovers.

그는 회복할 때까지 입원해야 한다.

---

35 remedy [rémədi] a successful way of dealing with a problem

n. 치료, 요법, 치료약 v. (병, 상처 등을) 치료하다, 고치다
remediable a. 치료할 수 있는, 구제할 수 있는

He realized the efficacy of the remedy.

그는 약의 효능을 실감했다.

---

36 resemble [rizémbl] to be similar to each other

v. ~을 닮다, ~와 공통점이 있다
resemblance n. 유사점, 닮음 | resemblant a. 닮은, 유사한

These pills resemble each other, but you have to distinguish each pill's use.

이 알약들은 서로 비슷하지만 각각의 효능을 구별해야 한다.

37 shortage [ʃɔ́ːrtidʒ] state of being not enough of something

n. 부족, 결핍
short a. 부족한, 결핍의 ǀ shorten v. 줄이다, 짧게 하다

Several vitamins shortages **cause serious diseases.**
여러 비타민의 결핍으로 심각한 질병을 유발할 수 있다.

38 side effect [sáid ifèkt] an extra and usully bad effect that a drug has on you, as well as curing illness or pain

n. (약물 등의) 부작용

The pharmaceutical company claims that the medicine must have no side effects.
그 제약회사는 그 약은 부작용이 없을 것이라고 주장한다.

39 stimulate [stímjulèit] to encourage something to begin or develop further

v. 자극하다, 활기를 띠게 하다
stimulation n. 자극, 흥분, 격려 ǀ stimulating a. 자극적인

His doctor said that a remedial exercise would stimulate **the circulation of the blood.**
그의 주치의는 재활운동이 혈액순환을 원활하게 할 것이라고 말했다.

40 suction [sʌ́kʃən] the process by which liquids, gases, or other substances are drawn out of somewhere

n. 빨기, 빨아들임, 흡입관
suck v. 빨다, 빨아 마시다

A suction **pipe that we use in a human body is kept clean.**
인체에 사용하는 흡입기는 청결을 유지되고 있다.

41 **surgery** [sə́:rdʒəri] medical treatment in which a surgeon cuts open body to repair or remove something inside

n. 외과적 처치, (외과) 수술, 외과

surgical a. 외과의, 수술상의 | surgeon n. 외과의사

Small cancers may be removed through simple surgery.

작은 암은 간단한 수술로 제거될 수 있다.

42 **symptom** [símptəm] a change in your body or mind that shows that you are not healthy

n. 징후, 증상

Many specialists advise that a fever must be a symptom **of illness.**

많은 전문가들은 열은 병의 징후라고 충고한다.

43 **tablet** [tǽblit] a small solid mass of medicine which you swallow

n. (약학에서) 정제

Children prefer tablets **to powdered medicines.**

아이들은 가루약보다 알약을 더 좋아한다.

44 **take** [téik] to eat, drink, etc. something

v. (약을) 복용하다, (음식을) 먹다

You must follow the description and take **it 30 minutes after each meal.**

식후 30분 후에 복용하라는 지시를 따라야 한다.

45 thoroughly [θə́:rouli] completely and perfectly

ad. 완전히, 철저히, 순전히
thorough a. 철저한, 완전한

This is the medical machine that checks out a patients' brain thoroughly.

이것은 환자의 뇌를 정밀 검사할 수 있는 의료기기이다.

46 unique [juːníːk, ju-] being the only one of kinds of something

a. 유일한, 대신할 것이 없는

In Korea, the doctor is the unique **specialist of heart disease.**

한국에서, 그 의사는 심장병에 대해서는 유일무이한 전문가이다.

47 vaccinate [vǽksənèit] to give a person or an animal a vaccine, in order to protect them against a disease

v. ~에게 백신 접종을 하다
vaccine n. 백신

It is far easier to vaccinate **cattle.**

소에게 백신 접종하는 것이 훨씬 쉽다.

48 vital [váitl] necessary for keeping one's life

a. 생명의, 생명 유지에 필요한

Contributing vital **organs of own body is not easy.**

자기 신체의 중요 기관을 기증하는 것은 쉬운 일이 아니다.

49 vitamin [vaítəmi(:)n] a chemical substance in food that is necessary for good health

n. 비타민

To take a lot of vitamin C is good for a cold.

비타민 C를 복용하는 것이 감기 증상에 좋다.

50 within [wiðín, wiθ-] inside time or a boundary, or surrounded by it

prep. (시간, 한계 등) ~이내의, ~의 범위 내에서

They say that you have to visit the nearest hospital within an hour when you feel a pain in your ears.

귀에 통증이 느껴지면 한 시간 이내로 가까운 병원을 방문하라고 그들은 말한다.

Check up

A 다음 빈 칸에 가장 알맞은 것을 고르시오.

1. Are you _____ to any medication?

 a. carsick   b. conscious   c. allergic   d. headache   e. crick

2. Atmospheric _____ dioxide warms things up a bit.

 a. oxygen   b. electricity   c. water   d. wind   e. carbon

3. A flu _____ has infected everyone in the classroom.

 a. DNA   b. pill   c. virus   d. satellite   e. feeble

4. He is on _____ for high blood pressure.

 a. prescription   b. antibiotic   c. injection
 d. medication   e. allergy

5. She looks a little _____ because of her disease.

 a. pale   b. healthy   c. smart   d. lonely   e. brave

B 다음 단어의 반의어를 고르시오.

1. vital **signs**

a. essential　　b. unnecessary　　c. critical　　d. indispensable

2. a unique **hero**

a. common　　b. special　　c. distinctive　　d. peculiar

3. stimulation **therapy**

a. arouse　　b. stir　　c. inspire　　d. stifle

4. recover **consciousness**

a. get better　　b. heal　　c. recuperate　　d. deteriorate

5. a painful **wound**

a. sore　　b. painless　　c. traumatic　　d. distressing

Lesson 3
Aerospace

|우주과학

01   **alien** [éiljən, -liən]   a creature from another world

a. 외국의, 외계의 n. 외계인, 우주인, 이방인

Do you think what you saw was an alien craft?

당신이 본 게 외계 우주선이라고 생각해요?

02   **asteroid** [ǽstərɔ̀id]   one of the very small planets that move around the sun between Mars and Jupiter

n. 소행성

Asteroids will hit the Earth.

소행성이 지구와 충돌할 것이다.

03   **black hole** [blǽk hóul]   an area in space that nothing, not even light, can escape from, because of gravity

n. 블랙홀

A black hole swallows other planet and anything around it .

블랙홀은 다른 행성과 주변의 모든 것을 삼켜 버린다.

04   **blast** [blǽst]   an explosion or a powerful movement of air caused by an explosion

n. 폭발, 센 바람, 돌풍, 폭풍 v. 망쳐 버리다, 폭파하다

27 schoolchildren were injured in the blast.

그 폭발 사고로 초등학생 27명이 다쳤다.

05 cosmology [kɑzmάlədʒi]   the scientific study of the universe and its origin and development

n. 우주론
cosmologic a. 우주론의

He is a leader in the fields of physics and cosmology.
그는 물리학과 우주론 분야의 선도자입니다.

06 cosmos [kάzməs]   the universe, especially when it is thought of as an ordered system

n. 우주, 질서, 조화
chaos n. 혼돈, 무질서

No one knows exactly how old the cosmos was.
아무도 우주의 나이가 얼마인지 정확히 알지 못한다.

07 crater [kréitər]   a round hole in the ground made by something that has fallen on it

n. 분화구

A meteor hit the earth and made a huge crater.
운석이 지구에 떨어져서 큰 분화구가 생겼다.

08 cycle [sáikl]   the fact of a series of events being repeated many times, always in the same order

n. 순환, 주기
cyclic a. 순환하는

The universe repeats the cycle of creation and extinction.
우주는 생성과 소멸의 순환을 반복한다.

09 **dense** [déns]   containing a lot of people, things, plants, etc. with little space between them

a. 밀집한, 빽빽한
density n. 밀도, 농도

A dense fog rolled over the city.
짙은 안개가 도시를 뒤덮었다.

10 **distance** [dístəns]   the amount of space between two places or things

n. 거리, 먼 거리
distant a. (거리가) 먼, 떨어진

The distance between the Earth and Mars is much more far than that of Earth and Venus.
지구와 화성 사이의 거리가 지구와 금성 사이의 거리보다 훨씬 더 멀다.

11 **Earth** [əːrθ]   the world; the planet that we live on

n. 지구, 대지, 흙

The earth moves around the sun.
지구는 태양의 주위를 공전한다.

12 **enormous** [inɔ́ːrməs, e-]   extremely large

a. 거대한
enormously ad. 막대하게, 엄청나게

The astronauts discovered an enormous underground chamber.
우주인들은 거대한 지하공간을 발견했다.

13 **exploration** [èkspləréiʃən] the act of travelling through a place in order to find out about it

n. 답사, 탐구
explore v. 탐험하다

The spaceship was sent to Mars for the purpose of exploration.

그 우주선은 화성을 탐사하기 위해 보내졌다.

14 **explorer** [iksplɔ́ːrər] a person who travels to unknown places in order to find out more about them

n. 탐험가

The ancient ruin was discovered by the explorer.

그 고대 유적은 탐험가에 의해서 발견되었다.

15 **heaven** [hévən] the place believed to be the home of God where good people go when they die

n. 하늘, 천국
heavenly a. 천국의

They call stars as the eyes of heaven.

그들은 별을 하늘의 눈이라고 부른다.

16 **infinite** [ínfənət] without limits; without end

a. 무한한
infinitely ad. 무한하게

We don't know the universe is infinite or not.

우리는 우주가 무한한지 어떤지 알지 못한다.

17   jet [dʒét]   a plane driven by jet engines

n. 제트기

Jet planes cruise at 600 miles per hour.

제트기는 시속 600마일의 속도로 비행한다.

18   Jupiter [dʒúːpətər]   the largest planet of the solar system, fifth in order of distance from the sun

n. 목성

Jupiter protects the Earth from falling away from the solar system.

목성은 지구가 태양계에서 떨어져 나가는 것을 막아 준다.

19   laboratory [lǽbərətɔ̀ːri]   a room or building used for scientific research, experiments, testing, etc.

n. 실험실

laboratorial a. 실험실의

The samples are sent to the laboratory for analysis.

샘플들은 분석을 위해 실험실로 보내진다.

20   lighten [láitn]   to become or make something become brighter or lighter in color

v. 가볍게 하다, 밝게 하다, 밝아지다

light a. 밝은, 연한 n. 빛, 불꽃

The sky began to lighten in the east.

동녘 하늘이 밝아 오기 시작했다.

21 **magnet** [mǽgnit] a piece of iron that attracts objects made of iron towards it, either naturally or because of an electric current that is passed through it

n. 자석
magnetic a. 자석의

Same poles of the magnet repel each other.

자석은 같은 극끼리는 서로 밀어낸다.

22 **Mars** [má:rz] the planet in the solar system that is fourth in order of distance from the sun

n. 화성
Martian n. (SF 소설 등의) 화성인

Mars is especially well known as a red-looking planet.

화성은 유난히 붉게 보이는 행성으로 유명하다.

23 **material** [mətíəriəl] a substance that things can be made from

n. 물질 a. 물질의, 물질적인
materially ad. 실질적으로, 물질적으로

The spaceship stopped by the planet to collect materials.

우주선이 자료를 수집하기 위해 행성에 잠시 착륙했다.

24 **Mercury** [mə́:rkjəri] the smallest planet in the solar system, nearest to the sun

n. 수성

Mercury is the nearest planet to the sun in solar system.

수성은 태양계에서 태양에 가장 가까이 있는 행성이다.

25 **meteor** [míːtiər, -tiɔ́ːr] a piece of rock from outer space that makes a bright line across the night sky as it burns up while falling through the earth's atmosphere

n. 유성, 유성체, 운석
meteoric a. 유성의

I prayed to the falling meteor.

나는 떨어지는 유성에 기도했다.

26 **Milky Way** [mílki wéi] the pale white band of stars that can be seen across the sky at night

n. 은하수, 은하계

A Greek said that the Milky Way was made of many stars.

은하수는 수많은 별들로 이루어져 있다고 한 그리스인이 말했다.

27 **mysterious** [mistíəriəs] strange and not known about something

a. 신비한, 불가사의한, 확실하지 않은
mystery n. 신비, 비밀, 미스테리

For the future, we tried to find out the secrets of the mysterious universe.

미래를 위해, 우리는 신비한 우주의 비밀을 밝히려 노력하고 있다.

28 **Neptune** [néptjuːn] a planet in the solar system that is 8th in order of distance from the sun

n. 해왕성

They thought that the Neptune was a very silent and cold planet because of the distance from the Sun.

해왕성은 태양과의 먼 거리 때문에 차갑고 조용한 행성이라고 생각했다.

29 **object** [ábdʒikt, -dʒekt]   a thing that can be seen and touched, but is not alive

n. 물건, 물체
objective a. 객관적인, 사실에 근거한 n. 목적, 목표

The objects in space float like a feather.

우주에서 물체들은 깃털처럼 떠다닌다.

---

30 **observatory** [əbzə́ːrvətɔ̀ːri]   a special building from which scientist watch the moon, stars, weather, etc.

n. 관측소, 천문대
observation n. 관찰, 관측 | observance n. (법률 등의) 준수

In this observatory, you can observe a solar eclipse regardless of weather.

여러분은 이 천문대에서 날씨에 상관없이 일식을 관찰할 수 있다.

---

31 **orbiting** [ɔ́ːrbitiŋ]   moving around a planet, moon or sun in a continuous curving path

a. 궤도를 선회하는
orbit n. 궤도

Some artificial satellites are orbiting regularly.

어떤 인공위성은 규칙적으로 궤도를 선회한다.

---

32 **planet** [plǽnət]   a large, round object in space that moves around a strar

n. 행성, 유성
planetary a. 행성의

Experts say that Mars is the planet in which creatures cannot live.

전문가들은 화성은 생명체가 살 수 없는 행성이라고 말한다.

33 Pluto [plúːtou] the planet in the solar system that is furthest from the sun

n. 명왕성

At first, Pluto was also authorized as a planet.

처음에는, 명왕성도 행성으로 인정되었다.

---

34 revolve [riválv] to go in a circle around the central point

v. (천체가) 공전하다, 선회하다, 회전하다

revolving a. 회전하는

A satellite comes to revolve because of a magnet called a planet.

위성은 행성이라 불리는 자석 때문에 공전하게 된다.

---

35 rotate [róuteit] to move or turn around a central fixed point

v. 회전하다

rotation n. 회전

Days and nights occur as the Earth rotates on its axis.

낮과 밤은 지구가 그 축을 따라 자전하면서 생겨난다.

---

36 Saturn [sǽtərn] a large planet in the solar system that has rings around it and is 6th in order of distance from the sun

n. 토성

The atmosphere of Saturn is made up of hydrogen and helium gas mainly.

토성의 대기는 주로 수소와 헬륨으로 이루어져 있다.

37 scientific [sàiəntífik] involving science; connected with science

a. 과학의, 과학적인

science n. 과학

Traveling to space is the result of scientific studies.

우주로의 여행은 과학적 연구의 결과물이다.

38 shuttle [ʃʌtl] a spacecraft that is designed to travel into space and back to earth several times

n. 우주왕복선

The mission of the space shuttle is to bring the astronauts back to Earth.

우주왕복선의 임무는 우주인을 지구로 귀환시키는 것이다.

39 solar system [sóulər sístəm] the sun and all the planets that move around it

n. 태양계

In the solar system, Venus is the nearest planet to Earth.

태양계에서 금성이 지구와 가장 가까운 행성이다.

40 spaceship [spéisʃìp] a vehicle that travels in space, carrying people

n. 우주선

The spaceship has dived safely into the Pacific Ocean.

우주선은 태평양에 안전하게 착수(着水)했다.

41 speculate [spékjəlèit] to guess about something's nature or identity

v. 추측하다, 예측하다
speculation n. 추측, 투기

We can only speculate how the universe is huge.

우주가 얼마나 거대한지 우리는 오로지 추측할 수밖에 없다.

42 sunbeam [sʌ́nbìːm] a stream of light from the sun

n. 태양 광선, 일광

You are so beautiful in the morning sunbeam.

당신을 아침 햇살 아래서 보니 무척 아름답습니다.

43 surround [səráund] to be all around something or someone

v. 둘러싸다, 에워싸다
surrounding n. 주변, 환경 a. 주위의

Police surrounded the builing.

경찰이 그 건물을 포위했다.

44 survey [sə:rvéi] an investigation of the opinions, behaviour, etc. of a particular group of people, which is usually done by asking them questions

n. 조사, 측량
surveyor n. 측량자

The results of the survey were quite astonishing.

그 조사의 결과는 매우 놀라운 것이었다.

| 45 | **telescope** [téləskòup] | a piece of equipment shaped like a tube, used for making distant objects look larger and closer |

n. 망원경, 확대 광학 기계

People had the telescope **developed to see more unfound planets.**

사람들은 확인되지 않은 별들을 더 많이 보기 위해 망원경을 개발했다.

| 46 | **universe** [júːnəvəːrs] | the whole of space and everything in it, including the earth, the planets and the stars |

n. 우주, 은하계, 성운

universal a. 만국의, 우주의, 보편적인

Even now a lot of scientists are trying to solve the riddle of the universe**.**

지금도 많은 과학자들은 우주의 수수께끼를 풀기 위해 애쓰고 있다.

| 47 | **Uranus** [júərənəs] | the planet in the solar system that is 7th in order of distance from the sun |

n. 천왕성

It was revealed that Uranus **has a great magnetic field.**

천왕성이 거대한 자기장을 가졌다는 것이 밝혀졌다.

| 48 | **vacuum** [vǽkjuəm, -kjə(ː)m] | a space that contains no air or other gas |

n. 진공, 진공상태

The astronauts who prepare for exploring space have to be trained in a vacuum**.**

우주 탐사를 준비하는 우주비행사들은 진공 상태에서 훈련을 해야만 한다.

49 **Venus** [víːnəs] the planet in the solar system that is second in order of distance from the sun

n. 금성

Venus is as big as the Earth.

금성은 지구와 크기가 비슷하다.

50 **wonder** [wʌ́ndər] to think about something and try to decide what is true, what will happen, what you should do, etc.

v. 이상하게 여기다, ~이 아닐까 생각하다　n. 경탄할 만한 것, 경이

wonderful a. 이상한, 불가사의한

I can't wait to experience the wonders of the universe.

나는 우주의 경이로운 세계의 경험이 기대된다.

A 다음의 단어와 뜻이 가장 가까운 것을 고르시오.

1. move in a cycle

a. direct   b. rotation   c. hurry   d. slow   e. parallel

2. at a distance

a. interval   b. remoteness   c. aloofness
d. coldness   e. stretch

3. lighten the color

a. ease   b. relieve   c. brighten   d. gladden   e. alleviate

4. speculate on the stock market

a. think   b. sold   c. split   d. gamble   e. dabble

5. a natural wonder

a. marvel   b. achievement   c. record
d. event   e. accident

B 다음 뜻을 모두 포괄하는 단어를 보기에서 고르시오.

dense ǀ crater ǀ heaven ǀ rotate

1. _____

a. a large hole in the top of a volcano

b. a large hole in the ground caused by the explosion of a bomb
   or by something large hitting it

2. _____

a. about something to move or turn around a central fixed point

b. regularly change the job or regularly change who does the job

3. _____

a. containing a lot of people, things, plants, etc. with little space
   between them

b. difficult to see through or breathe in

4. _____

a. the place believed to be the home for God where good people
   go when they die

b. a place or situation in which you are very happy

Computer

컴퓨터

01 **access** [ǽkses] the opportunity or right to see or use something or somebody

n. (장소, 사람 등에의) 접근, 출입, 이용할 권리 v. 접속하다, 접근하다
accessible a. 접근하기 쉬운, 이용할 수 있는

Access **has been denied to the named file.**

지정된 파일을 찾을 수 없다.

02 **appear** [əpíər] to move into a position where you can see someone or something

v. 나타나다, 출현하다, 나오다
apparent a. 또렷이 보이는, 식별할 수 있는
appearance n. 출현, 외관, 겉모습

You can find that the icons appears **on your screen.**

화면에 아이콘이 나타나는 것을 볼 수 있다.

03 **appropriate** [əpróuprièit] suitable, acceptable or correct for a particular situation

a. 적절한 v. 도용하다, 전용하다, 책정하다
inappropriate a. 부적절한

This program is most appropriate **for the work.**

이 프로그램은 그 일에 가장 적합하다.

04 **boot** [búːt] to prepare a computer for use by loading its operating system

v. (컴퓨터를) 기억장치로 스타트하다, 프로그램을 깔다

When you boot **your computer, you can get the information of the computer.**

컴퓨터를 부팅할 때 컴퓨터의 사양을 확인할 수 있다.

05 **browse** [bráuz] to look for information on computer, especially on the Internet

v. 대강 읽다, (웹 등의 정보를) 열람[검색]하다

My father browses **through the paper every morning.**

아버지는 아침마다 신문을 대강 훑어보신다.

06 **chat** [tʃǽt] to talk to each other in an informal and friendly way

v. 잡담하다, 수다 떨다, 채팅하다

I chat **with them on the Internet every night.**

매일 밤 그 사람들하고 인터넷으로 채팅을 합니다.

07 **command** [kəmǽnd, -máːnd] an instruction that you give to a computer

n. (컴퓨터에 대한) 명령어, 명령, 지시, 지휘

In DOS program, you must type the command **directly.**

도스에서는 명령을 직접 타이핑해야 한다.

08 **complex** [kəmpléks] having many different parts, and being often difficult to understand

a. 복잡한, 복합의, 합성의
complexity n. 복잡성, 복잡한 것

To work with computers you need to understand complex **mechanisms.**

컴퓨터에 관련된 일을 하려면 복잡한 메커니즘을 이해해야 한다.

09 **component** [kəmpóunənt, kɑm-] the parts that something is made of

n. (기계, 스테레오 등의) 구성 요소, 성분

A cell is generally equipped with four components.

세포는 일반적으로 4가지 물질로 구성되어 있다.

10 **connect** [kənékt] to join two things together

v. 연결하다, 접속하다
connection n. 연결, 접속

Today people enjoy surfing the Internet without connecting a wire.

오늘날 사람들은 선 연결 없이 인터넷 서핑을 즐긴다.

11 **cyber** [sáibər] related to a computer work; of a computer network

a. 컴퓨터와 관계 있는, 컴퓨터(네트워크)의

The National Police Agency announced that a cyber terror happens at least once a week.

사이버 공격이 적어도 일주일에 한 번은 일어난다고 경찰청이 발표했다.

12 **data** [déitə, dǽtə, dɑ́:tə] information that can be stored and used by a computer program

n. 데이터, 자료, 지식, 정보

By 5:00 p.m. the data base must be restored.

오후 5시까지는 데이터 베이스가 복구되어야 한다.

13 delete [dilíːt] to remove something that has been written down or stored in a computer

v. 삭제하다, 지우다

If the virus passed into your computer, you'd better backup important data before it's deleted.

바이러스가 컴퓨터에 침투하면, 중요한 데이터가 삭제되기 전에 백업하는 것이 좋다.

14 e-mail [íːmèil] a system of sending written messages electronically from one computer to another

n. 이메일, 전자 우편

He sends me a list of his friends' address by e-mail.

그는 나에게 자기 친구들의 주소를 이메일로 보내주었다.

15 engineer [èndʒiníər] a person whose job involves designing and building machines, roads, bridges, etc.

n. 기사, 기술자, 공학자
engineering n. 공학

The project will be executed by many experts and computer engineers.

그 프로젝트는 많은 전문가와 컴퓨터 기술자에 의해 실행될 것이다.

16 frequent [fríːkwənt] happening or doing something often

a. 자주 일어나는, 자주 있는, 빈번한
frequency n. 빈번, 자주 일어남 | frequenter n. 자주 가는 사람, 단골손님

You can customize any of five buttons as shortcuts for frequent tasks.

자주 사용하는 기능을 5개의 바로가기 키로 설정해 놓을 수 있다.

17   **identify** [aidéntəfài, id-]   to recognize someone or something, or distinguish them from others

v. 확인하다, 증명하다, 식별하다
identity n. 동일함, 정체, 신원, 신분 증명서

Some programs enable you to identify your computer's options.
일부 프로그램들은 당신의 컴퓨터 사양을 확인할 수 있게 해준다.

18   **imagine** [imǽdʒin]   to form a mental picture of something

v. 상상하다, 가정하다
imagination n. 상상, 상상력 ∣ imaginative a. 상상의, 상상력이 풍부한

Until the 1990's, we couldn't imagine that we would buy things at home.
1990년대까지만 해도 집에서 물건을 산다는 것은 상상도 못했다.

19   **indicate** [índikèit]   to show or point out

v. 나타내다, 보이다, 표시하다

From the indicating device in computer, digital image data is indicated.
컴퓨터 표시장치에서 디지털 이미지 데이터를 나타낸다.

20   **information** [infərméiʃən]   the facts and figures that are stored and used by a computer program

n. 정보, 데이터, 자료
inform v. 알리다, 통지하다

In DVDs, you can store 10 times more information than CDs.
DVD는 CD보다 10배나 많은 데이터를 저장할 수 있다.

21 **input** [ínpùt] to feed information into a computer

v. (정보 등을) 입력하다 n. 입력, 투입(량)

A scanner is the device that enables to input **the image files to your computer.**

스캐너는 컴퓨터에 이미지 파일을 입력할 수 있도록 하는 장치이다.

22 **insert** [insə́:rt] to put the object inside something

v. 끼워 넣다, 삽입하다
insertion n. 삽입, 끼워 넣음

It doesn't work when I insert **the CD.**

내가 CD를 넣으면 작동을 안한다.

23 **install** [instɔ́:l] to fit a piece of equipment or put it somewhere so that it is ready to be used

v. (소프트웨어 등을) 설치하다
installation n. 설치, 가설

To install **this software, enough room is necessary.**

이 프로그램을 설치하기 위해서는 충분한 공간이 필요하다.

24 **laptop** [lǽptàp] a small portable computer

n. 랩톱 컴퓨터(노트북)

The sales volume of laptops **increased about 3%.**

노트북의 판매량이 3% 정도 증가했다.

25 machine [məʃíːn] a piece of equipment with moving parts that uses power such as electricity to do particular job

n. 컴퓨터, 기계, 기계 장치
machinery n. (집합적) 기계류

Hardware is the machine that organizes a computer.

하드웨어는 컴퓨터를 구성하는 기계 장치이다.

26 messenger [mésəndʒər] a person or a program that takes a message to someone

n. (우편) 배달부, 심부름꾼, 전달자
message n. 전갈, 전언, 메세지

The mobile messenger is offered free.

모바일 메신저는 무료로 제공된다.

27 monitor [mánətər] a television or part of a computer with a screen on which you can see pictures or information

n. 모니터, 단말 스크린

The company announced that they would release the LCD monitor for experts.

그 회사는 전문가용 LCD모니터를 출시할 것이라고 발표했다.

28 network [nétwəːrk] a system of things which are connected and which operate together

n. 통신망, 네트워크

We can be connected with the Internet network anywhere.

우리는 어디서든지 인터넷 통신망으로 연결될 수 있다.

29 occur [əkə́:r] to happen; to exist in a particular place or situation

v. (일이) 일어나다, 생기다, 발생하다

occurrence n. 발생, 사건

A single irruption of a virus has never occurred **in 10 years.**

10년 동안 한 번도 바이러스 침입이 발생한 적이 없다.

30 online [ɑːnláin, ɔnláin] connected to the Internet

a. 온라인의, (단말기가 주컴퓨터)에 연결된

Many students are hooked on the online **games.**

많은 학생들이 온라인 게임에 중독되어 있다.

31 output [áutpùt] the information, result, etc. produced by a computer

n. 생산량, 산출량, 출력

A monitor is the machine that is the output **device of a computer.**

모니터는 컴퓨터의 출력 장치인 기계 장치이다.

32 particular [pərtíkjulər] specific, special

a. 특별한, 특정한, 특유의

particularly ad. 특히, 두드러지게

Computer programs are made up of the particular **languages that computers read.**

컴퓨터 프로그램은 컴퓨터가 읽는 특정한 언어로 만들어진다.

33 **password** [pǽswə:rd, pɑ́:s-]   a secret word or phrase that you must know before you can use a system or program

n. 암호

You'd better change your password frequently to prevent the theft of your personal information.

개인정보 도용을 막으려면 패스워드를 자주 바꾸는 것이 좋다.

34 **program** [próugræm, -grəm-]   a set of instruction in code that control the operations or functions of a computer

n. 프로그램

We can limitedly use shareware programs for free.

우리는 무료 셰어웨어 프로그램을 제한적으로 사용할 수 있다.

35 **proceed** [prousí:d]   to continue doing something that has already been started; to continue being done

v. 나아가다, 속행하다, 계속하다
process n. 진행, 속행

There was insufficient memory to proceed.

메모리가 부족하여 계속할 수 없다.

36 **promptly** [prɑ́:mptli]   without delay

ad. 즉시, 즉각적으로
prompt a. 재빠른, 날쌘

Today computers help us contact the world promptly.

오늘날 컴퓨터로 세계 소식을 즉시 접할 수 있다.

37 public [pʌ́blik] relating to all the people in a country or community

a. 공공의, 공중의, 일반 대중의 n. 공중, 대중

With a computer, Internet shopping became public.
컴퓨터로 인해, 인터넷 쇼핑이 대중화되었다.

38 purpose [pə́:rpəs] the reason for which it is made or done

n. 목적, 의도, 용도
on purpose 일부러, 고의로

Crackers pass into others' computers with a bad purpose.
크래커들은 나쁜 목적으로 다른 사람의 컴퓨터에 침입한다.

39 receive [risíːv] to get or accept something that is sent or given

v. 수신하다, (제공, 배달된 것 등을) 수취하다
receipt n. 영수증, 받음, 수취

We simply click to send and receive **an e-mail.**
단지 클릭만 하면 전자우편을 보내고 받는다.

40 respond [rispánd] to react to something by doing or saying something

v. 대답하다, 응답하다
response n. 반응, 응답, 대답
respondent a. 반응하는 n. 응답자

When you inquire of the customer service center on the board, a worker will respond **immediately.**
만약 게시판에 있는 고객센터에 문의하면 직원이 곧바로 대답해줄 것이다.

41 **send** [sénd] to arrange for something to be taken and delivered to someone

v. (편지 등을) 보내다, 발신하다
sender n. 발송인

The boss told her secretary to send an e-mail to the clients.

사장은 고객들에게 이메일을 보내라고 비서에게 말했다.

42 **sensor** [sénsɔːr, -sər] a device that can react to light, heat, pressure, etc.

n. (빛, 온도, 방사능 등의 자극을 신호로 바꾸는) 감지기, 감지 장치

V3 is the most reliable sensor that can inform the user of viruses.

V3는 사용자에게 바이러스를 알려줄 수 있는 가장 믿을 만한 감지 장치이다.

43 **setup** [sétʌp] the progress of installing computer hardware or software and making it ready to use

n. (프로그램 등의) 설치

Let me begin to guide the BIOS setup of this.

이 제품의 BIOS(바이오스) 셋업 가이드를 시작해보겠습니다.

44 **surf** [səːrf] to use the internet

v. 인터넷상의 정보를 찾아다니다

The boy is surfing the Internet.

그 소년은 인터넷을 서핑하고 있다.

45 upgrade [ʌpgréid] to improve or make equipment or services more efficient

v. 업그레이드하다, (제품의) 품질이나 성능을 향상시키다 n. 개량, 향상

If you want to do this program smoothly, you should upgrade your computer.

이 프로그램을 원활하게 사용하려면 컴퓨터를 업그레이드하는 것이 좋다.

46 various [vɛ́əriəs] having several different things of the type

a. 다양한, 여러 가지의, 다방면의

variety n. 다양(성), 종류, 갖가지 | variation n. 변화, 변동

The new computer which our company has made is including various functions.

우리 회사가 만든 새 컴퓨터는 다양한 기능들을 총망라하고 있다.

47 virtual [və́:rtʃuəl] made to appear to exist by the use of computer software

a. 가상 기억의, 허상의

virtually ad. 사실상, 실질적으로

You don't have to use a real CD any more because a virtual drive doesn't need a real one.

가상 드라이브는 실제의 CD가 필요 없기 때문에 더 이상 CD를 사용할 필요가 없다.

48 virus [váiərəs] instructions that are hidden within a computer program and are designed to cause faults or destroy data

n. 컴퓨터 바이러스, 바이러스, 병원체

A virus called DDOS hit the computation system of the USA and Korea lately.

최근에 DDOS라는 바이러스가 미국과 한국의 전산 시스템을 공격했다.

49 **web page** [wéb péidʒ] all the information that you can see in one part of a website

n. World Wide Web의 개별적인 컴퓨터 화면 문서

A homepage is usually composed with a lot of linked web pages.

보통 홈페이지는 링크된 많은 웹페이지로 구성된다.

---

50 **without** [wiðáut, wiθ-] not having or not using the thing mentioned

prep. ~이 없이, ~이 없는, ~이 없으면

Probably people feel uncomfortable without computers that now are inseparable with human beings.

이제 인간과는 떼어놓을 수 없는 컴퓨터가 없다면 아마도 사람들은 불편함을 느낄 것이다.

A 우리말과 같은 뜻이 되도록 빈 칸에 주어진 철자로 시작하는 단어를 쓰시오.

1. You can't a＿＿＿＿ the file without the password.

   암호 없이는 파일에 접근할 수 없다.

2. You are most a＿＿＿＿＿ for that job.

   당신은 그 일에 가장 적합합니다.

3. You must d＿＿＿ your personal information after using the computer in the public space.

   공공장소에서 컴퓨터를 사용한 뒤에는 반드시 개인정보를 지워야 합니다.

4. I＿＿＿＿ the disk if you want to install the program.

   그 프로그램을 설치하고 싶으면 디스크를 넣으세요.

5. Computer programs are made up of the p＿＿＿＿＿ languages that it can read.

   컴퓨터 프로그램은 컴퓨터가 읽을 수 있는 특정한 언어로 만들어졌다.

B 주어진 표현에 해당하는 단어를 보기에서 고르시오.

| proceed | component | virtual | respond | frequent |

1. _____ : the parts that something is made of

2. _____ : happening or doing something often

3. _____ : to continue doing something that has already
      been started

4. _____ : to react quickly or in the correct way to
      something or someone

5. _____ : made to appear to exist by the use of
      computer software

C 알맞은 반대말끼리 연결하시오.

1. appropriate   • disappear

2. complex   • inappropriate

3. connect •   • output

4. appear •   • simple

5. input •   • disconnect

Part 4

Politics

[정치]

overnment 정부 | **Law** 법 | **Thought** 사상 | **War & Peace** 전쟁과 평화

Lesson 1

Government

| 정부

01　abolish [əbáliʃ]　to officially end a law, a system or an institution

v. 폐지하다

abolishable a. 폐지할 수 있는 | abolishment n. 폐지

The government has to focus on abolishing the law which many people can escape.

정부는 많은 사람들이 빠져나갈 수 있는 법들을 폐지하는 것에 집중해야 한다.

02　achieve [ətʃíːv]　to attain or reach a goal through a lot of effort

v. 성취하다, (공적을) 세우다

achievable a. 완수할 수 있는 | achievement n. 업적, 공로

The president had achieved great things during his term of office.　그 대통령은 그의 임기 동안 큰 공을 세웠다.

03　administration [ədmìnəstréiʃən]　the government of a country at a particular time

n. 경영, 관리, 통치, 행정부

administer v. 관리하다, 운영하다 | administrator n. 행정관, 통치자

Most of the people wanted a new administration against the previous one.

대부분의 사람들이 이전의 행정부에 반대하여 새로운 행정부를 원했다.

04　affair [əfɛ́ər]　events that are of public interest or political importance

n. 사건, 직무, 업무

They faced on an affair of great importance, so they decided to have an urgent meeting.

그들은 중대 사건에 직면해서, 긴급 회의를 열기로 결정했다.

05　**agreement** [əgríːmənt]　an arrangement, a promise or a contract made with somebody

n. 동의, 일치, 협정
agree　v. 동의하다

The government will have a lot of benefits because of the Free Trade Agreement.
정부는 자유 무역 협정으로 인해 많은 이익을 얻게 될 것이다.

06　**aim** [eim]　to try or plan to achieve something

v. 목표로 하다, 겨누다　n. 목표, 의도
aimless　a. 목적 없는 | aimlessly　ad. 목적 없이

The aim of the conference is to improve working conditions this time.
이번 회의의 목적은 근무 환경을 개선하는 것이다.

07　**appointment** [əpɔ́intmənt]　an arrangement to meet

n. 약속, 지정, 임명
appoint　v. 약속하다, 임명하다

He took an appointment as the Korean ambassador to the US.　그는 주미 한국 대사로 임명되었다.

08　**approve** [əprúːv]　to agree to a plan, request, etc. officially

v. 승인하다
approvable　a. 승인할 수 있는 | approval　n. 찬성, 승인 | approved　a. 승인된

The budget was approved by the committee last week.
예산안은 지난주에 위원회에 의해 승인되었다.

09 **assembly** [əsémbli] a group of people gathered together for a particular purpose

n. 집회, 의회, 조립품
assemble v. 모으다, 수집하다 ㅣ assembly line (대량 생산의) 조립 라인

I left the message that the assembly hall was changed on your answering machine.
회의장이 바뀌었다는 메시지를 너의 자동응답기에 남겼다.

10 **attend** [əténd] to be present at an event

v. 출석하다, 참석하다, 수행하다
attendance n. 출석 ㅣ attendant n. 안내원 ㅣ attendee n. 출석자

At the end they decided to delegate Mr. Kim to attend a conference.
마침내 그들은 Mr. Kim을 대표로 회의에 참석시키기로 결정했다.

11 **authority** [əθɔ́:rəti, əθár-] power to make decisions or control others

n. 권위, 권력
authoritative a. 권위 있는, 당국의

The problem was that Mr. Jang exceeded his authority.
Mr. Jang이 월권 행위를 한 것이 문제였다.

12 **branch** [bræntʃ, brɑ:ntʃ] a local office or shop/store belonging to a large company or organization

n. 지사, 지부 v. 파생하다

The company has its branch offices all over the world.
그 회사는 전 세계에 지사를 두고 있다.

13 **candidate** [kǽndidèit, -dət]   a person who is trying to be elected or is applying for a job

n. 후보자, 지원자

There was a great speech by one of presidential candidates.

대통령 후보들 중 한 사람의 훌륭한 연설이 있었다.

---

14 **central** [séntrəl]   in the centre of an area or object

a. 중앙의, 중심의
center n. 중심, 중심지

We have to observe the decision of the central committee.

우리는 중앙 위원회의 결정을 따라야 한다.

---

15 **consider** [kənsídər]   to think about; regard as; allow for

v. 고려하다, 숙고하다, 간주하다
considerable a. 고려해야 할, 상당히 I **considerably** ad. 상당히, 꽤
considerate a. 신중한

He is considered as the best writer all over the world.

그는 전 세계에서 가장 훌륭한 작가로 고려된다.

---

16 **constitution** [kànstətjúːʃən]   general structure of body or mind

n. 구성, 조직, 헌법, 제정
constitute v. 구성하다, (법을) 제정하다 I **constitutional** a. 구조상의, 헌법상의

Mr. Garner who is interested in law wants to study about the constitution.

법에 관심이 있는 **Mr. Garner**는 헌법에 대해 공부하고 싶어한다.

17 **control** [kəntróul] to have power to make the decisions about how a country, place, etc. is run

v. 지배하다, 통제하다 n. 지배, 관리
controllable a. 조종할 수 있는 | controlled a. 통제된
controller n. 지배자, 감사관, 관리인

That country is controlled by one person who has gerat power. 저 나라는 강한 힘을 가진 한 사람에 의해 통치된다.

18 **corrupt** [kərʌ́pt] dishonest; to make spoil

a. 타락한, 부정한 v. 타락하다, 부패하다
incorrupt a. 청렴한, 타락하지 않은 | corruption n. 타락, 퇴폐

They insisted that the government was getting corrupted.
그들은 정부가 타락하고 있다고 주장했다.

19 **declare** [dikléər] to say something officially or publicly

v. 선언하다
declarable a. 선언할 수 있는 | declaration n. 선언, 신고

The government declared that the fare of transportation will be raised from next month.
정부는 교통비가 다음 달부터 오를 것이라고 선언했다.

20 **democracy** [dimɑ́krəsi] a system of a government in which every citizen in the country can vote to elect its government officials

n. 민주주의
democrat n. 민주주의자 | democratic a. 민주주의의

He has made an effort to keep democracy vital for 10 years.
그는 10년 동안 민주주의의 활력을 지키기 위해 노력해 왔다.

21 diplomat [dípləmæt] a person whose job is to represent his or her country in a foreign country

n. 외교관
diplomacy n. 외교, 외교술 | diplomatic a. 외교의
diplomatically ad. 외교적으로, 외교상

She really wants to be a diplomat in her future.
그녀는 장래에 외교관이 되기를 정말로 원한다.

22 discuss [diskʌ́s] to talk about something with another person or a group in order to exchange ideas or decide something

v. 논의하다, 토론하다
discussion n. 논의, 상의

Ellen made up her mind after she discussed it with others for a long time.
Ellen은 그것에 대해 다른 사람들과 오랫동안 토론한 후에 마음을 정했다.

23 duty [djúːti] work that you have to do for your job

n. 의무, 임무
on duty 당번인, 근무 중인

We're looking for a person who has a strong sense of duty.
우리는 강한 의무감을 가진 사람을 찾고 있다.

24 elect [ilékt] to choose somebody to do a particular job by voting for him/her

v. 선거하다, 뽑다
election n. 선거, 선정

He is the man who is elected as a representative of the White House. 그가 백악관의 대표자로 선출된 그 사람이다.

25 embassy [émbəsi] a group of officials who represent their government in a foreign country

n. 대사관
ambassador n. 대사

I am supposed to visit to the British Embassy in Seoul today.
난 오늘 서울에 있는 영국 대사관을 방문하기로 되어 있다.

---

26 enforce [infɔ́:rs, en-] to make sure that people obey a particular law or rule

v. (법률 등을) 시행하다, 집행하다
enforced a. 강제적인 | enforceable a. 시행 가능한

This is the result of enforcing the ban on the use of cell phones while driving.
이것이 운전 중 휴대전화 사용 금지를 시행한 결과이다.

---

27 exile [égzail, éks-] a person who is living in a foreign country because they can't live in their own country, usually for political reasons

n. 국외 추방, 망명, 망명자 v. 추방하다

He asserted his innocence, but he was exiled from his country in the end.
그는 결백을 주장했으나, 결국 국외로 추방되었다.

---

28 expectation [èkspektéiʃən] what you think or hope will happen

n. 기대, 예상
expect v. 예상하다, 기대하다, 기다리다 | expectant a. 기대하는

The election lasted for a long time beyond expectation.
선거가 예상외로 오랫동안 계속됐다.

29 focus [fóukəs] to give a special attention to one particular thing or person

v. 초점을 맞추다, 집중하다   n. 초점

The members are too busy to focus on the other matters.
회원들이 너무 바빠서 다른 문제들에 집중을 할 수가 없다.

30 interpret [intə́:rprit] to translate something immediately into another language

v. 설명하다, 통역하다
interpretation n. 해석, 통역

He interpreted for the foreigners during the whole meeting.
그는 회의 내내 외국인들을 위해 통역했다.

31 investigate [invéstəgeit] to try to find out the truth about or the cause of something such as a crime, accident, or scientific problem

v. 조사하다, 수사하다
investigation n. 조사, 연구 ∣ investigative a. 연구의, 조사의
investigator n. 연구자, 조사자

The government makes the police officers investigate the case thoroughly.
정부는 경찰이 그 사건을 철저히 조사하도록 했다.

32 legislation [lèdʒisléiʃən] the process of making and passing laws

n. 법률 제정, 입법 행위
legislate v. 법률을 제정하다 ∣ legislative a. 입법상의 ∣ legislator n. 입법자

There is only one organization which has the power of legislation.   법률 제정의 권한을 가진 기관은 오직 하나뿐이다.

33 **minister** [mínistər] a person who is in charge of a particular government department

n. 장관, 성직자, 외교 사절 v. 섬기다, 봉사하다

Mr. Kim is the new Minister of Justice.

Mr. Kim이 새로운 법무부 장관이다.

34 **neutral** [njú:trəl] not supporting or helping either side in disagreement, competition, etc.

a. 중립의 n. 중립국

neutralize v. 중립화하다 | neutrality n. 중립 | neutralization n. 중립화

According to the neutral policy line, the government didn't support any countries.

중립 정책 방침에 따라 정부는 어떤 나라도 지지하지 않았다.

35 **nominate** [námənèit] to officially suggest someone or something for an important position, duty, or prize

v. 지명하다, 임명하다

nomination n. 지명, 임명 | nominee n. 후보, 지명된 사람

She is nominated as a candidate for president.

그녀는 대통령 후보로 지명되었다.

36 **official** [əfíʃəl] a person who holds a position of authority in an organization

n. 공무원 a. 공식의

officer n. 장교, 경찰관 | officially ad. 공식으로

He was a government official, but he is a designer now.

그는 공무원이었지만, 지금은 디자이너이다.

37 **overthrow** [òuvərθróu] to remove a leader or a government from position of power by force

v. 뒤엎다, 전복하다, 폐지하다 n. 타도, 전복

The government is overthrown, so new policy will be expected soon.

정부가 전복됐으니 곧 새로운 정책이 예상될 것이다.

38 **parliament** [pɑ́ːrləmənt] the group of people who are elected to make and change the laws of a country

n. 의회
parliamentarian n. 의회[국회] 의원 | parliamentary a. 의회의

The parliament was convened because of the impeachment.

탄핵 때문에 의회가 소집되었다.

39 **policy** [pɑ́ləsi] a plan of action agreed or chosen by a political party, a business, etc.

n. 정책, 방침

The news was about the foreign policy.

그 소식은 외교 정책에 관한 것이었다.

40 **political** [pəlítikəl] connected with the state, government or public affairs

a. 정치의
politic a. 행동이 신중한, 현명한 | politically ad. 정치적으로 |
politician n. 정치가

He used to discuss the political issues.

그는 정치적인 문제들에 대해 토론하곤 했었다.

41 population [pὰpjuléiʃən] all the people who live in a country or area

n. 인구
populate vt. 거주시키다

The population of Korea has decreased for a few years.
한국의 인구가 몇 해 동안 줄고 있다.

42 president [prézədənt] the elected head of state in republic

n. 대통령
vice president n. 부통령

I thought that he deserved to be the next president.
난 그가 다음 대통령이 될 만하다고 생각했다.

43 promote [prəmóut] to help something to happen or develop

v. 진전시키다, 장려하다
promoter n. 촉진자 ㅣ promotion n. 승진
promotional a. 승진의 ㅣ promotive a. 진행시키는

To promote world peace, they prevent the whole world from having a nuclear weapon.
세계 평화를 촉진시키기 위해, 그들은 전 세계가 핵무기를 소유하려는 것을 저지하고 있다.

44 propose [prəpóuz] to suggest something for people to think about and decide upon

v. 제안하다
proposal n. 신청, 제안 ㅣ proposer n. 신청인, 제의자

He proposed new policy about the education part last week.
지난주 그는 교육 부문에 대한 새로운 정책을 제안했다.

45 refuse [rifjúːz]

to say firmly that you will not do something that someone asked you to do

v. 거절하다, 사절하다

refusable a. 거절할 수 있는 | refusal n. 거절, 사퇴 | refuser n. 거절자

The parliament had refused the proposal he mentioned last week.

의회는 그가 지난주에 언급했던 제안을 거절했다.

46 reject [ridʒékt] to refuse to accept or consider something

v. 거절하다, 무시하다

rejection n. 거절

His recommendation was rejected due to various reasons.

그의 추천은 다양한 이유 때문에 거절당했다.

47 representative [rèprizéntətiv]

a person who has been chosen to speak, vote or make decisions for someone else

n. 대표자, 대의원 a. 대표적인, 대리하는

represent v. 묘사하다, 대표하다 | representation n. 표현, 설명, 대표

The representative is very busy and has another meeting today.

그 대의원은 매우 바쁘고 오늘 또 다른 회의도 있다.

48 republic [ripʌ́blik] a country that is governed by a president and politicians elected by the people where there is no king or queen

n. 공화국
republican a. 공화국의 n. 공화주의자

It is not easy to establish a republic.
공화국을 수립하는 것은 쉬운 일이 아니다.

49 sovereignty [sάvərənti, sʌ́v-] the power that an independent country has to govern itself

n. 주권, 통치권
sovereign n. 주권자, 원수 a. 최고의 권력을 가진, 자주의, 독립의

The nation has the sovereignty in democratic countries.
민주주의 국가에서는 국민이 주권을 가지고 있다.

50 supreme [su:prí:m, sju:-] highest in rank or position

a. 최고의, 가장 중요한
supremacy n. 최고, 최상 ǀ Supreme Court 대법원

The human rights are the supreme one of the rights that we have to have.
인권은 우리가 가져야 할 권리 중에 가장 중요한 권리이다.

Check up

A 다음 각 문장의 단어가 본문에서 쓰인 의미를 고르시오.

1. It plans to abolish the ceilings completely by the end of the year.

    a. to officially end a law, a system or an institution

    b. to destroy entirely

2. The opposition party will take the Government to task for the affair.

    a. events that are of public interest or political importance

    b. a sexual relationship between two people

3. We aim to increase both exports and imports.

    a. to try or plan to achieve something

    b. to point or direct a weapon, a shot, a kick, etc. at something or somebody

4. They announced his appointment to the chief.

    a. an arrangement for a meeting at an agreed time and place

    b. the act of choosing a person for a job or position of responsibility

5. He also accepts the need to move assembly lines to cheaper locals.

   a. a group of people who have been elected to meet together regularly

   b. the process of putting together the parts of something such as a vehicle

B 알맞은 반대말끼리 연결하시오.

1. attend ·   · peripheral

2. central ·   · straight

3. control ·   · exempt

4. corrupt ·   · miss

5. enforce ·   · unrestraint

Lesson 2
Law

| 법

01 **accuse** [əkjúːz] to say that you believe someone is guilty of crime or of doing something bad

v. 고발하다, 책망하다
accusable a. 고소해야 할, 비난할 만한 I accusation n. 고발, 고소

Mr. Han accused her of stealing items from his house.
Mr. Han은 그의 집에서 물건을 훔친 것에 대해 그녀를 고소했다.

02 **allow** [əláu] to let someone do or have something

v. 허락하다, 참작하다
allowance n. 수당, 허용, 참작 I allowed a. 허가받은

All these factors must be allowed for.
이 모든 요소들이 감안되어야 한다.

03 **amend** [əménd] to change a law, document, statement, etc. slightly in order to correct a mistake or improve it

v. 수정하다
amendable a. 개정할 수 있는 I amendment n. 개정, 수정

It's necessary to amend a few laws with reflecting modern ideas. 현대의 생각들을 반영해서 몇 가지 법을 수정하는 것이 필요하다.

04 **arbitrary** [ɑ́ːrbətrèri] decided or arranged without any reason or plan, often unfairly

a. 멋대로인, 독단적인, 임의의
arbitrate v. 중재하다 I arbitration n. 중재 I arbitrator n. 중재인

They had been under the arbitrary rules for a few years.
그들은 몇 해 동안 독단적인 규율 아래 있었다.

05 attorney [ətə́ːrni] a lawyer

n. 변호사, 검사, 대리인
attorney general n. 법무 장관

The attorney is busy reviewing that case right now.

그 검사는 지금 그 사건을 검토 중이라 바쁘다.

06 ban [bǽn] to state officially that it must not be done, shown, or used

v. 금지하다 n. 금지

They decided to ban the use of plastic bags for environment.

그들은 환경을 위해 비닐봉지 사용을 금지하기로 결정했다.

07 basis [béisis] a principle on which an idea or theory is based

n. 기초, 근거
base v. ~에 기초를 두다 | basic a. 기초의, 근본의

These days many people work on a five day a week basis.

요즘엔 많은 사람들이 주 5일제로 근무한다.

08 blame [bléim] to think or say that someone or something is responsible for something bad

v. 비난하다, 죄를 ~에게 씌우다 n. 비난, 책망
blameful a. 비난할 만한 | blameless a. 결백한

Mrs. Garcia blamed him for the car accident that occurred last night.

Mrs. Garcia는 어젯밤 발생했던 자동차 사고에 대한 책임을 그에게 물었다.

09 coincidence [kouínsidəns] the fact of two things happening at the same time by chance and without any planning

n. 일치, 부합, 동시에 일어난 사건
coincide v. 동시에 일어나다 ㅣ coincident a. 일치하는

They tried to find out common things between the coincidences.
그들은 동시에 일어난 사건들 사이의 공통점을 찾으려고 노력했다.

10 commit [kəmít] to do something wrong or illegal

v. (죄를) 범하다, 위임하다
commitment n. 위탁, 위임 ㅣ committed a. 전념하는, 헌신적인
committee n. 위원회

He committed a great crime and he was under arrest.
그는 큰 범죄를 저질러서 체포되었다.

11 compel [kəmpél] to force someone to do something

v. 억지로 ~ 시키다, 강요하다
compelling a. 강제적인

She was compelled to stop doing that.
그녀는 그것을 하는 것을 멈추도록 강요당했다.

12 compensate [kámpenseit] to provide something good to balance or reduce the bad effects of damage, loss, etc.

v. ~에게 보상하다, 변상하다
compensation n. 배상, 보상금

He was compensated for the damages of the typhoon.
그는 태풍으로 인한 손상들에 대한 보상을 받았다.

13 **condemn** [kəndém]   to express very strong disapproval of someone, usually for moral reasons

v. 비난하다, 유죄 판결을 내리다
condemnable a. 비난할 만한 | **condemnation** n. 비난, 유죄 판결

The judge condemned him to death at the appellate court.
상고 법원에서 판사는 그에게 사형을 선고했다.

---

14 **confess** [kənfés]   to admit, especially formally or to the police, that you have done something wrong or illegal

v. 자백하다, 인정하다
confession n. 자백, 고백

Finally Thomas confessed his fault to the public.
결국 Thomas는 대중에게 그의 잘못을 인정했다.

---

15 **confine** [kənfáin]   to prevent it from spreading beyond that place or group

v. 제한하다, 가두다
confined a. 제한된 | **confinement** n. 제한, 감금

The bereaved family wanted to confine the convict in jail.
유가족들은 그 죄수를 감옥에 가두기를 원했다.

---

16 **conscience** [kánʃəns]   the part of your mind that tells you whether what you are doing is right or wrong

n. 양심, 선악의 판단력
conscientious a. 양심적인 | **conscientiously** ad. 양심적으로

This is the matter of conscience, not of the law.
이것은 법의 문제가 아니라 양심의 문제이다.

17 convict [kənvíkt]   to declare and state officially in court that someone is guilty of a crime

v. ~에게 유죄를 선고하다 n. 죄수
conviction n. 유죄의 판결

He was convicted **of the murder but he appealed in a high court.**

그는 살인의 유죄 판결을 받았으나 상소했다.

---

18 court [kɔ́ːrt]   a place where legal matters are decided by a judge and jury or by a magistrate

n. 법정, 안마당

I heard that he has to come into the court **tomorrow.**

난 그가 법원에 출두해야 한다고 들었다.

---

19 decision [disíʒən]   a choice or judgement that you make after thinking and talking about what is the best thing to do

n. 결정, 판단
decisive a. 결정적인, 중대한 | decisively ad. 결정적으로

The jury box was very quiet as they were waiting to be given the decision **of the case.**

배심원단은 사건의 판결을 기다리면서 매우 조용했다.

---

20 deny [dinái]   to say that something is not true

v. 부인하다, 거절하다
denial n. 부정, 부인, 거부

He denied **all of the evidences presented at that time.**

그는 그 당시에 제시된 모든 증거들을 부인했다.

21 detect [ditékt] to discover or notice something

v. 발견하다, 수색하다

detection n. 발견, 간파 ㅣ detective a. 검출용의 n. 탐정

More than 100 police officers were gathered to detect the clues of the accident.

100명이 넘는 경찰들이 그 사건의 단서를 찾기 위해 모였다.

22 evidence [évidəns] facts or information that prove something

n. 증거, 흔적

evident a. 명백한, 분명히 알 수 있는 ㅣ evidently ad. 분명하게

The private detective found an important piece of evidence.

그 사립탐정은 중요한 단서를 찾아냈다.

23 exception [iksépʃən] a person or thing that is not included

n. 제외, 예외

except v. 제외하다 prep. ~을 제외하고 ㅣ exceptionable a. 반대할 수 있는

He is one of those who believe that there is no rule without exception.

그는 예외 없는 규칙은 없다고 믿는 사람들 중 하나이다.

24 fine [fáin] penalty of money for a wrong doing

n. 벌금 a. 훌륭한, 멋진, (날씨가) 맑은 ㅣ finable a. 벌금에 처할 수 있는

My friend, Joe, was punished with a fine for drunk driving.

내 친구 Joe는 음주 운전으로 벌금형에 처해졌다.

25 **forbid** [fərbíd] to order someone not to do something

v. 금하다, 금지하다
forbidden a. 금지된 | forbiddance n. 금지

I'm sorry but more than three glasses of wine are forbidden during the flight.

죄송하지만 비행 동안 세 잔 이상의 와인은 금지되어 있습니다.

26 **guilty** [gílti] feeling, showing or involving guilt

a. 유죄의, 가책을 느끼는
guilt n. 죄책감, 유죄

I'm sure he is guilty.

난 그가 유죄라고 확신한다.

27 **identify** [aidéntəfài] to recognize someone or something and be able to say who or what they are

v. 확인하다, 증명하다, 동일시하다
identical a. 동일한, 똑같은 | identity n. 동일성, 주체성

They decided to identify the body because of some suspicious things.

그들은 몇 가지 수상한 점들 때문에 시체를 확인하기로 결심했다.

28 **illegal** [ilí:gəl] not allowed by the law

a. 불법의
illegality n. 불법, 위법 | illegally ad. 불법적으로

I've been ticketed for illegal parking just once before.

난 전에 딱 한 번 불법 주차 딱지를 발부받은 적이 있다.

29 innocent [ínəsənt] not guilty of crime

a. 결백한, 순진한
innocence n. 무죄, 결백

There is no reason to establish that he is innocent anymore.

더 이상 그가 결백하다는 것을 증명할 이유가 없다.

30 judge [dʒʌ́dʒ] to decide whether someone is guilty or innocent in a court

v. 재판하다, 판단하다   n. 판사, 재판관
judgment n. 재판, 판결 ǀ judgmental a. 재판상의

Don't judge a person by appearances when you meet someone.

누군가를 만날 때 외모로 사람을 판단하지 마라.

31 lawful [lɔ́ːfəl] allowed or recognized by law

a. 합법적인
lawfully ad. 합법적으로, 정당하게 ǀ unlawful a. 불법의, 비합법적인

There is no way to find out whether it is lawful or not.

그것이 합법적인지 아닌지 알아낼 방법이 없다.

32 legal [líɡəl] connected with the law

a. 법률(상)의, 합법의
legally ad. 법률적으로, 합법적으로

He is going to take legal steps about that case.

그는 그 사건에 대해 법적 조치를 취할 것이다.

33 limit [límit] to stop something from increasing beyond a particular amount or level

v. 제한하다, 한정하다 n. 제한, 한도
limited a. 한정된, 유한한 ǀ limitation n. 제한, 한정

Limit your answer to two minutes, please.
대답은 2분 이내로 제한하시오.

34 obey [əbéi] to do what you are told or expected to do

v. 복종하다, 준수하다, 따르다
obeyer n. 복종하는 사람 ǀ obedience n. 복종, 순종
obedient a. 순종하는, 말 잘 듣는

You should obey the rules when you come in.
여기에 들어오면 규칙에 따라야 한다.

35 observe [əbzə́:rv] to see or notice someone or something

v. 관찰하다, 감시하다, 준수하다
observant a. 주의 깊은 n. 준수자 ǀ observation n. 관찰, 주목
observatory n. 관측소, 기상대 ǀ observance n. (법률 등의) 준수

We should observe the rule whether we like it or not.
우리는 좋든 싫든 간에 규칙을 지켜야 한다.

36 offend [əfénd] to commit a crime or crimes

v. 죄를 범하다, 화나게 하다
offender n. 범죄자 ǀ offense n. 위반, 범죄 ǀ offensive a. 화나게 하는, 무례한

Since he offended a statute, he will be punished.
그는 규칙을 위반했기 때문에 벌을 받을 것이다.

37 penalty [pénəlti] a punishment for breaking a law, rule or contract

n. 벌금, 형벌, 위약금
penal a. 형벌의 | penalize v. 유죄를 선고하다, 벌주다

The penalty for doing this will be stricter than you thought.
이것을 한 것에 대한 벌은 너의 생각보다 더 엄할 것이다.

38 plead [pliːd] to speak out in someone's support or defence

v. 변호하다, 탄원하다
plead guilty 유죄(책임)을 인정하다

He canceled other cases to plead your case.
그는 너의 사건을 변호하기 위해 다른 사건들을 취소했다.

39 prevent [privént] to stop someone from doing something

v. 막다, 방해하다, 예방하다, 보호하다
preventive a. 예방의 | prevention n. 방지, 예방

There is nothing to prevent you from a spreading plague but to have an injection.
퍼지고 있는 전염병으로부터 널 지킬 방법은 주사를 맞는 것 이외에는 없다.

40 privilege [prívəlidʒ] to treat some people or things better than others

v. 특혜를 주다 n. 특권, 은혜, 면제
privileged a. 특권이 있는

It has been an issue for several weeks that Mr. Ford privileged his son from military service.
Mr. Ford가 아들을 군대에서 면제해주었다는 것이 몇 주 동안 이슈가 되고 있다.

41 **prohibit** [prouhíbit, prə-] to forbid something, especially by law

v. 금지하다, 방해하다

Secondly, make laws to prohibit **smoking in public.**

둘째로, 공공장소에서 흡연을 금하는 법을 제정해야 합니다.

---

42 **random** [rǽndəm] lacking any definite plan, aim or pattern

a. 되는대로의, 무작위, 멋대로
randomly ad. 무작위로

He made up a random **answer for the lawyer's question.**

그는 그 변호사의 질문에 되는대로 대답했다.

---

43 **reasonable** [ríːzənəbl] fair, practical and sensible

a. 이치에 맞는, 정당한
reasonably ad. 합리적으로, 정당하게

All of the merchants are allowed to make a price by reasonable **causes.**

모든 상인들은 정당한 이유들로 가격을 매기도록 허락되었다.

---

44 **regulate** [régjuleit] to control something by means of rules

v. 규제하다, 조절하다
regulation n. 규칙, 규정 l regulator n. 규정자, 조정자

She plays a role in regulating **traffic.**

그녀는 교통정리 역할을 하고 있다.

45 **release** [rilíːs] to let someone or something come out of a place where they have been kept or trapped

v. 풀어 놓다, 해방하다, 개봉하다

I heard that he will be released **from prison next week.**
그가 다음 주에 석방될 거라고 들었다.

46 **restrict** [ristríkt] to limit the size, amuont or range of something

v. 제한하다, 한정하다
restricted a. 한정된 | restriction n. 제한, 한정 | restrictive a. 제한하는, 한정하는

We restrict the number of students per class to 10.
우리는 학급당 학생 수를 10명으로 제한한다.

47 **testify** [téstəfai] to make a formal statement of what is true, especially in a court of law

v. 증명하다, 증언하다
testimony n. 증거, 증인 | testimonial n. 증명서, 추천장

He testified **that he saw that man break the window.**
그는 그 남자가 유리창을 깨는 것을 봤다고 증언했다.

48 **torture** [tɔ́ːrtʃər] to hurt people physically or mentally in order to punish them or make them say

v. 고문하다 n. 고문, 심한 고통
torturer n. 고문하는 사람 | tortured a. 고뇌하는, 무척 고통받는

He was tortured **into giving them the information.**
그는 고문을 당하고 그들에게 정보를 넘겨주었다.

49 **trial** [tráiəl] a legal process in which a judge examine information to decide whether someone is guilty of a crime

n. 공판, 재판

The trial will be held behind closed doors on June 5th.

공판은 6월 5일에 비공개로 열릴 것이다.

50 **witness** [wítnis] a person who sees something happen and is able to describe it to other people

n. 목격자, 증인, 증거 v. 목격하다, 증언하다
witness stand n. 증인석

I didn't know that I'm the only witness of the car accident.

난 내가 그 자동차 사고의 유일한 목격자라는 것을 몰랐다.

Check up

A 우리말과 같은 뜻이 되도록 빈 칸에 주어진 철자로 시작하는 단어를 쓰시오.

1. They a_____ him of murder.

그들은 그를 살인 혐의로 기소했다.

2. There is a b_____ on smoking on the street.

길거리에서 흡연을 금하고 있다.

3. C_____ your sins to God and he will forgive you.

신에게 죄를 고백하면 용서 받을 것이다.

4. There is no e_____ that he is guilty.

그가 유죄라는 증거는 없다.

5. It is i_____ to offer a bribe to the official.

공무원에게 뇌물을 주는 것은 불법이다.

B 주어진 표현에 해당하는 단어를 보기에서 고르시오.

| ban | basis | blame | compensate | court |

1. _____ : criticize; condemn; attack; denounce; censure

2. _____ : foundation; base

3. _____ : offset; counter; cancel out; make up for something

4. _____ : tribunal; courtroom; court of law; courthouse

5. _____ : prohibit; bar; forbid; outlaw

C 우리말은 영어로, 영어는 우리말로 바꾸시오.

1. confine

2. 죄수; ~에게 유죄를 선고하다

3. 부인하다, 거절하다

4. detect

5. fine

6. 유죄의, 가책을 느끼는

7. 확인하다, 증명하다

8. illegal

9. lawful

10. 복종하다, 준수하다

Lesson 3
Thought
|사상

01 **advocate** [ǽdvəkeit] a person who supports or speaks in favour of someone or of a public plan or action

n. 대변자, 지지자 v. 변호하다, 옹호하다
advocacy n. 변호, 옹호 | advocator n. 옹호자, 주창자

She was a strong advocate for children.
그녀는 아이들의 든든한 지지자였다.

02 **argue** [ɑ́:rgju:] to speak angrily to someone because you disagree with them

v. 논쟁하다, 주장하다
argument n. 논쟁, 언쟁, 논거

She always argues with her mother whenever something happens.
그녀는 무슨 일이 생길 때마다 어머니와 다툰다.

03 **aware** [əwέər] knowing or realizing something

a. (~을) 알고 있는, 눈치 채고 있는
awareness n. 의식, 인식 | unaware a. 알지 못하는, 눈치 채지 못한

She became aware that he is the man who hit her after Mr. John's statement.
그녀는 Mr. John의 진술 후에 그가 그녀를 친 그 남자란 것을 알았다.

04 **belief** [bilí:f] a strong feeling that something or somebody exist or is true

n. 믿음, 확신, 신앙
believe v. 믿다

It is important to have the belief that they can believe and depend on.
믿고 의지할 수 있는 신앙을 갖는 것은 중요하다.

05 capitalism [kǽpətəlizm]

an economic and political system in which businesses belong mostly to private owners, not to the government

n. 자본주의 (체제)
capitalist n. 자본가, 자본주의자 I capitalistic a. 자본가의, 자본주의의
capital n. 수도, 자본금, 자산

I'm going to study about the period when capitalism **began to lead to economic growth.**

난 자본주의가 경제 성장을 이끌기 시작했던 시기에 대해 공부할 것이다.

06 communism [kάmjunizm]

a political system in which government controls the production of all food and goods, and there is no privately owned property

n. 공산주의
communist n. 공산주의자, 공산당원 I communistic a. 공산주의자의
communitarian n. 공동 사회의 일원

After the collapse of communism, **people expect that there will be a lot of change of the society.**

공산주의의 붕괴 후, 사람들은 많은 사회 변화가 있을 거라고 기대한다.

07 compatible [kəmpǽtəbl]

able to exist or be used together without causing problem

a. 모순이 없는, 호환성의
compatibility n. 양립성, 정합성 I compatibly ad. 모순없이, 적합하게
incompatible a. 양립하기 힘든, 상반되는

If certain religion is compatible **with democracy, I can believe that.**

만약 어떤 종교가 민주주의와 양립할 수 있다면, 그것을 믿을 수 있다.

| 08 | compromise | [kámprəmàiz] | to reach an agreement in which everyone involved accepts less than what they wanted at first |

v. 타협하다, 화해하다 n. 타협, 화해, 절충안

It is the biggest problem not to compromise **each other at all.**

서로 전혀 타협하지 않는 것이 가장 큰 문제이다.

| 09 | conflict | [kánflikt] | a state of disagreement or argument between people, groups, countries, etc. |

n. 투쟁, 충돌 v. 투쟁하다, 충돌하다

conflicting a. 서로 다투는, 충돌하는 ㅣ confliction n. 다툼, 충돌

We had much conflict **between our employer and the employees last year.**

작년에 우리 회사에서는 노사 분규가 잦았다.

| 10 | conscience | [kánʃəns] | the moral sense of right and wrong that determines someone's thoughts and behavior |

n. 양심, 도의심

conscientious a. 양심적인 ㅣ conscientiously ad. 양심적으로

Conscience **is the inner voice that warns us somebody may be looking.**

양심은 누군가가 우리를 (지켜) 보고 있을지 모른다고 타일러 주는 내부의 소리이다.

11 conservative [kənsə́:rvətiv] unwilling to accept changes and new ideas

a. 보수적인 n. 보수주의자
conservation n. 보호, 관리, 유지 | conservable a. 보존할 수 있는

A conservative party and a radical party are always on the rival situations.
보수 정당과 진보 정당은 항상 경쟁 관계에 있다.

12 contemporary [kəntémpərèri] belonging to the same time

a. 같은 시대의, 현대의 n. 같은 시대의 사람

Shakespeare is the best writer among the contemporary writers.
셰익스피어는 동시대 작가들 중 최고의 작가이다.

13 contradict [kɑntrədíkt] to disagree with something, especially by saying that the opposite is true

v. 부인하다, 반박하다, 모순되다
contradiction n. 부정, 반대, 모순

He contradicted her, but she didn't care about it.
그는 그녀의 말에 반박했지만, 그녀는 신경 쓰지 않았다.

14 controversial [kɑntrəvə́:rʃəl] causing a lot of angry public discussion and disagreement

a. 논쟁을 좋아하는
controvert vt. 논의하다, 논쟁하다

All of the members try to avoid the controversial matter.
모든 회원들이 논쟁의 여지가 있는 문제를 피하려고 한다.

15 **convict** [kənvíkt]   to decide and state officially in court that somebody is guilty of a crime

vt. ~에게 유죄를 선고하다
conviction n. 유죄 판결, 설득 ㅣ convictive a. 설득력 있는
convince v. 확신시키다

Last Saturday, he was convicted in his case by the juries.
지난주 토요일, 그는 배심원들에 의해 그의 사건에 대해 유죄 판결을 받았다.

16 **critical** [krítikəl]   expressing disapproval of someone or something and saying what you think is bad about them

a. 비평의, 평론의, 비판적인
critically ad. 비평적으로, 혹평하여 ㅣ criticise v. 비평하다, 평론하다
criticism n. 비평, 비판

He assumes a critical attitude of the current government.
그는 현 정부에 비판적인 태도를 취한다.

17 **debate** [dibéit]   to discuss a subject formally when you are trying to make a decision

v. 토론하다, 논쟁하다 n. 토론, 논쟁
debater n. 토론가, 토의가 ㅣ debating n. 토론(하기)

They fought each other when they debated the topic.
그들은 그 화제에 대해 토론했을 때 서로 다투었다.

18 determine [ditə́ːrmin] to officially decide something

v. 결심하다, 결정하다
determination n. 결심, 결정 | determined a. 굳게 결심한, 단호한
determiner n. 결정하는 사람

He firmly determined to act on a right way with her advice.

그는 그녀의 충고로 옳은 쪽으로 행동하기로 결정했다.

19 dispute [dispjúːt] to argue or disagree strongly with someone about something

v. 논쟁하다, 반론하다 n. 논의, 토론, 논쟁
disputation n. 논쟁, 논의 | disputer n. 논쟁자

Dr. Kim used to dispute which way is better with those who have different ideas from his.

김박사는 자신의 의견과 다른 사람들과 어느 쪽이 더 나은지에 대해 논쟁하곤 했다.

20 emphasis [émfəsis] special importance that is given to something

n. 강조, 중요성
emphasize v. ~을 강조하다 | emphatic a. 강조된
emphatically ad. 강조하여, 단호히

For years so many people have put emphasis on establishing their own identity.

수년 동안 많은 사람들은 그들만의 주체성 확립에 대해 강조해왔다.

21   **expose** [ikspóuz]   to show something that is usually hidden

v. 폭로하다, 드러내다, 발표하다
exposition n. 설명, 제시, 폭로 | exposed a. 노출된
exposure n. 폭로, 드러남

It was exposed **through the news that the famous singer had died of a heart attack.**
유명한 가수가 심장 마비로 죽었다는 것이 뉴스를 통해 발표되었다.

22   **faith** [féiθ]   belief and trust in God

n. 신앙, 신뢰, 신용, 신념
faithful a. 충실한, 성실한, 믿을 만한 | faithfully ad. 성실하게, 성숙하게
faithfulness n. 충실, 진실 | faithless a. 충실하지 못한, 신앙이 없는

Why don't you have faith **for yourself?**
너 자신을 위해 신앙을 가지는 건 어때?

23   **fancy** [fǽnsi]   to like or want something, or want to do something

v. 상상하다, 좋아하다 n. 공상, 좋아함 a. 상상의, 화려한
fanciful a. 공상에 잠긴, 변덕스러운, 기발한

Sorry but, I don't fancy **going out tonight.**
미안하지만 오늘밤엔 나가고 싶지 않다.

24 fundamental [fʌndəméntl] basic and underlying

a. 기초의, 근본의
fundamentality n. 기본성, 중요성 I fundamentally ad. 본질적으로

The fundamental truth of all of the religions is same.
모든 종교의 근본적인 진리는 같다.

25 grant [grǽnt, grɑ́:nt] to give someone something or allow someone to have something

v. 주다, 인정하다 n. 허가, 양도

They grew up enough to grant your favor.
그들은 너의 부탁을 들어줄 만큼 충분히 자랐다.

26 ideology [àidiɑ́ləʤi, ìd-] a set of beliefs on which an economic or political system is based

n. 관념학, 이데올로기, 공론
ideologic a. 관념적인 I ideologist n. 관념론자

There can be differences about ideology among people.
사람들 사이에는 이데올로기의 차이가 있을 수 있다.

27 insist [insíst] to demand that something happens or that someone agree to do something

v. 주장하다, 강요하다
insistence n. 주장, 강조, 강요 I insistent a. 주장하는, 눈에 띄는

He always insists that we have to be kind to the old.
그는 항상 우리가 노인들에게 친절해야 한다고 주장한다.

28 **liberal** [líbərəl] wanting or allowing a lot of political and economic freedom and supporting gradual social, political or religious change

a. 자유주의의, 관대한 n. 자유주의자
liberty n. 자유, 허가 | liberalize v. 완화하다

She is liberal **with her money.**

그녀는 돈에 관해서는 관대하다.

---

29 **logic** [ládʒik] a way of thinking about something that seems correct and reasonable

n. 논리, 논리학, 이치
logical a. 논리적인

There is a leap in your logic.

당신의 논리에는 비약이 있다.

---

30 **mental** [méntl] connected with or happening in the mind

a. 마음의, 정신의, 지적인
mentalism n. 심리주의 | mentality n. 사고방식

The mental **health is the most important thing.**

정신적인 건강이 가장 중요한 것이다.

---

31 **motivate** [móutəvèit] to be the reason why someone does something or behaves in a particular way

v. ~에게 동기를 주다
motivation n. 자극, 동기 부여 | motive n. 동기 a. 동기의, 원동력이 되는

The poem I read a long time ago, motivated **me to be a writer.**

오래 전에 읽었던 그 시가 나에게 작가가 될 수 있도록 동기를 주었다.

32 **optimistic** [ὰptəmístik] expecting good thing to happen or something to be successful

a. 낙천주의의, 낙관적인
optimism n. 낙천주의 | optimist n. 낙관주의자
optimize v. 낙관하다

It is necessary to have an optimistic **view when regarding the future.** 장래를 낙관하는 것은 필요한 것이다.

33 **patriot** [péitriət] someone who loves their country and is willing to defend it

n. 애국자
patriotic a. 애국적인 | patriotism n. 애국심

Do you think you are a patriot?
넌 네가 애국자라고 생각하니?

34 **pessimistic** [pèsəmístik] expecting bad things to happen or something not to be successful

a. 비관적인, 염세적인
pessimism n. 염세주의 | pessimist n. 비관론자, 염세주의자

She committed suicide since she had a pessimistic **view of her own life.**
그녀는 그녀의 삶을 비관하였기 때문에 자살했다.

35 **prejudice** [prédʒudis] an unreasonable dislike of a particular group of people or things

n. 선입관, 편견, 침해 v. ~에 편견을 갖다
prejudiced a. 선입관을 가진

Many women still encounter prejudice **in the work place.**
아직도 많은 여성들이 직장에서 편견에 부딪히고 있다.

36   **profound** [prəfáund]   showing great knowledge or understanding

a. (학문이) 깊은, 충심의
profoundly ad. 깊게, 매우

I have taken a profound interest in psychology since I was a high school student.

나는 고등학교 때부터 심리학에 깊은 관심이 있어 왔다.

37   **progressive** [prəgrésiv]   in favour of new ideas, modern methods and changes

a. 전진하는, 진보적인 n. 진보주의
progress n. 전진, 진보 v. 전진하다 | progressively ad. 점진적으로

He is the man with the most progressive ideas I know.

그는 내가 아는 가장 진보적인 사람이다.

38   **purpose** [pə́ːrpəs]   the intention, aim or function of something

n. 목적, 취지 v. 작정하다
purposeful a. 목적이 있는, 고의의 | purposeless a. 무의미한, 목적이 없는
on purpose 고의로, 일부러

Have a fixed purpose, and you'll be improving as much as you want.

확고한 목적을 가져라, 그러면 네가 원하는 만큼 향상될 것이다.

39 radical [rǽdikəl] in favor of complete political change

a. 근본적인, 급진적인 n. 급진주의자
radically ad. 근본적으로, 완전히

The radical party showed their radical aspects compared with others.

진보당은 다른 당에 비해 과격한 양상을 보여주었다.

40 rational [rǽʃənl] based on reason rather than emotions

a. 이성적인, 합리적인, 추론의 n. 합리적인 것
rationalism n. 이성론, 합리주의 | rationalize v. 합리화하다

His reaction was a very rational action when compared with Mr. Jones.

Mr. Jones와 비교하면 그의 반응은 매우 이성적인 행동이었다.

41 recognition [rèkəgníʃən] the act of remembering who is when you see a person

n. 알아봄, 인지, 인정
recognize v. 알아보다, 인지하다 | recognizable a. 인식할 수 있는

Her exclusive attitude turned into a generous attitude by recognition of different ideas.

다른 생각들을 인정함으로써 그녀의 배타적인 태도는 관대한 태도로 바뀌었다.

42 **reject** [ridʒékt] to refuse to accept or consider something

v. 거절하다, 무시하다
rejection n. 거절, 기각

I remember that he rejected her suggestion in a word
three years ago.

3년 전 그가 그녀의 제안을 한마디로 거절했던 것을 기억하고 있다.

43 **revolution** [revəlúːʃən] an attempt, by a large number of people, to change the government of a country, especially by violent action

n. 혁명, 변혁, 공전
revolutionary a. 혁명의, 회전하는 | revolutionize v. 혁명을 일으키다

The revolution of the whole nation against the
government will cause many big problems.

정부에 반대하는 전 국민의 혁명은 많은 큰 문제들을 일으킬 것이다.

44 **severe** [səvíər] very bad or very serious

a. 엄한, 엄격한, 심한
severely ad. 심하게, 엄하게 | severity n. 격렬, 엄격

Her father was very severe when she was a little girl.

그녀의 아버지는 그녀가 어렸을 때 매우 엄하셨다.

45 **skeptical** [sképtikəl] doubtful; inclined to be incredulous

a. 의심 많은, 회의적인
skeptic n. 회의론자 a. 회의론자의

He is skeptical about that girl weeping behind the church.
그는 교회 뒤에서 울고 있는 저 소녀를 의심한다.

46 **socialism** [sóuʃəlìzm] a set of political and economic theories based on the belief that everyone has an equal right to a share of a country's wealth and that the government should own and control main industries

n. 사회주의 (운동)
socialist n. 사회주의자

The socialism was spread in a wink.
사회주의는 순식간에 퍼졌다.

47 **suppose** [səpóuz] to think or believe that something is true or possible

v. 가정하다, 추측하다, 전제로 하다
supposed a. 상상된, 가정의 | supposition n. 상상, 추측, 가정

Nobody supposed that he might commit such a cruel crime.
아무도 그가 그런 끔찍한 범죄를 저질렀을 거라고 상상하지 못했다.

48 **swear** [swɛ́ər] to make a serious promise to do something

v. 맹세하다, 증언하다 n. 맹세, 선서

I swear that I will tell the truth.
진실을 말할 것을 맹세한다.

49　**sympathy** [símpəθi]　the feeling of being sorry for someone

n. 동정, 공감, 호의
sympathetic a. 동정심 있는 ǀ sympathetically ad. 동정하여
sympathize v. 동정하다, 공명하다, 동감하다

I know a woman of wide sympathies.

포용력이 있는 여성을 알고 있다.

50　**symbolism** [símbəlìzm]　the use of symbols to represent ideas, especially in art and literature

n. 상징화, 상징, 상징주의
symbol n. 상징, 기호 ǀ symbolical a. 상징적인, 표상하는
symbolize v. 상징하다 ǀ symbolization n. 기호화, 상징화

She is one of those who are addicted to symbolism.

그녀는 상징주의에 빠져 있는 사람들 중 하나이다.

C h e c k u p

A 괄호 안의 단어 중 문맥상 적절한 것을 고르시오.

1. She is an (advocate/advocation) of children's right.

2. I (ascribe/argue) with my brother all the time.

3. Not many are (award/aware) of the old and the poor.

4. Many people expect the collapse of (communism/democracy).

5. The labor union doesn't offer an acceptable (compromise /compromising).

B 보기에서 알맞은 단어를 골라 관용어를 완성하시오.

sympathy	fancy	purpose	mental	suppose
faith	prejudice	swear	grant	recognition

1. enough to _____ by : 아주 조금

2. beyond _____ : 옛 모습을 찾아볼 수 없을 정도로

3. have a _____ against : ~을 까닭 없이 싫어하다

4. be _____ d to do : (관습, 법, 의무로) ~하기로 되어 있다

5. after a person's _____ : ~의 마음에 드는

6. take ~ for _____ ed : 당연한 일로 생각하다

7. by one's _____ : 맹세코, 단연코

8. answer the _____ : 목적에 알맞다, 쓸모 있다

9. go _____ : 머리가 이상해지다, 바보 같은 짓을 하다

10. express _____ for : ~을 위문하다, 조의를 표하다

C 다음 영영풀이에 해당되는 단어를 골라 쓰시오.

| determine | expose | critical | emphasis | dispute |

1. to show something that is usually hidden

2. to discover the facts about something

3. expressing disapproval of something and saying what you think is bad

4. special importance that is given to something

5. an argument or a disagreement between two people, groups or countries

Lesson 4
War & Peace
| 전쟁과 평화

01 **assault** [əsɔ́:lt] the crime of physically attacking someone

n. 갑작스런 습격, 공격 v. 폭행하다, 괴롭히다

They lost the fortress to the enemy's assault.

그들은 적의 습격에 요새를 점령당했다.

---

02 **attack** [ətǽk] to deliberately use violence to hurt a person or damage a place

v. 공격하다, 습격하다 n. 공격, 습격
attacker n. 공격자

When you attack **someone, you should know all about him or her.**

누군가를 공격할 땐, 그나 그녀에 대해 모든 걸 알아야 한다.

---

03 **battle** [bǽtl] a fight between armies, ships or planes, especially during a war

n. 전투, 싸움, 승리 v. 싸우다, 투쟁하다
battlefield n. 싸움터, 전장

He was wounded in the battle **20 years ago.**

그는 20년 전 전투에서 부상을 당했다.

---

04 **betray** [bitréi] to hurt someone who trusts you, especially by not being loyal or faithful to them

v. 배반하다
betrayal n. 배신, 밀고 | betrayer n. 배신자

If you betray **your country, we'll give you anything you want.**

만약 당신이 당신의 나라를 배반한다면, 우리는 당신이 원하는 것은 무엇이든 주겠다.

05 blast [blǽst, blάːst] an explosion or a powerful movement of air caused by an explosion

n. 폭발, 강한 바람 v. 폭발하다, (음악) 쾅쾅 울리다
blasted a. 폭파된 | blasting n. 폭파

No one was wounded in the second blast.

두 번째 폭발에서 다친 사람은 아무도 없었다.

06 bomb [bάm] a weapon designed to explode at a particular time or when it is dropped or thrown

n. 폭탄, 핵무기 v. 폭격하다
bombard v. 포격하다 | bomber n. 폭격기

I'm experimenting and researching a new bomb which can lead us to victory.

나는 우리를 승리로 이끌어 줄 수 있는 새로운 폭탄을 실험 · 연구 중이다.

07 capture [kǽptʃər] to catch a person or an animal and keep them as a prisoner in a confined space

v. 붙잡다, 사로잡다 n. 포획, 생포

Being captured by the enemy, I kept thinking about how to escape from them.

적들에게 생포되자 어떻게 그들로부터 도망칠지 계속 생각했다.

08 casualty [kǽʒuəlti] a person who is injured or killed in a war or in an accident

n. 불상사, 사망자, 부상자

Suddenly the Star Department Store was destroyed, and it had heavy casualties.

갑자기 Star 백화점이 무너졌고, 많은 사상자가 발생했다.

09 **cease** [siːs] to stop happening or existing; stop doing something

v. 그치다, 중지하다
ceaseless a. 끊임없는 | ceaselessly ad. 끊임없이

You'd better cease the plan of sending spies to the enemy.
적에게 스파이를 보내는 계획을 중단하는 게 낫겠다.

10 **civilian** [sivíljən] a person who is not member of the armed forces or the police

n. 일반 국민 a. 민간의
civil a. 시민의, 국내의

They solved the problem between the civilians with conversation.
그들은 국민들과의 대화로 문제를 해결했다.

11 **combat** [kəmbǽt, kámbæt] to fight against someone or something

v. 싸우다, 투쟁하다 n. 전투, 투쟁
combatant n. 전투원, 투사 a. 전투를 하는 | combative a. 투쟁적인

Don't combat with your classmates for anything.
어떠한 이유로든 반 친구들과 싸우지 마라.

12 **commander** [kəmǽndər] an officer in charge of a military operation or organization

n. 지휘자, 사령관
command v. 명령하다, 지휘하다 n. 명령, 지휘 | commanding a. 지휘하는, 당당한

Mr. Purple was appointed as a lieutenant commander.
Mr. Purple은 해군 소령으로 임명되었다.

13 compulsory [kəmpʌ́lsəri] required by the rule, law etc.

a. 의무적인, 강제적인
compulsion n. 강요, 강박 | compulsive a. 강제적인
compulsorily ad. 강제적으로

As the education in elementary school is compulsory
education, everyone has the right to go to elementary
school including him.

초등학교 교육은 의무 교육이기 때문에, 그를 포함한 모든 사람들이 초등학교에
다닐 권리가 있다.

14 conventional [kənvénʃənl] following what is traditional or the way something has been done for a long time

a. 관습적인, 전통적인, 재래식의
convention n. 집회, 정기총회, 관습, 관례
conventional weapons n. 재래식 무기

We'll never beat the competition with conventional
methods.

틀에 박힌 방법으로는 경쟁에서 이길 수 없다.

15 defeat [difíːt] to win against someone in a war, competition, sports game, etc.

v. 좌절시키다 n. 패배, 좌절

He's defeated **all his enemies since he became the**
commander.

그가 지휘관이 된 이래로 그는 모든 적들을 이겨왔다.

16 **defend** [diফénd] to protect someone or something from attack

vt. 막다, 지키다, 방어하다
defence n. 방어, 변호 I defender n. 방어자

He didn't know how to defend his army from the enemy
at that time.
그는 그 당시 적들로부터 그의 군대를 어떻게 방어해야 할지를 몰랐다.

17 **demolish** [dimáliʃ] to destroy something accidentally

vt. 폭파하다, (건물을) 헐다
demolition n. 파괴

Mr. Jim found their shelter, and planned to demolish it.
Mr. Jim은 그들의 은신처를 발견하고 그것을 폭파시킬 계획을 세웠다.

18 **disarm** [disáːrm] to take weapons away

v. 무장 해제하다
disarming a. 흥분을 가라앉히는, 무장 해제시키는

They disarmed him of his weapons as soon as they saw him.
그들은 그를 보자마자 무장 해제시켰다.

19 **discipline** [dísəplin] to train or force to behave in an ordered and controlled way

vt. 훈련하다, 훈계하다, 징벌하다 n. 규율, 훈육
disciplinary a. 훈련상의

The soldier disciplined the captive for his resistance.
그 군인은 그 포로가 반항해서 벌을 주었다.

20   disguise [disgáiz]   to change your appearance so that people cannot recognize you

v. 변장하다 n. 변장, 분장
disguised a. 변장한 | in disguise 변장한

He put on a large hat and glasses as a disguise and no one would recognize him.
그는 변장술로 큰 모자와 안경을 썼는데 아무도 그를 알아보지 못했다.

21   drift [dríft]   a slow steady movement form one place to another

n. 표류, 흐름 v. 표류하다

The boat was on the drift in the sea.
바다에서 보트가 표류했다.

22   emergency [imə́:rdʒənsi]   a sudden serious and dangerous event or situation which needs immediate action to deal with it

n. 비상사태, 비상시

The government declared a state of national emergency.
정부는 국가 비상사태를 선언했다.

23   enemy [énəmi]   a person who acts or speaks against someone or something

n. 적, 경쟁자

They were trained to attack the enemy planes whenever they found them.
그들은 적기를 발견할 때마다 공격하도록 훈련받았다.

24 **explode** [iksplóud] to burst or make something burst loudly and violently, causing damage

v. 폭발하다, 격발하다, 폭파시키다
explosive a. 폭발(성)의, 폭발적인 | explosively ad. 폭발적으로
explosion n. 폭발, 파열

This bomb can explode if you press this button.
네가 이 버튼을 누르면 이 폭탄은 폭발할 수 있다.

25 **flee** [fli:] to leave somewhere very quickly, in order to escape from danger

v. 달아나다, 도망치다

At the end they started to flee for refuge.
결국 그들은 피난 가기 시작했다.

26 **forceful** [fɔ́:rsfəl] powerful; effective; influential

a. 힘이 있는, 힘센, 단호한, 강력한
force n. 힘 vt. 강요하다

The effect of this forceful poem is enhanced by contrast.
이 힘찬 시의 효과는 대조법에 의해 고조된다.

27 **fortress** [fɔ́:rtris] a building or place that has been made stronger and protect against attack

n. 요새

All you have to do is just to focus on defending our fortress.
네가 해야 할 일은 우리 요새 방어에 집중하는 것뿐이다.

28 **frontier** [frʌntíər, frɑn-] a line that separate two countries

n. 국경 a. 국경의

It is difficult to overpass the militarized frontier.

무장된 국경 지대를 넘는 것은 어렵다.

29 **hardship** [hɑ́ːrdʃìp] something that makes your life difficult or unpleasant, especially lack of money

n. 곤란, 결핍, 고충

She realized many things as she went through hardships .

그녀는 고난을 겪으면서 많은 것을 깨달았다.

30 **honorable** [ɑ́nərəbl] deserving or winning honor and respect

a. 고결한, 명예로운

honor n. 명예, 명성, 존경 | honorably ad. 장하게, 명예롭게

He is very honorable **and respected by all.**

그는 매우 명예롭고, 모두로부터 존경받는다.

31 **hostile** [hɑ́stl, -tail] very unfriendly or aggressive and ready to argue or fight

a. 적(군)의, 적대하는

hostility n. 적개심, 적대 행위

Both two countries have kept their hostile **attitude towards each other.**

두 나라는 서로 적대적인 태도를 유지해왔다.

32 independence [indipéndəns]　freedom from political control by other countries

n. 독립, 자주
independency n. 독립, 독립심 | independent a. 독립한, 자주의

India declared their independence from British in 1947.
1947년에 인도는 영국으로부터 독립을 선언했다.

---

33 interruption [intərʌ́pʃən]　process of interrupting or state of being stopped

n. 중단, 방해
interrupt v. 가로막다, 방해하다 | interrupted a. 가로막힌, 중단된

I prefer to think without interruptions.
나는 방해받지 않고 생각하기를 좋아한다.

---

34 intervene [intərvíːn]　to become involved in a situation in order to affect the outcome

v. 사이에 끼다, 방해하다
intervener n. 중재자, 간섭자 | intervention n. 조정, 중재, 간섭

It seems inappropriate for us to intervene at this stage.
이 단계에서 우리가 끼어드는 것은 부적절한 것 같다.

---

35 invade [invéid]　to enter a country, town, etc. using military force in order to take control of it

v. 침략하다, 침입하다
invader n. 침략자, 침입자 | invasion n. 침략, 침입

That country has been invaded more than 100 times during their history.
저 나라는 그들의 역사동안 100회 이상 침략을 받았다.

36 monument [mɑ́njumənt] something built to remind people of famous person or event

n. 기념비(탑), 기념물
monumental a. 기념비의, 기념이 되는

The monument commemorating the general Kim is set up there.
김장군을 기념하는 기념비가 저기에 세워져 있다.

37 navy [néivi] the part of a country's armed forces that fight at sea

n. 해군
naval a. 해군의

He wanted to join the navy, and his dream came true.
그는 해군에 들어가기를 원했고, 그의 꿈은 이루어졌다.

38 patrol [pətróul] going around an area or a building at regular times to check that it is safe and that there is no trouble

n. 순찰, 순찰병 v. 순찰하다

The thief was caught by the police officer on patrol.
그 도둑은 순찰 중인 경찰에 의해 잡혔다.

39 poverty [pɑ́vərti] the state of being extremely poor

n. 빈곤, 가난

Painless poverty is better than embittered wealth.
고통없는 빈곤이 괴로운 부(富)보다 낫다.

40 **resistance** [rizístəns] dislike or opposition to plan an idea, etc.

n. 저항, 반항

resist v. 저항하다, 반항하다 I resistant a. 저항하는, 반항하는

He made a stubborn resistance against the enemy.

그는 적에게 꿋꿋하게 저항했다.

41 **riot** [ráiət] a situatuion in which a group of people behave in a violent way in a public place, often as a protest

n. 폭동, 소동 v. 폭동을 일으키다

In fact, he is the man who instigated the riot.

사실 그 폭동을 부추겼던 사람은 그이다.

42 **strategy** [strǽtədʒi] a plan that is intended to achieve a particular purpose

n. 전략, 병법, 용병학

strategic a. 전략의 I strategically ad. 전략상으로

If you have a great strategy, you'll win the war.

훌륭한 전략이 있다면 그 전쟁에서 이길 것이다.

43 **surrender** [səréndər] to give up something or someone because you are forced to

vt. 넘겨주다 vi. 항복하다, 포기하다 n. 항복

They couldn't agree to surrender their sovereignty to England.

그들은 영국에 그들의 주권을 넘겨주는 것에 동의할 수 없었다.

44 territory [térətɔ:ri]   land which is controlled by a particular country or ruler

n. 영토, 지역
territorial a. 영토의, 토지의

They tried to invade our territory 100 years ago.
그들은 100년 전에 우리의 영토를 침범하려고 했었다.

---

45 trap [trǽp]   a trick that is intended to catch or deceive someone

n. 올가미, 덫 v. 덫으로 잡다, 속이다
trapper n. 덫을 놓는 사람 ㅣ trappy a. 함정이 있는

He was caught in a trap by his mistake.
그는 실수로 함정에 빠졌다.

---

46 triumph [tráiəmf, -ʌmf]   a great success, achievement or victory

n. 승리, 대성공 v. 승리를 거두다, 이기다
triumphant a. 승리를 거둔, 성공한 ㅣ triumphantly ad. 의기양양하여

We won a triumph over China in the war.
우리는 전쟁에서 중국을 이겼다.

---

47 victim [víktim]   a person who has been attacked, injured or killed as the result of the crime, a disease, an accident, etc.

n. 희생(자), 산 제물
victimize vt. 희생시키다

She is the real victim of the war, not them.
그들이 아니라 그녀가 그 전쟁의 진짜 희생자이다.

48 warrior [wɔ́:riər, wár] a person who fights in a battle or war

n. 전사, 용사 a. 전사의

We could win the war by the sacrifice of many warriors.

많은 용사들의 희생으로 그 전쟁을 이길 수 있었다.

49 warship [wɔ́:rʃip] a ship used in a war

n. 군함, 전함

They don't have enough warships**, so we can win this battle.**

그들은 충분한 군함이 없으니까 우리가 이 전쟁을 이길 수 있다.

50 weapon [wépən] an object such as knife, gun, bomb, etc. that is used for fighting or attacking someone

n. 무기, 흉기

weaponry n. 무기류

The new weapons **were introduced at the exhibition.**

새로운 무기들이 전시회에서 소개되었다.

Check up

A 다음 내용이 설명하고 있는 단어를 〈보기〉에서 골라 그 기호를 쓰시오.

> a. assault   b. battle   c. betray   d. blast   e. capture

1. a fight between armies, ships or planes, especially during a war

2. an explosion or a powerful movement of air caused by an explosion

3. to catch a person or an animal and keep them as a prisoner or in a confined space

4. the crime of attacking somebody physically

5. to give information about something to an enemy

B 알맞은 반대말끼리 연결하시오.

1. casualty •

2. civilian •

3. compulsory •

4. defeat •

5. disarm •

• 불의의 재난, 부상자

• 패배, 좌절

• 무장 해제하다

• 일반 국민, 민간의

• 의무적인, 강제적인

C 다음 빈 칸에 의미상 가장 알맞은 단어를 보기에서 골라 쓰시오.

| discipline | disguise | drift | emergency | enemy |

1. military _____ : 군기, 규율

2. _____ needs : 비상시 필수품

3. be one's own worst _____ : 자신을 가장 괴롭히는 요소가 되다

4. throw off one's _____ : 정체를 드러내다, 가면을 벗어버리다

5. _____ along through life : 허송세월하다

D 다음 영영풀이에 알맞은 단어를 고르시오.

1. a great success, achievement or victory (triumph / defeat)

2. to admit that you have been defeated (resist / surrender)

3. the state of being poor (wealth / poverty)

4. very unfriendly or aggressive (hostile / amicable)

5. deserving or winning honer and respect

(dishonorable / honorable)

Part 5

Economy

[경제]

Lesson 1
Economy
| 경제

01 **attain** [ətéin] to succeed in getting something, usually after a lot of effort

v. 달성하다, 성취하다
attainment n. 달성, 도달 ㅣ attainable a. 도달할 수 있는

The government attained its goal last year.

정부는 작년에 목표를 달성했다.

02 **available** [əvéiləbl] able to be used; able to be bought or found easily

a. 이용할 수 있는, 유효한

There are no more seat available.

더 이상 좌석이 없다.

03 **bargain** [báːrgən] to discuss the conditions of a sale, agreement, etc. for example to get a lower price

v. 협상하다, 흥정하다   n. 매매, 흥정, 거래
bargaining n. 협상, 흥정

The government let the merchants bargain with the producers about the price.

정부는 상인들이 생산자들과 가격 흥정을 하도록 했다.

04 **barter** [báːrtər] to exchange goods and services for other goods and services rather than using money

v. 물물 교환하다, 교환하다   n. 물물 교환

Once upon a time you could barter salt for everything.

옛날에는 소금으로 모든 것을 교환할 수 있었다.

05 boom [búːm] a sudden increase in trade and economic activity

n. (사업 · 경제의) 붐, 호황, 대유행, 쾅 하는 소리
booming a. 쾅 하고 울리는, 급속히 발전하는

The hotel business is destined for a boom again, I think.
내 생각에는 호텔 사업이 다시 호황을 누릴 것이다.

06 budget [bʌ́dʒit] a plan specifying how money will be spent and allocated during a particular period of time

n. 예산 v. 예산을 세우다
budgetary a. 예산상의

The government needs to balance the budget each year.
정부는 해마다 예산 균형을 맞출 필요가 있다.

07 business [bíznis] the activity of making, buying, selling or supplying goods or services for money

n. 사무, 상업, 일, 상점
businesslike a. 사무적인, 실제적인 | businessman n. 실업가, 상인

He is going to stay here on business for three days.
그는 3일 동안 사업상 여기에 머물 것이다.

08 calculate [kǽlkjulèit] to use numbers to find out a total number, amount, distance, etc.

v. 계산하다, 추산하다, 어림잡다
calculated a. 계산된, 계획적인 | calculating a. 타산적인, 계산적인
calculation n. 계산, 추정 | calculator n. 계산기

You must calculate the budget for next year.
너는 내년 예산을 추산해야 한다.

09 commodity [kəmɑ́dəti] a product or a raw material that can be bought and sold

n. 상품, 일용품, 필수품

It was announced through the news that the price of
commodities **will raise from next month.**

다음달부터 생활필수품 가격이 오를 것이라고 뉴스에 발표되었다.

10 consume [kənsúːm] to use something, especially fuel, energy or time

v. 소비하다, 소모하다, 소멸하다
consumable a. 소비할 수 있는 I consumer n. 소비자
consuming a. 소비하는, 절실한 I consumer goods 소비재

Consuming **causes the cycle of economy market.**

소비하는 것이 경제 시장의 순환을 일으킨다.

11 consumption [kənsʌ́mpʃən] the act of using energy, food or materials

n. 소비(량), 소모

Consumption **makes the market active unless too much.**

너무 과하지만 않다면 소비는 시장을 활기차게 만든다.

12 deal [díːl] an agreement, especially in business, on particular conditions for buying or doing something

n. 협정, 거래, 분량 v. 분배하다, 다루다, 취급하다
dealer n. 상인

I'm still under consideration if I will close a deal **or not.**

나는 거래를 끝낼 것이지 아닌지 아직도 고려 중이다.

13 **decide** [disáid] to think carefully about the different possibilities that are available and choose them

v. 해결하다, 결심하다, 결정하다
decisive a. 결정적인, 결단력 있는 | decision n. 결심, 결정

He decided to use the traditional market instead of the convenience store.
그는 편의점 대신 재래 시장을 이용하기로 결정했다.

14 **deflation** [difléiʃən] a reduction in the amount of money in a country's economy, so that prices fall or stop rising

n. 통화 수축, 디플레이션, 공기 빼기
deflate v. (통화를) 수축하다, (물가를) 끌어내리다, 공기를 빼다,

To pull the economy out of the long deflation, the government held the urgent meeting.
오랜 디플레이션 현상에서 벗어나기 위해 정부는 긴급 회의를 열었다.

15 **delay** [diléi] to make someone late or force them to do something more slowly

v. 미루다, 연기하다, ~을 늦추다 n. 지연

You can have more time by delaying the meeting.
너는 회의를 늦춤으로써 시간을 벌 수 있다.

16 **demand** [dimǽnd] to ask for something very firmly

v. 요구하다, 청구하다 n. 요구, 청구, 수요
demanding a. 힘든, 요구가 많은

The nation demanded a improvement of inflation in an instant.
국민은 즉각 인플레이션의 개선을 요구했다.

17 discount [dískaunt] to take the amount or percentage off the usual price

v. 할인하다 n. 할인
discountable a. 할인할 수 있는 ㅣ discount market 할인시장

They are planning to discount all of the items at 50 percent for two hours in the morning.

그들은 오전 2시간 동안 모든 상품들을 50% 할인할 계획을 세우고 있다.

18 distribute [distríbju:t] to give things to large number of people

v. 분배하다, 배포하다
distribution n. 분배, 배급 ㅣ distributor n. 분배자, 배급자

To distribute some supplies to the sufferers can be helpful for them to recover.

이재민들에게 지급품을 분배하는 것은 그들이 복구하는 데에 도움이 될 수 있다.

19 durable [djúərəbl] likely to last for a long time without breaking or getting weaker

a. 튼튼한, 영속성이 있는
durability n. 영속성, 내구성 ㅣ duration n. 기간

The parts of the machine which experience a lot of friction have to be made from durable materials.

마찰이 많은 기계 부품은 내구성 있는 소재로 만들어야 한다.

20 earn [ə́:rn] to get money for work that you do

v. 벌다, 획득하다
earning n. 소득

To earn a lot of money, you have to change your lazy habits first.

돈을 많이 벌기 위해서는 우선 네 게으른 버릇부터 바꿔야 한다.

21 economy [ikάnəmi] the system according to which the money, industry, and trade of a country or region are organized

n. 경제, 절약

economic a. 경제학의 ㅣ economical a. 경제적인

The Korean economy has gotten better recently.

최근 한국 경제가 나아지고 있다.

.

22 employ [implɔ́i, em-] to give someone a job to do for payment

v. 고용하다, ~에 종사하다

employee n. 고용인, 종업원 ㅣ employer n. 고용주, 사용자

She was employed as a secretary of the chairman.

그녀는 회장 비서로 고용되었다.

23 endure [indʒúər, en-] to experience and deal with something that is painful or unpleasant, especially without complaining

v. 견디다, ~을 참다, 인정하다

endurable a. 참을 수 있는 ㅣ endurance n. 내구성, 참을성

Can you endure it, if it is so painful?

이것 때문에 엄청난 고통이 와도 견딜 수 있겠니?

24 estimate [éstəmət, -mèit] to form an idea of the cost, size, value, etc. but without calculating it exactly

v. 평가하다, 견적내다 n. 평가, 견적

estimable a. 평가할 수 있는 ㅣ estimated a. 견적의, 추측의

estimation n. 판단, 평가, 견적

Estimate how much it would cost to repair it.

그것을 수리하는 데에 얼마나 비용이 드는지 견적을 내라.

25 exceed [iksíːd] to be greater than a particular number or amount

v. 넘다, 초과하다, 지나치다
exceeding a. 엄청난, 대단한 | exceedingly ad. 매우

Drivers must not exceed **a maximum of 55 miles an hour.**
운전자들은 시속 55마일의 최고 속도를 초과하지 말아야 한다.

26 income [ínkʌm] money received over a period of time as payment for work or as interest or profit from shares or investment

n. 수입, 소득
incomer n. 들어오는 사람, 새 가입자 | incoming n. 수입, 소득 a. 들어오는, 후임의

Mr. Robin always pays a lot of income **tax.**
Mr. Robbin은 항상 많은 소득세를 낸다.

27 inflation [infléiʃən] a general increase in the prices of goods and services in a country

n. 인플레이션, 통화 팽창
inflate v. 부풀게 하다, (물가를) 올리다 | inflated a. 부풀은, 팽창한

They focused on the wage inflation.
그들은 임금 인플레이션에 주목했다.

28 item [áitəm] one thing on a list of things to buy, do, talk about, etc.

n. 항목, 품목
itemize v. 조목별로 쓰다, 항목으로 나누다

To make a list of items **that you have to buy is a good habit for saving money.**
사야 할 제품 목록을 만드는 것은 돈을 절약하는 좋은 습관이다.

29 labor [léibər]   work, especially physical work

n. 노동 a. 노동의 v. 열심히 일하다, 노동하다
laboring a. 노동에 종사하는 l laborious a. 힘 드는, 일 잘하는

Many people are gathering into the labor market.

많은 사람들이 노동 시장으로 모이고 있다.

30 luxury [lʌ́kʃəri, lʌ́gʒə-]   a thing that is expensive but not essential

n. 사치(품) a. 사치스러운, 고급의
luxuriant a. 풍부한 l luxurious a. 사치스러운 l luxuriously ad. 사치스럽게

There are much more people who live in luxury than you think.

네가 생각하는 것보다 훨씬 많은 사람들이 호화스럽게 살고 있다.

31 market [má:rkit]   a place where goods are bought and sold, usually outdoors

n. 시장, 매매 v. 물건을 사다, 시장에 내놓다
marketability n. 시장성 l marketable a. 시장성이 있는

He usually visits a meat market after his work as he really likes meat.

그는 고기를 정말 좋아해서 퇴근 후 자주 식육점에 간다.

32 multinational [mʌltinǽʃənl]   existing in or involving many countries

a. 다국적의, 다국적 회사의 n. 다국적 기업

These days the multinational companies contribute to the economy of our country.

요즘 다국적 기업들아 우리나라 경제에 기여하고 있다.

33 **necessity** [nəsésəti] a thing that you must have and cannot manage without

n. 필요, 필요성, 필연성, 필수품
necessary a. 필요한 ㅣ necessarily ad. 필연적으로

His works tell us the necessity for invention.

그의 작품은 발명의 필요성을 말해주고 있다.

34 **obtain** [əbtéin] to get something, especially by making an effort

v. 획득하다, 얻게 하다, 달성하다
obtainable a. 얻을 수 있는

He works hard to obtain knowledge through studying.

그는 연구를 통해 지식을 얻으려고 열심히 일한다.

35 **possess** [pəzés] to have or own something

v. 소유하다
possession n. 소유, 재산 ㅣ possessive a. 소유의

What she possesses is just a house and a car.

그녀가 가지고 있는 것은 단지 집과 차뿐이다.

36 **practical** [prǽktikəl] connected with real situations rather than ideas or theories

a. 실용적인, 실제의
practicable a. 실제적인, 실용적인, 사용할 수 있는
practically ad. 실제로, 사실상

That position requires practical experience and fluent English skills.

그 자리는 실무 경험과 유창한 영어 실력을 필요로 한다.

37 purchase [pə́:rtʃəs] to buy something

v. 구입하다, 사다, 획득하다 n. 구입, 매입
purchaser n. 사는 사람, 구매자

He does not know where to purchase **an item.**

그는 그것을 어디서 사야할지 모른다.

38 relieve [rilíːv] to remove or reduce an unpleasant feeling or pain

v. 경감하다, 구원하다
relieved a. 안도하는 I reliever n. 구제자

I want to contribute a lot of money to relieve **the poor from poverty.**

빈곤으로부터 빈민을 구제하기 위해 많은 돈을 기부하고 싶다.

39 sale [séil] an act or the process of selling something

n. 판매, 매매, 할인 판매
on sale 판매되는, 구입할 수 있는 I salesman n. 판매원

We are looking forward to starting the bargain sale **of the Star department store.**

우리는 Star 백화점의 특가 판매 시작을 굉장히 기대하고 있다.

40 satisfaction [sæ̀tisfǽkʃən] the pleasure that you feel when you do something or get something that you wanted or needed to do or get

n. 만족, 만족을 주는 것
satisfy v. 만족시키다 I satisfactory a. 만족스러운

The motto of my company is customer satisfaction.

우리 회사의 모토는 고객 만족이다.

41 **slight** [sláit] very small in degree or quantity

a. 근소한, 약간의, 가냘픈
slightly ad. 약간

The price of oil showed a slight decline today.
오늘 기름 값이 다소 감소하는 추세를 보였다.

42 **slump** [slʌ́mp] to fall in price, value, number etc. suddenly and by a large amount

v. 쿵 떨어지다, 폭락하다. n. 쿵 떨어짐, 불황

It showed that it is getting out of the worldwide slump.
그것은 세계적인 불황에서 벗어나고 있음을 보여 주었다.

43 **statistic** [stətístik] a collection of information shown in numbers

n. 통계치(량), 통계 자료
statistical a. 통계적인, 통계학상의 | statistically ad. 통계적으로
statistics n. 통계학

This statistic lets us know that watching TV too much can
be harmful for teenagers.
이 통계는 TV를 너무 많이 시청하는 것이 청소년들에게 해로울 수 있다는 것을
알려준다.

44 **supplement** [sʌ́pləmənt] to add something to something in order to improve it or make it more complete

v. 보충하다, 증보하다 n. 추가, 보충
supplemental a. 보충의, 추가의 | supplementary a. 보충하는, 추가의
supplementation n. 보충, 추가

Gestures are often used to supplement the verbal message.
제스처는 종종 음성 메시지를 보충하는 데 사용됩니다.

45 supply [səplái]

to provide someone with something that they need or want, especially in large quantities

v. 공급하다, 대신하다 n. 공급, 배급
supplier n. 공급자, 보충자 | demand and supply 수요와 공급

The city supplies free meals for the old who live alone, three times a week.

시에서는 혼자 사는 노인들에게 일주일에 세 번 무료 식사를 제공한다.

46 unemployed [ʌnimplɔ́id]   without paid empolyment; jobless

a. 실직한, 한가한
unemployment n. 실직, 실업률

He spent more than a year unemployed.

그는 실직 상태로 1년 넘는 시간을 보냈다.

47 utilize [júːtəlaiz]   to use something for a particular purpose

v. 이용하다, 소용되게 하다
utilization n. 이용

He has utilized the facilities since he moved in here.

그는 여기에 이사 온 후로 그 편의 시설을 이용해 왔다.

48 warrant [wɔ́ːrənt, wɑ́r-]   to promise that something is true

v. 정당화하다, 보증하다 n. 권한, 인가, 정당한 이유, 보증
warranty n. 정당한 이유, 보증, 담보

I can warrant the quality of the item, trust me.

난 그 제품의 품질을 보증할 수 있다. 나를 믿어라.

49　　wealth　[wélθ]　a large amount of money, property, etc. that a person or country owns

n. 부, 재산, 풍부

wealthy　a. 부유한, 풍부한

The wealth can't be a standard of one's happiness.

부가 행복의 척도가 될 순 없다.

50　　workforce　[wə́:rkfɔ:rs]　all the people who work for a particular company, organization, etc.

n. 전 종업원, 노동력

They couldn't help downsizing the workforce.

그들은 노동력 감축을 하지 않을 수 없었다.

Check up

A 다음 중 유의어가 아닌 것을 고르시오.

1. available

a. for sale   b. on the market   c. unavailable   d. on sale

2. business

a. work   b. preserve   c. job   d. trade

3. delay

a. postpone   b. rush   c. put off   d. defer

4. demand

a. obviate   b. require   c. want   d. need

5. distribute

a. dispense   b. deal   c. gather   d. pass out

B 주어진 표현에 해당하는 단어를 보기에서 고르시오.

| durable | deal | employ | estimate | income |

1. _____ : hire, recruit, sign, contract, engage

2. _____ : guess, judge, reckon, calculate, gauge

3. _____ : wage, pay, salary, earnings

4. _____ : long, serviceable, imperishable

5. _____ : agreement, contract, pact

C 우리말은 영어로, 영어는 우리말로 바꾸시오.

1. workforce   2. 구입하다, 사다, 획득하다

3. 정당한 이유, 보증   4. statistic

5. 근소한; 경시하다   6. 소유하다

7. relieve   8. unemployed

9. multinational   10. 소비, 소모

Lesson 2
Agriculture
|농업

01 abundant [əbʌ́ndənt] existing in large quantites

a. 풍부한, 많은
abundance n. 풍부, 다수

Oranges are abundant in this district.
이 지방은 오렌지가 풍부하다.

02 acre [éikər] a unit for measuring an area of land

n. 에이커

He plowed up two acres of field a day.
그는 하루 2에이커만큼의 땅을 갈아엎었다.

03 agriculture [ǽgrikʌ̀ltʃər] a science or practice of farming

n. 농업, 농사
agricultural a. 농업의, 농사의

The number of the young who work in agriculture is increasing.
농업에 종사하는 젊은이들의 수가 점점 늘고 있다.

04 ample [ǽmpl] enough or more than euough

a. 충분한, 넓은
amplify vt. 확대하다, 자세히 설명하다

He chose that land because it can provide ample grass for cows.
그는 소들에게 충분한 풀을 제공할 수 있기 때문에 그 땅을 선택했다.

05 arise [əráiz] to happen

v. 일어나다, 생기다

A conflict arose between the farmers and the retailers because of the price.

가격 때문에 농부들과 소매 상인들 간의 분쟁이 일어났다.

06 bare [bέər] not covered by any clothes

a. 발가벗은, 빈
barely ad. 겨우, 간신히, 거의…없이

Here is filled with trees bare of leaves.

여기는 잎이 진 나무들로 가득하다.

07 barren [bǽrən] not good enough to produce crops or fruit

a. 불모의, 메마른 n. 불모지
barrenness n. 불모, 무익

It can't be possible to cultivate something in a barren land.

메마른 농토에서 경작하는 것은 불가능하다.

08 breed [bríːd] a to keep animals or plants in order to produce young ones in a controlled way

v. (새끼를) 낳다, 사육하다, 양육하다 n. 품종
breeder n. 번식하는 동식물, 양육자 I breeding n. 번식, 부화

Mr. Robin breeds cattle for living.

Mr. Robin은 생계로 소를 사육한다.

09 **caterpillar** [kǽtərpilər] a small creature like a worm with legs that develops into a butterfly or moth

n. 모충, 애벌레

Caterpillars turn into butterflies after spending time in a cocoon.

애벌레는 고치로 지낸 후에 나비로 변한다.

10 **cattle** [kǽtl] cows and bulls that are kept as farm animals for their milk or meat

n. 소

My ranch had 1,000 cattle, but just half of them remained now.

내 목장에는 1,000마리의 소가 있었지만 지금은 반만 남았다.

11 **circumstance** [sə́ːrkəmstæns] the conditions and facts that are connected with and affect a situation, or an action

n. 주위의 사정, 상황

circumstantial a. 주위 사정에 따른, 이차적인, 부수적인

As he moved, he tried to let his chickens adapt to new circumstances.

그는 이사를 해서 그의 닭들이 새로운 환경에 적응하도록 하고 있다.

12 **clear** [klíər] easy to see through

a. 밝은, 맑은, 명백한 v. 명백히 하다, ~을 제거하다

clearly ad. 밝게, 뚜렷하게, 분명히

You can start to work after the mist clears away.

안개가 걷혀야 너는 일을 시작할 수 있다.

13 **constant** [kánstənt] happening all the time or repeatedly

a. 불변의, 끊임없이
constantly ad. 끊임없이, 항상 | inconstant a. 변덕스러운

It needs the constant **temperature to grow.**

이것은 자라기 위해 일정한 온도가 필요하다.

14 **cope** [kóup] to deal successfully with something difficult

v. 대항하다, 잘 처리하다

He did anything he could do to cope **with the poverty.**

그는 가난을 극복하려고 그가 할 수 있는 어떠한 것이라도 했다.

15 **creek** [kríːk, krík] a narrow place where the sea comes a long way into the land

n. 작은 천, 작은 만

There are a lot of different kinds of plants around the creek.

하천 근처에는 많은 종류의 식물이 있다.

16 **crop** [kráp] a plant that is grown in large quantities, especially as food

n. 수확, 농작물 v. 수확하다, 작물을 심다

The California orange crop **is more than twice as big as last year.**

캘리포니아 오렌지 수확량이 지난해보다 두 배 이상 많다.

17 cultivate [kʌ́ltəvèit]　to prepare and use land for growing plants or crops

v. 경작하다, 재배하다, 양식하다
cultivation n. 경작, 재배 | cultivated a. 경작된

I cultivated this land into a fertile one where I can grow crops.
나는 이 땅을 작물을 재배할 수 있는 비옥한 땅으로 경작했다.

18 dairy [déəri]　a place on a farm where milk is kept and where butter and cheese are made

n. 낙농업, 우유 제조장 a. 유제품의

A dairy farm is hardly ever seen these days.
요즘은 낙농장이 잘 보이지 않는다.

19 dam [dǽm]　a barrier built across a river in order to stop the water from flowing

n. 댐, 둑 v. 댐을 세우다

If you build a dam across the river, it will be able to produce clean energy.
네가 강에 댐을 만들면 청정 에너지를 생산할 수 있을 것이다.

20 dawn [dɔ́ːn]　the time of day when light first appears

n. 새벽, 처음 v. 날이 새다, 보이기 시작하다

Working at the farm continues from the dawn to the late night.
농장에서 일하는 것은 새벽부터 늦은 밤까지 계속된다.

21 **drain** [dréin] to empty by removing all the liquid

v. 배수하다, 흘러 나가다 n. 배수, 방수

drainage n. 배수, 하수, 하수도 ǀ **drainer** n. 하수 공사하는 사람, 배수구

The water drained through a small hole in the hose.

물이 호스의 작은 구멍으로 샜다.

22 **enormous** [inɔ́ːrməs, e-] extremely large

a. 거대한, 방대한

enormously ad. 몹시, 엄청나게

He doesn't care about anything unless it has an enormous scale. 그는 큰 규모가 아니라면 신경쓰지 않는다.

23 **feed** [fíːd] to give food to a person or an animal

v. 먹을 것을 주다, 기르다 n. 먹이, 사료

She starts her day with feeding her cat.

그녀는 고양이 밥을 주는 것으로 하루를 시작한다.

24 **fertile** [fɔ́ːrtl] able to produce good crops

a. (땅이) 기름진

fertilize v. (땅을) 기름지게 하다 ǀ **fertilization** n. 비옥화, 다산화

fertilizer n. 비료

Africa is the well blessed continent, fertile and with huge resources.

아프리카는 축복받은 대륙이다. 땅은 비옥하고, 천연자원이 풍부하다.

25   flock [flák] a group of birds, sheep, or goats

n. 무리, 떼 v. 떼를 짓다

The flock of crows over there makes me feel unhappy.

저 위에 까마귀 떼를 보니 기분이 좋지 않다.

26   generous [dʒénərəs] larger or more than the usual size or amount

a. 관대한, 후한, 마음이 넓은, 많은

generously ad. 관대하게, 풍부하게

This land maybe has generous potential natural sources.

이 땅엔 많은 잠재적인 천연자원이 있을 것이다.

27   grain [gréin] the small hard seeds of food plant such as wheat, rice, etc.

n. 곡물, 낟알 v. 낟알로 만들다

You have to let your children know the value of a grain of rice.

너는 아이들에게 쌀 한 톨의 가치를 알게 해주어야 한다.

28   graze [gréiz] to eat grass that is growing in a field

v. (가축이) 풀을 뜯어 먹다, 방목하다 n. 방목, 목축

grazing n. 목초(지)

I think it will be good for the cattle to graze all around.

내 생각에는 소들을 주위에 방목하는 것이 좋을 것이다.

29 **harvest** [hɑ́:rvist]　the crops that have been gathered

n. 수확　v. 수확하다

I couldn't have an abundant harvest because of the drought.

나는 가뭄 때문에 큰 수확을 거두지 못했다.

30 **hay** [héi]　grass that has been cut and dried and is used as food for animals

n. 건초　v. 건초로 하다, 건초를 만들다

Inside the hay is a nice place for hide-and-seek.

건초더미 안은 숨바꼭질하기에 좋은 장소다.

31 **herd** [hə́:rd]　a large group of animals of one kind that live together

n. 짐승의 떼, 군중　v. 모으다, 모이다

The herd of sheep saw the fox and ran away fast.

양 떼는 여우를 보고 재빨리 도망갔다.

32 **irrigate** [írəgèit]　to supply water to an area of land through pipes or channels so that crops will grow

v. 물을 대다, 관개하다
irrigation n. 관개

He couldn't think about anything except for how to irrigate to his field.

그는 밭에 물을 댈 방법 외에는 어떤 것도 생각할 수 없었다.

33 lack [lǽk] to not have something that you need or not have enough of it

v. 결핍하다, ~이 결핍되다 n. 부족, 결핍
lacking a. 부족하여 prep. ~이 없으면

If the plants lack sunlight, they can't grow well.
식물들은 햇빛이 부족하면 잘 자랄 수 없다.

34 livestock [láivstɑ̀k] the animals kept on a farm

n. 가축, 가축류

Come to the Green Ranch, you'll see lots of livestock.
Green 목장에 와라, 많은 가축을 볼 것이다.

35 overcome [òuvərkʌ́m] to succeed in dealing with or controlling a problem that has been preventing you from achieving something

v. 이기다, 극복하다

She overcame injury to win the Olympic gold medal.
그녀는 부상을 극복하고 올림픽 금메달을 땄다.

36 peasant [péznt] a farmer who owns or rents a small piece of land

n. 농부, 영세 농민
peasantry n. 소작농

The city began the various programs for the poor peasants.
시에서는 영세 농민을 위한 다양한 프로그램을 시작했다.

37 **plant** [plǽnt] to put plants or seeds in the ground to grow

v. (식물을) 심다 n. 식물, 농작물
plantable a. 경작할 수 있는 ㅣ planter n. 경작자

She wants to plant some flowers in her garden.
그녀는 정원에 꽃을 심고 싶어한다.

38 **plantation** [plæntéiʃən] a large piece of land, especially in a tropical country, where crops such as rubber, coffee, tea, or sugar are grown

n. 농원, 재배지

I'm planning to visit the coffee plantation on my vacation.
난 방학 때 커피 농장을 방문할 계획이다.

39 **plow** [pláu] a piece of farm equipment used to turn over the earth so that seed can be planted

n. 쟁기 v. 갈다

Could you tell me how to use the plow?
쟁기 사용법 좀 알려 줄래?

40 **ranch** [rǽntʃ] a large farm used for raising animals, especially cattle, horses, or sheep

n. 대목장, 농원 v. 목장을 경영하다 ㅣ rancher n. 목장주

This ranch provides more activities than others including riding a horse, hiking and a cowboy show.
이 목장은 말타기, 하이킹과 카우보이 쇼를 포함해서 다른 곳보다 많은 활동을 제공한다.

41 reap [ríːp] to cut and collect a crop of grain

v. 베어내다, 수확하다, 성과를 거두다

Reaping the field was delayed because of the heavy rain.
폭우 때문에 수확이 지연되었다.

42 scatter [skǽtər] to throw or drop things in different directions so that they cover an area of ground

v. 흩뿌리다, 뿔뿔이 흩어지다

Let me help you scatter seeds over the fields.
밭에 씨 뿌리는 것 도와 줄게.

43 seed [síːd] the small, hard part of a plant from which a new plant grows

n. 씨, 종자 v. 씨를 뿌리다

It was so difficult to get the seeds of this plant.
이 식물의 씨를 구하는 것은 너무 어려웠다.

44 soil [sɔ́il] the top layer of the earth in which plants, trees, etc. grow

n. 흙, 땅, 토양

The rich soil is an important asset for you to grow some crops.
기름진 땅은 네가 작물을 재배하는 데 있어서 중요한 자산이다.

45 sow [sóu] to plant or spread seeds in or on the ground

v. (씨를) 뿌리다
sower n. 씨 뿌리는 사람, 유포자

Spring is generally the proper time for sowing **seeds.**
봄이 일반적으로 씨 뿌리기에 적당한 시기이다.

46 stable [stéibl] a building in which horses are kept

n. 마구간

To clean the stable **is his responsibility, ask him not me.**
마구간을 청소하는 것은 그의 담당이니 나 말고 그에게 물어봐라.

47 sterile [stéril] not good enough to produce crops

a. 불모의, 무균의
sterilize v. 살균하다 | sterilization n. 살균, 단종

The sterile **soil is much cheaper than the fertile one in statistics.**
통계적으로 메마른 땅이 비옥한 땅보다 훨씬 값이 싸다.

48 transplant [trænsplǽnt] to move growing plant and plant it somewhere else

v. 이식하다, 옮겨 심다, 이주시키다 n. 이식, 이주
transplantation n. 이식, 이식한 식물

These plants are transplanted **from the flower-pot to the garden.**
이 식물들은 화분에서 정원으로 이식되었다.

49   weed [wíːd]   to remove unwanted plants from a garden or other place

v. 잡초를 없애다   n. 잡초
weeder n. 풀 뽑는 사람 l weedless a. 잡초가 없는
weedy a. 잡초가 많은

Make sure that you have to weed the garden after playing soccer.

축구하고 나서 정원에 있는 잡초를 뽑아야 한다는 것을 명심해라.

50   yield [jiːld]   to produce an animal product such as meat or milk, or a crop

v. (농작물 등을) 산출하다, 양보하다   n. 수확량

The apple tree yields poorly this year.

올해는 사과 작황이 좋지 못하다.

A 다음 단어가 본문에서 쓰인 의미를 고르시오.

1. an ample bosom

   a. enough or more than enough

   b. large, often in an attractive way

2. doubts arise

   a. to happen; to start to exist

   b. to get out of bed; to stand up

3. have one's head bare

   a. just enough; the most basic or simple

   b. not covered by any clothes

4. make barren soil fertile

   a. not good enough for plants to grow on it

   b. not able to produce children or young animals

5. breed misunderstanding

   a. to produce young

   b. to cause a particular feeling or condition

B 알맞은 반대말끼리 연결하시오.

1. weed   •   • fertile

2. sterile   •   • stingy

3. lack   •   • starve

4. generous •   • cultivated plant

5. feed   •   • have

Lesson 3

Industry

|산업

01 **absorb** [əbsɔ́ːrb, -zɔ́ːrb] to receive or take something in as part of oneself

v. 흡수하다, 병합하다
absorbed a. 흡수된, 열중한 | absorption n. 흡수, 병합

As the company absorbed another one, it became the largest company in Korea.
그 회사가 다른 회사와 병합함에 따라 우리나라에서 가장 큰 회사가 되었다.

02 **acquisition** [æ̀kwəzíʃən] the act of getting something, especially knowledge, a skil, etc.

n. 획득, 습득, 취득물
acquire v. 습득하다, 획득하다

She'll check the new acquisition of the company.
그녀가 회사에 새로 들어온 물품들을 확인할 것이다.

03 **alternative** [ɔːltə́ːrnətiv, æl-] a thing that you can choose to do or have out of two or more possibilities

n. 양자택일, 대안 a. 양자택일의, 대신의
alternate a. 교대의 n. 대리인 v. 교체하다 | alternatively ad. 양자택일로, 대신에

Since that plan is the only alternative, we can't help choosing it.
그 계획이 유일한 대안이기 때문에 그것을 선택할 수밖에 없다.

04 **architecture** [áːrkətèktʃər] the art and study of designing buildings

n. 건축학, 건축물, 건축 양식
architect n. 건축가, 건축 기사 | architectural a. 건축술의, 건축상의

The development of architecture brings us modern life.
건축학의 발전은 우리에게 현대적인 삶을 가져다 주었다.

05 **barrier** [bǽriər] an object like a fence that prevents people from moving forward from one place to another

n. 장벽, 장애

They have a problem with removing a trade barrier.
그들은 무역 장벽을 제거하는 데에 어려움을 겪고 있다.

06 **briefing** [bríːfiŋ] a meeting in which people are given instructions or information

n. 상황 설명회, 브리핑, 요약 보고
brief a. 짧은, 간단한 | briefly ad. 짧게, 간단히

You're supposed to attend the briefing at 3 o'clock today.
너는 오늘 3시에 상황 설명회에 참석해야 한다.

07 **coastal** [kóustəl] of or near a coast

a. 근해의
coast n. 연안, 해안 | coastguard n. 연안 경비대

We're planning to build a coastal industrial complex on the west coast.
우리는 서해안에 해안 공업 단지를 지을 계획을 하고 있다.

08 **collapse** [kəlǽps] to fall down or fall in suddenly

vi. (건물 등이) 무너지다 vi. 붕괴시키다

You'd better repair the building before it collapses.
너는 건물이 무너지기 전에 보수를 하는 것이 나을 것이다.

09 commerce [kámərs] trade, especially between countries

n. 상업, 통상
commercial a. 상업의, 공업용의 | commercially ad. 상업적으로
commercialize v. ~을 상업화하다

Seoul must be the center of commerce since there is a
gathering of all kinds of things to be seen.
모든 종류의 것들이 모여 있는 것을 보면 서울은 상업 중심지임에 틀림없다.

10 cooperative [kouɑ́pərətiv] involving doing something together or woking together with others towards a shared aim

a. 협력적인, 협동의
cooperate v. 협력하다, 협동하다 | cooperation n. 협력, 협동

The employees are pretty cooperative although not good
at working fast. 직원들은 빨리 일하지는 못하지만 매우 협조적이다.

11 corporate [kɔ́ːrpərət] belonging to or relating to a coporation

a. 법인 (조직)의
corporation n. 법인, 지방 자치제

This store has used a different name from the corporate one.
이 가게는 법인 이름과 다른 이름을 사용해 왔다.

12 criterion [kraitíəriən] a standard or principle by which is judged, or with the help of which a decision is made

n. 표준, 기준, 척도

I have some unique criterions to trade with other
countries. 나는 다른 나라와 거래를 하는 독특한 판단 기준을 가지고 있다.

13　**crucial** [krúːʃəl]　extremely important

a. 결정적인, 중대한

Your statement can be the crucial point of this project.
너의 말은 이 프로젝트의 중요한 요점이 될 수 있다.

14　**decline** [dikláin]　to say no politely when someone wants you to do something

v. 거절하다, 기울다, 내려가다　n. 기움, 쇠퇴
declination n. 기울기, 경사

He declined to discount the price of the items without
thinking once more.
그는 한 번 더 생각해 보지도 않고 물건 값을 할인하는 것을 거절했다.

15　**design** [dizáin]　to make a drawing or plan of something that will be made or built

v. 디자인하다, 설계하다, 계획하다　n. 디자인, 도안, 설계
designed a. 계획적인
designer n. 디자이너, 도안가, 설계자

I designed that house in the shape of the mushroom.
나는 저 집을 버섯 모양으로 설계했다.

16　**efficient** [ifíʃənt]　producing satisfactory results with no waste of time, money, or energy

a. 능률적인, 효과가 있는, 유능한
efficiency n. 능률, 효율 ㅣ **efficiently** ad. 능률적으로

An efficient heating system can be the most important
part of building houses.
효과적인 난방 시스템은 집을 짓는 일에 있어서 가장 중요한 부분이라 할 수 있다.

17 enterprise [éntərpràiz] a company or business

n. 기획, (모험적인) 사업
enterpriser n. 기업가 | enterprising a. 진취력이 있는

The government enterprises are sneaking into the small markets instead of the private ones.

공기업이 민영기업 대신 작은 시장으로 스며 들어오고 있다.

18 exchange [ikstʃéindʒ] to give something and get another thing else instead of it

v. 교환하다, 환전하다 n. 교환, 환전
exchangeable a. 교환할 수 있는

I'd like to exchange this sweater.

이 스웨터를 교환하고 싶습니다.

19 expand [ikspǽnd] to become greater in size, number or importance

v. 넓히다, 확장하다, 퍼지다
expanded a. 넓어진, 확대된

By expanding the hospital, we'll move to Star Avenue.

병원 확장에 따라 Star거리로 이사갈 것이다.

20 expend [ikspénd] to use or spend a lot of time, money, energy, etc.

v. 들이다, 소비하다
expendable a. 소비되는 | expenditure n. 지출

He expended the rest of his life on building the largest museum in Korea.

그는 남은 여생을 우리나라에서 가장 큰 박물관을 짓는 데에 열중했다.

21 facility [fəsíləti] buildings, services, equipment, etc. that are provided for a particular purpose

n. 시설, 편의
facilitate v. 용이하게 하다, 돕다

The apartment has good looks and wide space while it has poor transportation facilities.

그 아파트는 좋은 외관과 넓은 공간이 있는 반면 교통이 불편하다.

22 factory [fǽktəri] a building or groups of buildings where goods are made

n. 공장 a. 공장의

The H&C Company supplies the factory the fuel.

H&C 회사는 그 공장에 연료를 공급한다.

23 fishery [fíʃəri] an area of water where fish are caught in large quantities

n. 어업, 어장
fisher n. 어부 | fishman n. 어부, 낚싯배

If you visit the oyster fishery, you can get oysters at a low price.

네가 굴 양식장에 가면 싼 값에 굴을 살 수 있다.

24 forest [fɔ́(:)rist, fɑ́r-] a plant community extending over a large area and dominated by trees

n. 숲, 산림, 산림지
forestry n. 임학, 산림학

The rain forest is being systematically destroyed.

열대 우림이 체계적으로 파괴되고 있다.

25 fortune [fɔ́ːrtʃən] chance or luck

n. 운, 행운, 재산, 부
fortunate a. 운이 좋은, 행운의 ㅣ fortunately ad. 다행히도

Sometimes good fortune is the essential element for success in business.
가끔 행운은 사업 성공의 필수 요소이기도 하다.

26 goods [gúdz] things that are produced to be sold

n. 상품, 물품, 소유물, 소질

His careful personality is proper to the position of handling the fragile goods.
그의 조심스러운 성격은 깨지기 쉬운 물품들을 다루기에 적당하다.

27 growth [gróuθ] the process of growing physically, mentally or emotionally

n. 성장, 발전, 증대
grower n. 재배자 ㅣ grown a. 성장한, 재배한

You can also see the industrial growth, if you learn the history. 네가 역사를 배우면, 산업 발전도 알 수 있다.

28 industry [índəstri] the production of goods from raw materials, especially in factories

n. 산업, 공업, 근면, 연구
industrial a. 산업의, 공업의 n. 산업 근로자 ㅣ industrialize v. 산업(공업)화하다

The development of the broadcasting industry helped people express themselves more in various ways.
방송 산업의 발달은 사람들에게 더 다양한 표현이 가능하도록 해주었다.

29　interior [intíəriər]　the inside part of something

n. 내부, 실내 a. 안의, 내면의

What you have to do is just the interior design.

네가 해야 할 일은 실내 디자인뿐이다.

30　manufacturer [mæ̀njufǽktʃərər]　a person or company that produces goods in large quantities

n. 제조업자
manufactory n. 제작소, 공장
manufacture n. 제조 공업, 제품 v. 제조하다
manufacturing a. 제조업에 종사하는 n. 제조

He has the very unique item manufactured by a lot of manufacturers with new technology to surprise all of you.

그는 너희들 모두를 놀라게 할 만한 신기술로 많은 제조업자들이 만든 독특한 제품을 가지고 있다.

31　merge [mə́:rdʒ]　to combine or make two or more things combine to form a single thing

v. 합병하다, 융합하다
mergee n. 합병의 상대방 | mergence n. 몰입, 융합, 합병
merger n. 합병, 합동

Show me what benefits we will have if we merge with Green Company.

만약 Green회사와 합병을 하면 우리가 어떤 이득을 보는지 말해 봐라.

32 mine [main] a deep hole or holes in the ground that people dig so that they can remove coal, good, etc.

n. 광산, 광업

mining n. 채광, 광업 a. 광업의, 광업의 | miner n. 광산업자, 광부

Her father worked for the coal mine a few years ago.

그녀의 아버지는 몇 년 전에 탄광업에 종사하셨다.

33 monopoly [mənɑ́pəli] the complete control of trade in particular goods or the supply of a particular service

n. 전매, 독점

The company has a monopoly on the chicken sales all over the country.

그 회사가 나라 전체에 걸쳐 닭 유통을 독점하고 있다.

34 offer [ɔ́ːfər, ɑ́-] to say that you are willing to do something

v. 제공하다, 제출하다, 제의하다 n. 제공, 제의

Can you offer supplies to us by tomorrow?

내일까지 물품을 납품할 수 있겠니?

35 potential [pəténʃəl] likely to develop into something in the future

a. 가능한, 잠재하는 n. 가능성, 잠재성

potentiality n. 잠재하는 것, 가능성 | potentially ad. 가능성 있게, 잠재적으로

We have to research the potential energy instead of the energy run dry.

우리는 고갈되는 에너지 대신 잠재적인 에너지를 찾아야 한다.

36 prevail [privéil] to exist or be very common at a particular time or in a particular place

v. 우세하다, 극복하다, 보급되다
prevailing a. 우세한, 보급되는

Using the credit card prevails **these days.**
신용카드를 사용하는 것은 요즘 보편화되어 있다.

---

37 produce [prədjúːs] to make things to be sold, especially in large quantities

v. 생산하다, 제조하다
producer n. 생산자, 프로듀서 | product n. 생산품, 성과
production n. 생산, 산출 | productive a. 생산적인

He has planned to produce **a book since he was a university student.**
그는 대학 시절부터 책을 출판할 계획을 세워왔다.

---

38 profit [práfit] the money that you make in business or by selling things, especially after paying the cost involved

n. 이익, 이득 v. 이익을 얻다
profitable a. 이익이 되는 | nonprofit a. 비영리적인 | profitless a. 무익한

The meeting was held for the plan to maximize profits**.**
이익을 극대화하려는 계획 때문에 회의가 열렸다.

---

39 recall [rikɔ́ːl] to remember something

v. 상기하다, 생각나게 하다, 철회하다

I can't recall **meeting her before.**
나는 전에 그녀를 만난 기억이 안 난다.

40 **recession** [riséʃən] a difficult time when there is less trade, business, activity, etc. in a country than usual

n. 경기 후퇴, 불경기
recessional a. 퇴거의, 휴식의 I recessive a. 후퇴하는
recessionary a. 경기 후퇴의, 불경기와 관련된

As the recession lasts for a long time, people are getting stressful. 불경기가 지속되면서 사람들은 점점 스트레스를 받고 있다.

41 **reduction** [ridʌ́kʃən] an act of making something less or smaller

n. 축소, 저하
reduce v. 변화시키다, 줄이다, 낮추다 I reductive a. 감소하는

I'd like to avoid the personnel reduction, but I can't.
인원 감축은 피하고 싶으나 그럴 수 없다.

42 **resource** [ríːsɔːrs, -zɔːrs] things that it has and can use to increase its wealth, such as coal, oil, or land

n. 자원, 수단, 기력

I can dare to say here is the heaven of natural resources.
나는 감히 이곳이 천연 자원의 천국이라 말할 수 있다.

43 **scheme** [skíːm] a plan or system for doing or organizing something

n. 계획, 음모 v. 계획하다
schema n. 개요 I schematic a. 도식적인

They adopted the scheme of paving this road last Thursday.
그들은 지난주 목요일에 이 도로를 포장하는 계획을 채택했다.

44   secondary [sékəndèri] less important than something else

a. 제 2위의 n. 제 2차적인 것
second a. 제 2의, 둘째의

Mining, architecture, and manufacturing are the secondary **industries.**

광업, 건축업, 제조업은 2차 산업이다.

45   sector [séktər] a part of an area of activity, especially of country's economy

n. 부분, 분야, 부채꼴
section n. 부분 | **sectoral** a. 부채꼴의

The banking sector **is getting bigger than ever before.**

금융 분야가 전보다 더 커지고 있다.

46   stock [sták] a share in a company

n. 주식, 재고품, 저장 v. 들여놓다, 비축하다

I always hear the news about the stock.

난 항상 주식에 대한 뉴스를 듣는다.

47   strike [stráik] a period of time when an organized group of employees of a company stops working

n. 동맹 파업 v. 치다, 충돌하다

The workers are on strike **for their better work condition.**

근로자들은 더 나은 근무 환경을 위해 파업 중이다.

48 surplus [sə́ːrplʌs, -pləs] more than what is needed or used

a. 잔여의, 과잉의 n. 나머지, 잉여금

The government decided to build much more houses for the surplus **population.**

정부는 과잉 인구를 위해서 집을 훨씬 더 많이 짓기로 결정했다.

49 swift [swíft] happening or done very quickly or immediately

a. 빠른, 신속한
swiftly ad. 신속히, 즉시 I swiftness n. 빠름, 신속함

The bereaved families call for the swift **action of the government.**

유가족들은 정부의 즉각적인 조치를 요구한다.

50 tariff [tǽrif] a tax that is paid on goods coming into or going out of a country

n. 관세(표) v. 관세를 부과하다
revenue tariff 수입 관세

The fare is decided according to the airline passenger tariff**.**

운임은 국제 항공 운임표에 따라 결정된 것이다.

A 우리말과 같은 뜻이 되도록 빈 칸에 주어진 철자로 시작되는 단어를 쓰시오.

1. The government states that it'll a _____ a small firm into large cartel.

   정부는 소규모 회사를 큰 기업 연합에 합병시키겠다고 발표했다.

2. The citizens look forward to getting an appropriate a _____ .

   시민들은 적절한 대안을 기다리고 있다.

3. This building is the result of mixing Roman and Modern a _____ .

   이 건물은 로마와 현대 건축 양식의 결합의 결과이다.

4. My father c _____ from a heart attack yesterday.

   아버지가 어제 심장마비로 갑자기 쓰러지셨다.

5. It isn't e _____ to doing many things at the same time.

   동시에 많은 일을 하는 것은 효율적이지 않다.

B 주어진 표현에 해당하는 단어를 보기에서 고르시오.

| crucial | design | efficient | expand | interior |

1. _____ : systematic, orderly, tidy, businesslike

2. _____ : important, critical, material, decisive

3. _____ : internal, domestic, inland, indoor

4. _____ : format, layout, configuration, arrangement

5. _____ : widen, extend, enlarge, broaden

C 우리말은 영어로, 영어는 우리말로 바꾸시오.

1. surplus   2. 빠른, 신속한

3. scheme   4. 부채꼴, 부분, 분야

5. tariff   6. 경기 후퇴, 불경기

7. profit   8. 우세하다, 극복하다, 보급하다

9. monopoly   10. 합병하다, 융합하다

Lesson 4

Trade

| 무역

01　**adjust** [ədʒʌ́st]　to change something slightly to make it more suitable for a new set of conditions or to make it work better

v. 조절하다, 조정하다
adjusted a. 조정된, 보정된 I adjustment n. 조절, 조정

He adjusted the size of the TV according to the contract.
그는 계약에 따라 TV 크기를 조정했다.

02　**arbitration** [aːrbətréiʃən]　the official process of setting an argument or disagreement by someone who is not involved

n. 중재, 조정, 재정
arbitrary a. 임의의, 멋대로인 I arbitrate v. 중재하다
arbitrator n. 중재자

Both side in the dispute have agreed to go to arbitration.
분쟁 양측이 중재를 받기로 합의했다.

03　**arrival** [əráivəl]　an act of coming or being brought to a place

n. 도착, 도달 a. 도착의
arrive v. 도착하다, 도달하다

Check the arrival item list and take the receipt.
도착 물품 목록을 확인하고 영수증을 챙겨라.

04　**cancel** [kǽnsəl]　to decide that something that has been arranged will not now take place

v. 취소하다, 중지하다 n. 취소
cancellation n. 취소

You can't cancel your order after you signed on it.
서명을 하고 난 후에는 주문을 취소할 수 없다.

05 certificate [sərtífikət]   an official document that states that facts are true

n. 증명서 v. ~에게 증명서를 주다
certification n. 증명, 보증 ∣ certified a. 보증된, 공인된

Don't forget you must enclose the certificate **of origin with the documents.**

서류에 원산지 증명서를 동봉해야 하는 것을 잊지 마라.

06 charter [tʃɑ́:rtər]   a written statement describing the right that a particular group of people should have

n. 특허장, 전세계약, 헌장 a. 특허에 의한 v. ~에게 특허를 주다
chartered a. 특허를 받은, 공인된, 용선 계약된

The bareboat charter **was admitted last month.**

선체 용선 계약이 지난달에 승인이 되었다.

07 circulation [sə̀:rkjuléiʃən]   the movement of something around an area or inside a system or machine

n. 순환, 유통, 발행 부수, 통화
circulate v. 순환하다, 유통시키다, 배부하다 ∣ circulating a. 순환하는

The new bill will be put into circulation **next month.**

새 화폐가 다음 달부터 유통될 것이다.

08 collateral [kəlǽtərəl]   property or something valuable that you promise to give to someone if you cannot pay back money that you borrow

n. 담보 물건 a. 서로 나란한, 담보로 내놓은

You can't get a bank loan without collateral.

무담보로 은행에서 대출을 받을 수 없다.

09 condition [kəndíʃən]   the state that something is in

n. 상태, 상황, 조건
conditional a. 조건부의

Let us know when you fulfill the necessary conditions.

필수 조건을 갖추면 알려줘라.

10 confirm [kənfə́ːrm]   to state or show that something is definitely true or correct, especially by providing evidence

v. 굳게 하다, 확인하다
confirmation n. 확인, 확정 ǀ confirmed a. 확인된

To confirm **the agreement you have to keep in touch with him.**

협정을 승인하기 위해 그와 계속 연락해야 한다.

11 container [kəntéinər]   a large metal or wooden box of a standard size in which goods are packed so that they can easily be lifted onto a ship, train, etc. to be transported

n. 그릇, 컨테이너
contain v. 담고 있다, 포함하다 ǀ contained a. 억제하는

Why don't you change your old containers **to transport the goods?**

상품 수송하는 오래된 컨테이너들을 바꾸는 건 어때?

12 contract [kɑ́ntrækt] an official written agreement

n. 계약 v. 계약하다, 줄어들다
contracted a. 계약된 I contraction n. 수축, (약혼을) 맺음
contractor n. 계약자 I contractual a. 계약상의

That is a conditional contract that was established yesterday.

그것은 어제 체결된 조건부 계약이다.

13 deadline [dédlàin] a point in time by which something must be done

n. 최종 기한

We had to hurry because the deadline was around the corner.

제출일이 임박하여 우리는 서둘러야만 했다.

14 delay [diléi] not to do something until a later time or to make something happen at a later time

v. 늦추다, 미루다 n. 지연

The arrival of goods was delayed because of the heavy rain.

심한 비 때문에 물품 도착이 지연되었다.

15 deliver [dilívər] to take goods, letters, packages, etc. to a particular place or person

v. 배달하다, 넘겨주다
deliverable a. 인도 가능한 I delivery n. 배달, 납품 I deliverance n. 구출, 구조

Deliver the package with the shipment by August 10.

8월 10일까지 그 소포를 배편으로 배달하라.

16   **demand** [dimǽnd]   to ask for something very firmly

v. 요구하다, 청구하다   n. 요구, 청구
demandable   a. 요구할 수 있는 | demanding   a. 요구가 지나친

He demanded a wage increase.

그는 임금 인상을 요구했다.

17   **endure** [indjúər]   to experience and deal with something that is painful or unpleasant, especially without complaining

v. 참다, 견디다
enduring   a. 참을성 있는 | endurable   a. 참을 수 있는, 견딜 만한
endurance   n. 인내

Stupidly, he had endured the illness to save money.

미련하게도, 그는 돈을 아끼기 위해 아픈 것을 참았다.

18   **engagement** [ingéidʒmənt]   an arrangement to do something at a particular time, especially something official or connected with your job

n. 약속, 계약
engage   v. 약속하다, 약혼하다 | engaged   a. 약속된, 예약된

It's impossible to break off the engagement during the procedure.

진행 중에는 해약하는 것이 불가능하다.

19   **export** [ikspɔ́ːrt]   to sell products or raw materials to another country

v. 수출하다   n. 수출
exportation   n. 수출, 수출품 | exporter   n. 수출업자, 수출 회사

We can export the products to the foreign countries from next year.

우리는 내년부터 외국에 물품을 수출할 수 있다.

20　finally [fáinəli]　after a long time, especially when there has been some difficulty or delay

ad. 최후로, 드디어, 최종적으로
final a. 최후의, 마지막의 | finalize v. 완성하다, 끝내다

She had a really tough time, but she made a contract finally.

그녀는 정말 힘든 시기를 보냈지만 마침내 계약을 성사시켰다.

21　freight [fréit]　goods that are carried by ship, train, or aircraft, and the system of moving these goods

n. 화물 운송, 운송료 v. 화물을 싣다
freighter n. 화물선, 운송업자 | air freight n. 항공 화물

I must pay the freight for the equipment in advance.

나는 먼저 장비에 대한 운송 비용을 지불해야 한다.

22　holiday [hálədèi]　a period of time when you are not at work or school

n. 휴일, 공휴일 a. 휴일의, 휴가 중인

It will take 30 days except for the holidays.

공휴일을 제외하고 30일이 걸린다.

23　import [impɔ́ːrt]　to bring a product, a service, an idea, etc. into one country from another

v. 수입하다 n. 수입(품)
importable a. 수입할 수 있는

Korea imports a lot of things from foreign countries.

우리나라는 외국으로부터 많은 것들을 수입한다.

24 invitation [invətéiʃən] a spoken or written request to someone to do something or to go somewhere

n. 초대, 초대장
invite v. 초대하다 | inviter n. 초대자

You don't have to bring the invitation to the meeting.

회의에 초대장을 가져올 필요는 없다.

25 invoice [ínvɔis] a list of goods that have been sold or work that has been done, showing what you must pay

n. 송장

I'm making out the invoice of the goods which will be sent next week.

다음 주에 보내질 물품 송장을 만들고 있다.

26 load [lóud] something that is being carried by person, vehicle, etc.

n. 적재, 짐 v. 짐을 싣다
loading n. 적재 | loaded a. 짐을 실은

Let's distinguish between the ship that has been loaded and the ship without a load.

짐을 실은 배와 짐이 없는 배를 분류하자.

27 local [lóukəl] belonging to or connected with the particular place or area where you live

a. 공간의, 지방의
locality n. 장소 | localize v. ~의 위치를 알아내다

All of the local products are gathering to that market.

모든 지방 생산품들이 저 시장으로 모이고 있다.

28 necessary [nésəsèri] needed for a purpose or reason

a. 필요의, 필연의 n. 필수품

necessarily ad. 반드시 | **necessity** n. 필요, 필수품

There are lots of necessary documents for the export.

수출에 필요한 서류가 많다.

29 negotiate [nigóuʃièit, -si-] to bring about an agreement by formal discussion

v. 협정하다, 협상하다

negotiation n. 교섭, 협상 | **negotiable** a. 협정할 수 있는

She has special skills to negotiate with the buyers.

그녀는 바이어들과 협상하는 데에 특별한 기술을 가지고 있다.

30 notification [nòutəfikéiʃən] the act of giving or receiving official information about something

n. 통지(서), 공고(문)

notifiable a. 통지해야 할 | **notify** v. ~에게 통지하다

Only the notification in writing can be available.

서면으로 된 통지만이 유효하다.

31 order [ɔ́:rdər] to ask for goods or services to be supplied

v. 명령하다, 주문하다, 정돈하다 n. 순서, 명령, 주문

ordered a. 정연한 | **orderly** a. 정돈된, 질서 있는

You can order many things at once, just remember the code number.

한 번에 많은 물건들을 주문할 수 있다. 코드 번호만 기억해라.

32 **package** [pǽkidʒ] something wrapped in paper, packed in a box

n. 소포, 꾸러미 v. 짐을 꾸리다
pack n. 꾸러미 v. 포장하다 **| packer** n. 짐 꾸리는 사람, 포장업자

Its weight is about 20kg per a package **of the goods.**

무게는 상품 꾸러미당 약 20kg이다.

33 **payment** [péimənt] the act of paying something or of being paid

n. 지불, 납입, 지불 금액
pay v. 지불하다 **| payable** a. 지불할 수 있는

They made payment **in part, and more than a half remained.**

그들은 일부만 지불했고, 반 이상이 남았다.

34 **postpone** [poustpóun] to delay or put off something till later

v. 연기하다, 미루다

The delivery is postponed **until next Wednesday by the storm.**

배달이 태풍 때문에 다음 주 수요일로 연기되었다.

35 **protest** [prətést, próutest] to say or do something to show that you disagree with or disapprove of something

v. 항의하다, 주장하다
protestation n. 항의, 주장 **| protester** n. 항의자, 주장자
protestant n. 신교도

The organization protested **against the action of the government.**

그 조직은 정부의 조치에 항의했다.

36 quantity [kwɑ́ntəti] an amount or a number of something

n. 양, 분량, 다수
quantify v. ~의 양을 정하다 ǀ quantitative a. 양의
quantitatively ad. 양적으로

I measured the quantity of the load last night.
내가 어제 짐의 양을 쟀다.

---

37 receipt [risíːt] a piece of paper showing that goods or services have been paid for

n. 영수증 v. 영수증을 발행하다

If you don't keep the receipt, there can be some problems.
만약에 영수증을 보관하지 않으면 문제가 생길 수 있다.

---

38 regular [régjulər] following pattern, especially with the same time and space in between each thing and the next

a. 정기적인, 규칙적인
regularity n. 규칙적임, 정연함 ǀ regulation n. 규정, 규칙
regularize v. 조직화하다, 질서 있게 하다

The company stopped their regular order suddenly.
그 회사는 갑자기 정기 주문을 그만두었다.

---

39 reimburse [rìːimbə́ːrs] to pay back money to someone which they have spent or lost

v. 변상하다
reimbursement n. 변상, 상환

If any problems happen during delivery, the expense will be reimbursed.
배달 중 문제가 발생하면 비용은 상환될 것이다.

40 revolve [riválv] to go in a circle around a central point

v. 회전하다, 선회하다, 초점을 맞추다
revolving a. 회전하는 l revolver n. 연발 권총, 회전장치

The earth revolves around the sun.
지구는 태양의 주위를 회전한다.

---

41 shipment [ʃípmənt] the process of sending goods from one place to another

n. 선적, 수송

Are there more goods ready for the shipment?
선적 대기 중인 물품이 더 있나요?

---

42 square [skwέər] a shape with four equal sides and four right angles

n. 정사각형, 제곱 a. 정사각형의 v. 정사각형으로 만들다

The square boxes are easy to pile high.
정사각형의 상자들이 높이 쌓기 편하다.

---

43 stipulate [stípjulèit] to state clearly and firmly that something must be done, or how it must be done

v. 규정하다, 약정하다, 조건으로 요구하다
stipulation n. 약정, 규정 l stipulator n. 약정자

It is stipulated in the document that the delivery of the goods can be delayed by natural disasters.
물품 인도는 자연 재해에 의해 지연될 수 있다고 서류에 명시되어 있다.

44 trade [tréid]

the activity of buying, selling, or exchanging goods or services between people or countries

n. 무역, 상업 a. 무역의 v. 매매하다, 교환하다
trader n. 상인, 무역업자 ㅣ trading n. 상거래, 무역

The Free Trade Agreement between Korea and the U.S.A. was concluded last year.

우리나라와 미국 간의 자유 무역 협정이 작년에 체결되었다.

45 transmit [trænsmít, trænz-]

to pass something from one person to another

v. 부치다, 전하다, 송신하다
transmission n. 송달, 회송, 전달 ㅣ transmitter n. 양도자, 송신기

She had some problems transmitting the invoice, so she tried to transmit it again.

그녀는 송장을 보내는 데에 문제가 생겨서 다시 시도했다.

46 transport [trænspɔ́ːrt]

to carry people or goods from one place to another using vehicles, roads, etc.

v. 수송하다, 운송하다 n. 수송, 운송
transportable a. 수송할 수 있는 ㅣ transportation n. 수송, 운송

The truck is used to transport cars.

그 트럭은 차를 운반하는 데 사용되고 있다.

47	transship [trænsʃíp]	to transfer or be transferred from one vessel or vehicle to another

v. 다른 배로 옮기다, 갈아타다

These goods will be transshipped **at the east coast.**

이 물건들은 동해안에서 다른 배로 옮겨질 것이다.

48	treaty [tríːti]	formal agreement between two or more nations

n. 조약, 협정

I couldn't confirm an unfair treaty **such as that.**

그것처럼 불공평한 협정을 승인할 수 없었다.

49	unpaid [ʌnpéid]	not yet paid

a. 지불하지 않은, 미납의

The goods were delivered unpaid, **so you must pay by tomorrow.**

물건들이 미납 상태로 인도되었으니 내일까지 비용을 지불해야 한다.

50	voyage [vɔ́iidʒ]	a long journey by water or in space

n. 항해 v. 항해하다
voyager n. 항해 여행자

The ship is regarded as the one that has taken the longest voyage.

그 배는 가장 오랫동안 항해한 배라고 생각된다.

Check up

A 괄호 안의 단어 중 문맥상 적절한 것을 고르시오.

1. She usually (adjusts / adjustment) a thermostat in the room.

2. They nearly (arrived / arrival) on time.

3. You have to hand out a (certificate / certificated) of birth.

4. The victims have been out of (circulative / circulation) since the accident happened.

5. He is a (confirmed / confirm) bachelor.

B 알맞은 단어를 골라 적절히 변형하여 완성하시오.

contract	delay	deliver	demand	engagement
exchange	freight	holiday	invitation	load

1. be _____ of : (아이를) 낳다; (시를) 짓다

2. advanced _____ : 운임 선불

3. meet one's _____ : 채무를 이행하다

4. _____ cut : 협정 파기

5. on _____ : 휴업하다, 일을 쉬다

6. the rate of _____ : 외환 시세, 환율

7. on the _____ of : ~의 초대로

8. have a _____ on one's mind : 마음에 걸리는 일이 있다

9. admit of no _____ : 잠깐의 여유도 주지 않다

10. _____ money with menaces : 공갈, 갈취

C 다음 영영풀이에 해당하는 단어를 골라 쓰시오.

necessary	negotiate	notification	postpone	protest

1. official information about something

2. needed for a purpose or a reason

3. the expression of strong disagreement with or opposition to something

4. to arrange for an event, etc. to take place at a later time or date

5. to try to reach an agreement by formal discussion

Lesson 5

Finance

|금융

01 **account** [əkáunt] an arrangement that someone has with a bank to keep money and take some out

n. 예금 계좌, 예금 잔고
accountant n. 회계원, 회계사 ｜ accounting n. 회계, 회계 보고

We should not tell fishers our account number and security number.
우리는 보이스 피싱 전화에 계좌 번호와 비밀 번호를 말해 주어서는 안된다.

02 **accumulate** [əkjú:mjulèit] to gradually get more and more money, knowledge, etc. over a period of time

v. (장기간에 걸쳐 조금씩) 모으다, 축적하다
accumulation n. 축적, 누적 ｜ accumulative a. 적립식의, 누적의

The interest will be accumulated at the end of each year.
매해 연말에 이자가 적립될 것이다.

03 **analysis** [ənǽləsis] the detailed study or examination of something in order to understand more about it

n. 분석, 해석, 분해
analyze v. 분석하다, 해독하다 ｜ analyst n. 분석가, 해석가

An analysis is one of the ways of writing articles.
분석은 글쓰기의 한 방법이다.

04 **approximate** [əpráksəmeit] almost correct or accurate

a. 대략의, 비슷한, 근사한
approximately ad. 대체로, 대략적으로

The car mechanic gave me an approximate cost for the whole cost.
자동차 수리공은 대략적인 전체 비용을 나에게 알려 주었다.

05   asset [ǽset] a person or thing that is valuable or useful to someone or something

n. 자산, 재산
assess v. 사정하다, 평가하다 ㅣ assessment n. (과세를 위한) 평가, 사정

The one of the most important assets **in maintaining a relationship is honesty.**

인간 관계를 유지하는 데 있어서 가장 중요한 자산 중 하나는 정직이다.

06   banking [bǽŋkiŋ] the business activities of banks

n. 은행업, 은행 업무
banking account n. 계좌 ㅣ bank loan 은행 융자(금)

Nowadays, you can do all your banking **at an ATM or on the Internet.**

오늘날에는 ATM이나 인터넷으로 모든 은행 업무를 처리할 수 있다.

07   bankrupt [bǽŋkrʌpt, -rəpt] without enough money to pay what you owe

a. 파산한, 지불할 능력이 없는
bankruptcy n. 파산 ㅣ go bankrupt 파산하다

A number of companies have gone bankrupt **in the aftermath of the recession.**

경기 후퇴 여파로 많은 회사들이 도산하고 있다.

08   bulk [bʌlk] sold or moved in large quantities

a. 대량의, 대형의 n. (~의) 대부분, 규모
bulky a. 부피가 큰

Will you give a discount on bulk **purchase?**

대량 구입하면 할인을 받을 수 있습니까?

09 **charge** [tʃɑ:dʒ] the amount of money that somebody asks for goods and services

n. 청구금액, 요금, 짐, 부담, 책임, 비난 v. 청구하다, 부과하다, 부담을 주다

Many people tend to download music files from the Internet free of charge.

많은 사람들이 무료로 인터넷에서 음악을 내려받는 것을 좋아하는 경향이 있다.

10 **credit** [krédit] faith placed in something

n. 신뢰, 신용, 명성, 외상
creditable a. 신용할 만한 | creditability n. 신용할 만함, 명예가 됨

Credit cards are convenient to buy goods, but bad to save money.

신용 카드는 물건을 사기에는 좋지만 돈을 절약하기에는 좋지 않다.

11 **currency** [kə́:rənsi, kʌ́r-] the system of money that a country uses

n. 통화, 통화 유통액
current a. 현행의, 통용되는 | currently ad. 지금, 일반적으로

European currency is called the Euro.

유럽 통용 화폐는 유로라고 불린다.

12 **debt** [dét] a sum of money that someone owes

n. 부채, 빚, 채무

When you owe money, it means you are in debt.

당신이 돈을 빌려 쓰면 부채가 생기게 된다.

13 decrease [diːkríːs]   to become or make something become smaller in size, number, etc.

v. 줄다, 감소하다 n. 감소
decreasing a. 감소하는 | decreasingly ad. 점점 줄어드는, 감소하는

Stress can decrease the ability to remember.

긴장은 기억력을 감소시킬 수 있다.

14 deliberate [dilíbərət]   to think very carefully about something, usually before making a decision

v. 심의하다, 숙고하다 a. 신중한, 고의의
deliberative a. 깊이 생각하는, 심의하는 | deliberation n. 심의, 신중함

He spoke in a slow and deliberate way.

그는 천천히 신중한 태도로 말을 했다.

15 deposit [dipázit]   a sum of money that is given as the first part of a larger payment

n. 예금액, 예금

She has a large deposit in the bank.

그녀는 은행에 많은 예금이 있다.

16 disapprove [disəprúːv]   to think that someone or something is not good or suitable

v. 반대하다, 승인하지 않다
disapproval n. 불승인, 불찬성 | disapprovingly ad. 불찬성하여, 못마땅하여

Almost all of the religions disapprove of suicide.

거의 모든 종교들이 자살에 반대한다.

17 **divide** [diváid] to separate something into parts and distribute it

v. 나누다, 쪼개다, 분할하다
divisible a. 나눌 수 있는, 가분의 | division n. 분할, 분배, 부분

The last series of *Harry Potter* is divided into 2 movies.
해리포터 시리즈의 마지막 편은 2개의 영화로 나누어져 있다.

18 **endow** [indáu] to give a college, hospital etc. a large sum of money that provides it with an income

v. 기부하다, 증여하다 , (능력, 자질을) 부여하다
endowment n. 기증, 기부

We are all endowed with a talent.
우리는 모두 재능을 부여받았다.

19 **equivalent** [ikwívələnt] equal in value, amount, importance, etc.

n. 동등물, 상당하는 것 a. 동등한, 상당하는
equivalence n. 같음, 등가

The expression has no satisfactory English equivalent.
그 표현에 해당하는 적절한 영어는 없다.

20 **evaluate** [ivǽljuèit] to form an opinion of the value from investigating or thinking

v. 평가하다, 어림하다, 사정하다
evaluation n. 평가, 사정 | evaluator n. 평가자

Sincerity is an important factor when employers evaluate employees.
고용주들이 사원을 평가할 때 성실함은 중요한 요소이다.

21 expire [ikspáiər]   to be no longer valid because the period of time for which it could be used has ended

v. 만기가 되다, (기간이) 끝나다
expiration n. 만기, 종결 | expired a. 만기가 된, 기간이 다 된, 종결된

If your visa is expired**, you cannot travel overseas.**
만약 당신의 비자가 만료되면 해외 여행을 할 수 없다.

22 finance [fáinæns]   money used to run a business, an activity or a project

n.자금, 재정, 재무
financial a. 재정상의, 재무의 | financing n. 융자, 재정

The finance **committee monitors a company's expenditure.**
재무 위원회는 회사의 지출을 감시한다.

23 flexible [fléksəbl]   able to change to suit new conditions or situations

a. 융통성 있는, 탄력적인
flexibility n. 유연성, 융통성, 탄력성 | flexibly a. 유연하게, 융통성 있게

Children's muscles are flexible **so they can pronounce foreign language better than adults.**
아이들의 근육은 유연해서 어른들보다 외국어를 더 잘 발음할 수 있다.

24 fund [fʌnd]   an amount of money that has been saved or has been made available for a particular purpose

n. 기금, 축적 v. 자금을 제공하다, 투자하다
fundamental a. 기본의, 근본적인

A scholarship fund **will be a great help to those who are smart but poor.**
장학금은 똑똑하지만 가난한 학생들에게 큰 도움이 될 것이다.

25 guarantee [gæ̀rəntíː] to promise to do something

v. 보증하다 n. 담보(물), 보증
guarantee fund n. 보증 기금

A positive attitude always guarantees **a better result than negative one.**

긍정적인 태도는 부정적인 태도보다 항상 나은 결과를 보장한다.

26 immovable [imúːvəbl] impossible to change or persuade

a. 고정된, 움직일 수 없는
immovably ad. 확고하게, 흔들림 없이

Christians have an immovable **opposition to abortion.**

기독교인들은 낙태에 대해 확고한 반대 입장을 가지고 있다.

27 impose [impóuz] to force somebody to pay money such as tax

v. (세금, 의무, 벌 등을) 과하다, 부과하다

A new task has been imposed **on an immovable property.**

부동산에 새로운 세금이 부과되었다.

28 increase [inkríːs] to become or make something greater in amount, number, value, etc.

v. 늘다, 증가하다, 증가시키다 n. 증가
increasing a. 증가하는 l increasingly ad. 점점, 더욱 더

The number of the victims could increase.

희생자는 더욱더 늘어날 것으로 보인다.

29 **interest** [íntərəst, -tərèst]   extra money that you pay back when you borrow money or that you get when you invest money

n. (원금에서의) 이자, 이익 v. 흥미를 일으키게 하다
interested a. 이해 관계가 있는

A rise in interest rates would cause some problems.

이자율 상승은 몇 가지 문제를 불러 일으킬 수도 있다.

30 **lease** [líːs]   to use or let someone use something, especially property or equipment, in exchange for rent or regular payment

v. 임대하다, 임차하다 n. 임대, 리스

What are the conditions of the lease?

임대 조건이 무엇입니까?

31 **loan** [lóun]   the act of lending something, especially money

n. 대부, 임대

A loan from a bank is convenient but expensive.

은행에서의 대출은 편리하지만 비싸다.

32 **monetary** [mánətèri, mʌ̀n-]   connected with money, especially all the money in a country

a. 화폐의, 통화의
IMF(International Monetary Fund) 국제통화기금

Monetary policy affects economy a lot.

통화 정책은 경제에 많은 영향을 미친다.

33 multiply [mʌ́ltəplài] to add a number to itself a particular number of times

v. 곱하다
multiple a. 복합적인

Multiply **three by four and it equals twelve.**

3곱하기 4는 12이다.

34 numerous [njú:mərəs] existing in large numbers

a. 다수의, 많은, 셀 수 없이 많은
numerously ad. 다수로, 수없이 많이

There are numerous **things we can do to protect our environment.**

우리가 환경을 보호하기 위해서 할 수 있는 일들이 아주 많이 있다.

35 option [ápʃən] something that you can choose to have or do

n. (소유 여부를 선택할 수 있는) 선택권, 선택
optional a. 마음대로의, 선택 가능한, 임의의 ㅣ optionally ad. 마음대로

Is there another option **possible?**

또 다른 선택의 여지가 있습니까?

36 owe [óu] to have to pay someone for what you have already received or return money that you borrowed

vt. 빚지고 있다, ~의 은혜를 입고 있다

I owe **you once.**

내가 너한테 한 번 신세졌다.

37   **proper** [prápər]   appropriate or correct

a. 적당한, 알맞은
properly ad. 적당히, 알맞게 | **improper** a. 부적절한

Proper **exercise is good for your health.**
적당한 운동은 네 건강에 좋다.

38   **property** [prápəti]   a thing or things owned by somebody

n. 재산, 소유권
property right n. 재산권

Many people became unemployed as the property **market collapsed.**
자산 시장이 붕괴하면서 많은 사람들이 직장을 잃었다.

39   **proportion** [prəpɔ́ːrʃən]   a part or share of a whole

n. 부분, 비율, 크기, 균형
proportional a. 균형 잡힌 | **proportionally** ad. 비례하여, 어울리게

The proportion **of men to women in Korea is too high.**
한국의 남성 비율은 여성에 비해서 너무나 높다.

40   **rate** [réit]   a measurement of speed at which something happens

n. 요금, 비율, 등급
ratio n. 비, 비율

The infection is spreading at a terrific rate.
전염이 급속도로 퍼지고 있다.

41 refund [riːfʌ́nd, ríːfʌ̀nd] to pay back money

v. 환불하다, 상환하다 n. 환불, 상환
refundable a. 환불할 수 있는, 환불 가능한

No receipt, no refund.
영수증 없이는 환불이 불가능하다.

42 register [rédʒistər] to put somebody or something on an official list

v. 등록하다, 기재하다
registration n. 기재, 등기, 등록

You have to register **until today if you participate the seminar.**
세미나에 참가하고 싶으면 오늘까지 등록해야 합니다.

43 save [seiv] to keep money in a bank so that you can use it later

v. (돈을) 모으다, 저축하다, 구하다

Saving **a little everyday adds up to a lot in the long run.**
매일 조금씩 절약하면 나중에 큰 돈이 된다.

44 signature [sígnətʃər] the unique way of writing somebody's own name

n. 서명, 사인
sign v. 서명하다, 사인하다

When you write your signature **on the document, you have to really be careful.**
서류에 서명을 할 때는 정말 신중해야 한다.

45 sum [sʌ́m] entire cost of money

n. 총계, 총액, 합계
summate v. 더하다, 합계하다 ㅣ summation n. 요약, 합계하기

The sum of the change in my pockets are about ten
thousand won.
주머니 속 잔돈의 합계는 대략 만원이었다.

46 term [tə́ːrm] a period of time that lasts for, an arranged or limited time

n. 기간, 기한
termless a. 무기한의 ㅣ termly ad. 정기적으로

The human brain has a long term memory and a short
term memory.
인간의 두뇌는 장기 기억과 단기 기억을 가지고 있다.

47 thrift [θríft] the act of saving money or something

n. 절약, 검약
thrive v. 번영하다, 번성하다, 부자가 되다 ㅣ thrifty a. 검약하는, 아끼는

Economist call it "the paradox of thrift".
경제학자들은 그것을 "절약의 역설" 이라고 불렀다.

48 valid [vǽlid] legally or officially acceptable

a. 유효한, 법적으로 유효한
validate v. 정당성을 입증하다 ㅣ validity n. 정당함

This ticket is valid on the day of issue only.
이 표는 발행 당일에만 유효하다.

49 venture [véntʃər] a business that involves taking risks

n. 모험적 사업, 위험성이 있는 사업

venturous a. 모험을 좋아하는, 대담한, 무모한

It is a bold venture starting a business in this condition.

이러한 조건에서 사업을 시작하는 것은 대담한 모험이다.

50 withdraw [wiðdrɔ́ː, wiθ-] to take money out of a bank account

v. (돈을 은행에서) 인출하다

withdrawal n. 인출, 회수 ㅣ withdrawn a. 회수한, 철회한

How much do you want to withdraw?

얼마나 인출하시겠습니까?

Check up

A 다음 내용이 설명하고 있는 단어를 〈보기〉에서 골라 그 기호를 쓰시오.

| approximate | bankrupt | charge | debt | deliberate |

1. bust, insolvent, broke

2. close, inexact

3. loss, liability, arrears, debit

4. intended, conscious, intentional, willful, calculated, premeditated

5. fine, ask, levy, bill, invoice

B 단어와 한글 뜻을 알맞게 짝지으시오.

1. deposit · · 기부하다, 증여하다

2. endow · · (세금, 벌 등을) 부과하다

3. expire · · 담보, 보증

4. guarantee · · 예금액, 예금

5. impose · · 만기가 되다, (기간이) 끝나다

C 다음 빈 칸에 의미상 가장 알맞은 단어를 보기에서 골라 쓰시오.

interest | lease | loan | owe | rate

1. raise a _____ : 공채를 모집하다

2. _____ for delinquency : 연체 이자

3. at an easy _____ : 싼 값으로, 쉽게

4. by _____ : 임대로

5. _____ a person one : ~에게 은혜를 갚다

D 영영풀이에 알맞은 단어를 고르시오.

refund | signature | sum | thrift | withdraw

1. your name as you usually write it

2. an amount of money

3. to move back or away from a place or situation

4. a sum of money that is paid back to you

5. the habit of saving money and spending it carefully

Lesson 6
Occupation
| 직업

01 **agent** [éidʒənt] a person who does someone else's job or who represents somebody

n. 대리인
agency n. 대리점

The untrained agents cannot provide their customer with good service.

교육받지 않은 직원들이 손님들에게 좋은 서비스를 제공할 수 없다.

---

02 **amateur** [ǽmətʃər, ǽmətəːr] a person who takes part in a sport or other activity for enjoyment, not as a job

n. 아마추어 a. 아마추어의

Some actors are amateur car racers in their spare time.

몇몇 배우들은 여가 시간에 아마추어 자동차 경주자로 활동한다.

---

03 **ambition** [æmbíʃən] the desire or determination to be successful, rich, powerful

n. 야망, 야심
ambitious a. 야망을 품은, 야심이 큰

His ambition knows no limit.

그의 야망은 끝이 없다.

---

04 **apply** [əplái] to make a formal request for something, especially for a job

n. 지원하다, 신청하다, 적용되다
applicant n. 응모자, 신청자, 지원자 | application n. 신청, 적용, 지원

Law must be applied regardless of somebody's gender and race.

법은 성별과 인종에 상관없이 적용되어야 한다.

05 astronomer [əstránəmər] a scientist who studies astronomy

n. 천문학자

astronomy n. 천문학 | astronomical a. 천문의

Some astronomers **do not accept the "big-bang" theory.**

일부 천문학자들은 빅뱅이론을 인정하지 않는다.

06 athletic [æθlétik] connected with sports such as running, jumping and throwing

a. 운동의, 경기의, 강건한, (몸이) 탄탄한

athlete n. 운동 선수 | atheletics n. 운동 경기

Her family is very athletic.

그녀의 가족은 모두 운동 신경이 좋다.

07 attendant [əténdənt] a person whose job is to serve or help in a public place

n. 시중드는 사람, 안내원 a. 시중드는

attendance n. 시중, 수행, 간병 | attend v. 섬기다, 따라가다, 수행하다

She wants to be a flight attendant.

그녀는 비행기 승무원이 되고 싶어한다.

08 author [ɔ́:θər] a person who writes books as a job

n. 작가

You can find a book by its name or author**'s name.**

책 제목이나 작가 이름으로 책을 찾을 수 있다.

09 **award** [əwɔ́:rd] to give something to someone as a payment, prize, etc.

v. 수여하다 n. 상, 상금, 상패
awardee n. 수상자 l awarder n. 시상자

A gold medal will be awarded to the winner.

금메달이 우승자에게 수여될 것입니다.

10 **banker** [bǽŋkər] a person who has a bank or has an important job at a bank

n. 은행가, 은행원
bank n. 은행 l bank account 계좌 l banking 은행업무

They married their daughter to a banker.

그들은 딸을 은행가와 결혼시켰다.

11 **businessman** [bíznismæ̀n] a person who works in business especially at a high level

n. 실업가, 상인, 사업가

He proved himself a capable businessman.

그는 자신이 유능한 사업가임을 입증했다.

12 **career** [kəríər] the period of time that someone spent their life working or doing a job

n. 이력, 경력

Many of sports star players begin their career in their early age.

많은 스포츠 스타들이 어린 나이에 그들의 경력을 시작한다.

13 chemist [kémist]   a person who studies chemistry; a person who sells medicine

n. 화학자, 약사
chemical n. 화학 약품 I chemistry n. 화학

He is a world famous chemist.

그는 전 세계적으로 유명한 화학자이다.

14 chief [tʃi:f]   a person with a high rank or the highest rank in a company or an organization

n. 우두머리, 두목, 장
chiefly ad. 주로

The chief of a family is usually a father.

가장은 대개 아버지이다.

15 conference [kánfərəns]   a large official meeting, usually lasting for a few days, at which people with the same work or interests come together to discuss their view

n. 협의, 회의
confer v. 협의하다, 의논하다, 상담하다 I conferrable a. 협의 가능한

The meeting will be held in the conference room.

회의는 회의실에서 열릴 것이다.

16 correspondent [kɔ:rəspándənt]   a person who reports news from a particular country or on a particular subject for a newspaper, a television or radio station

n. 특파원, 통신원
correspondence n. 통신, 왕래 I correspond v. 일치하다, 상응하다

He used to be a correspondent for New York Times in Korea.   그는 뉴욕 타임지의 한국 특파원이었다.

17 **crew** [krú:] a group of people who work in a ship, plane, etc.

n. (집합적) 승무원
wrecking crew n. 구조대

The airplane has a crew of thirty.

그 비행기 승무원은 30명이다.

18 **earn** [ə́:rn] to get something, especially money by doing your job

n. 벌다, 획득하다
earn a living (생계비를) 벌다 ㅣ earning n. 소득, 벌기

Women earn less than men on average.

평균적으로 여성들의 소득이 남성보다 적다.

19 **efficient** [ifíʃənt] doing something well without waste of money, time, and effort

a. 능률적인, 효과가 있는
efficacy n. 효능, 효험 ㅣ efficiency n. 능력, 능률

It is not efficient to hire poorly trained workers.

미숙련 노동자를 고용하는 것은 능률적이지 않다.

20 **employee** [implɔ́ii:] a person who is paid to work for someone

n. 고용인, 종업원
employed a. 취업 상태의 ㅣ employer n. 고용주 ㅣ employ v. 고용하다

If you want to succeed in your career, be a valued and respected employee.

직업적으로 성공하고 싶다면, 가치 있고 존경 받는 사원이 되어라.

21 employer [implɔ́iər]   a person or company that pays people working for them

n. 고용주
employment n. 고용, 사용, 이용 ᅵ employment agency n. 직업 소개소

The employer is planning to hire 20 more people for the assembly line.

고용주는 조립 부분에 20명의 사람을 더 고용할 계획이다.

22 excellent [éksələnt]   extremely good

a. 우수한, 뛰어난
excel v. 빼어나다, 타고나다, 남을 능가하다 ᅵ excellence n. 우수, 탁월성

She is the excellent employee I told you the other day.

그녀가 내가 전에 말했던 우수한 사원이다.

23 experience [ikspíəriəns]   the knowledge and skill that somebody have learned during doing something

n. 경험, 경험한 일 vt. 경험하다, 체험하다
experienced a. 경험이 있는, 노련한, 숙련된

All knowledge rests on experience.

모든 지식은 경험에 근거한다.

24 fluent [flúːənt]   able to speak, read or write a language easily and well

a. 유창한, 거침이 없는
fluency n. 유창함, 능숙도 ᅵ fluently ad. 유창하게

Many politicians have fluent tongues.

많은 정치가들이 말을 잘한다.

25 · **form** [fɔ́ːrm] an official document containing spaces for answers

n. 신청 용지, 문서 양식, 서식
formal a. 공식적인, 격식 차린, 형식적인 ǀ format n. 구성, 판형

When you submit this homework, confirm your paper to a standard form.

이 과제를 제출할 때는, 규정 양식에 형식을 일치시켜라.

26 **gardener** [gɑ́ːrdnər] a person who is paid to work in someone else's garden

n. 원예사, 정원사
garden n. 정원 ǀ gardening n. 원예

The gardener **is leaning over, doing his watering.**

정원사가 몸을 구부려 물을 주고 있다.

27 **historian** [histɔ́ːriən] a person who writes and studies history; an expert in history.

n. 사학자, 역사가
history n. 역사 ǀ historical a. 역사적인

Sometimes the facts are changed by the historians.

가끔씩 역사학자들에 의해 사실이 바뀌기도 한다.

28 **interview** [íntərvjùː] a formal meeting at which someone is asked questions to see if they are suitable for a particular job or for a course of study at a college, university, etc

n. 면접, 인터뷰
interviewer n. 면접관 ǀ interviewee n. 면접자

The most important thing about an interview **is not to be late.**

면접에서 가장 중요한 것은 늦지 않는 것이다.

29 journalist [dʒə́ːrnəlist] a person who writes news stories for the mass media

n. 저널리스트
journal n. 신문, 잡지, 일지

Sometimes journalists refuse to disclose the sources of their information.

때때로 언론인들은 정보의 출처를 밝히기를 거부한다.

30 lawyer [lɔ́ːjər] a person who is qualified to advise people about the law

n. 변호사
lawsuit n. 소송, 고소 ǀ law n. 법

She wants to consult with a lawyer of good reputation.

그녀는 평판이 좋은 변호사와 상담하기를 원한다.

31 magistrate [mǽdʒəstrèit] an official who acts as a judge in the lowest court of law

n. 행정 장관, 치안 판사

A country magistrate in ancient Korea had undisputed power.

옛날 한국의 고을 원님은 막강한 힘을 가지고 있었다.

32 musician [mjuːzíʃən] a person who plays musical instrument or write music, especially as a job

n. 음악가
music n. 음악 ǀ musical n. 뮤지컬 a. 음악적인

We came to the conclusion that Beethoven is the greatest musician.

우리는 베토벤이 가장 위대한 음악가라는 결론을 내렸다.

33 obvious [ábviəs] easy to see or understand

a. 명백한
obviousness n. 명백함 | obviously ad. 명백하게, 확실히

This is too obvious to require any argument.

이것은 논의하기에는 너무나 명백하다.

34 official [əfíʃəl] a person who is in a position of authority in a large organization

n. 공무원 a. 공식의
office n. 공직, 사무실, 사무소 | officiate v. 직무를 행하다, 직권을 행사하다

Every official has gone home.

모든 공무원들이 집에 갔다.

35 operate [ápərèit] to control or use a machine or make it work

v. 작동하다, 조종하다
operation n. 작용, 움직임 | operational a. 사용할 수 있는, 사용 가능한

Cars will operate on alternative fuels in the future.

미래에는 자동차들이 대체 연료로 작동할 것이다.

36 passionate [pǽʃənət] having or showing strong feelings of enthusiasm for something or belief in something

a. 열정적인, 열렬한
passion n. 열정, 격정, 정열 | passionately ad. 열렬하게, 격정적으로

A passionate kiss uses all 34 facial muscles.

열정적인 키스는 34개의 안면 근육을 사용한다.

37　personality [pə̀ːrsənǽləti]　the various aspects of person's character

n. 개성, 성격
personal a. 개인적인, 개인의 l **person** n. 개인

We need to have a job that suits our personality.
적성에 맞는 직업을 선택해야 한다.

38　physician [fizíʃən]　a doctor, especially who is an expert in general medicine

n. 내과 의사, 의사
physical a. 물리적인, 물질의 l **physics** n. 물리학, 물리적 현상

Mother nature is the best physician.
자연이 가장 좋은 의사다.

39　profession [prəféʃən]　a kind of job that need special training and education

n. 직업
professional a. 직업의, 직업상의, 프로의
professionally ad. 전문적으로, 직업적으로, 직업상

Playing computer games is just a hobby, not a profession.
컴퓨터 게임을 하는 것은 단순한 취미이지 직업이 아니다.

40　quality [kwáləti]　the degree or extent of excellence of something

n. 품질, 소질, 자질
qualification n. 자격

Quality is as important as quantity in studying foreign languages.
외국어를 공부하는 데 있어서 질은 양만큼 중요하다.

41 **recruit** [rikrúːt] a person who newly joined a company, an organization, the army, etc.

n. 신입 vt. (신입을) 모집하다

recruitment n. 신규 모집, 채용, 보충

The new recruit made a butchery of the work.

그 신입 사원은 서툴러서 일을 엉망으로 만들었다.

42 **resume** [rézuměi] a short written account of your education and previous jobs that you send to an employer when you're looking for a new job

n. 이력서

A resume includes information regarding age, education and experience.

이력서에는 나이, 학력과 경력이 포함된다.

43 **retire** [ritáiər] to stop doing one's job, especially because of age

v. 은퇴하다

retirement n. 은퇴, 퇴직, 퇴역 | retired a. 은퇴한, 퇴직한

What would you do when you retire?

은퇴하면 무엇을 하실 생각이에요?

44 **salesman** [séilzmən] a person whose job is selling goods

n. 판매원

Sociability is an important asset to a salesman.

사교성은 판매원에게는 중요한 자산이다.

45 skillful [skílfəl]

being good at doing something that needs special ability or training

a. 기술이 좋은, 솜씨가 좋은
skill n. 솜씨, 익숙함

Skillful diplomacy will lead country to a bright future.

능숙한 외교는 나라를 밝은 미래로 이끌 것이다.

46 staff [stæf, stάːf] the people who work for an organization

n. (집합적) 직원

In an emergency situation, you should follow staff member's directions.

응급 상황에서는 직원의 지시를 따르세요.

47 value [vǽljuː] worth in monetary terms

n. 가치
valuable a. 금전적 가치가 있는 | valuation n. 평가, 평가액

The value of the dollar is falling.

달러 가치가 하락하고 있다.

48 veteran [vétərən]

a person who has a lot of experience and knowledge about something

n. 베테랑, 숙련공

Veteran players saved their team from defeat yesterday.

베테랑 선수들이 어제 그들의 팀을 패배에서 구해냈다.

49 visible [vízəbl] able to be seen

n. 눈에 보이는, 명백한, 현저한

visibly ad. 눈에 띄게, 역력히 ｜ visibility n. 눈에 보임, 가시도

Some things are not visible **but valuable.**

어떤 것들은 눈에 보이지는 않지만 소중하다.

50 workaholic [wə:rkəhɔ́:lik]   a person who works very hard and hardly do anything else

n. 일 중독자, 일 벌레

workaholism n. 일 중독

He seems to be a complete workaholic.

그는 완전히 일 중독자 같다.

Check up

A 다음 단어의 유의어가 아닌 것을 고르시오.

1. agent

a. spy　　　　b. officer　　　c. representative　d. infantary

2. apply

a. defy　　　　b. impose　　　c. enforce　　　d. put into

3. athletic

a. active　　　b. healthy　　　c. fit　　　　　d. feeble

4. attendant

a. assistart　　b. absenter　　c. aide　　　　d. helper

5. award

a. punishment　b. prize　　　c. reward　　　d. medal

B 주어진 표현에 해당하는 단어를 보기에서 고르시오.

| chief | earn | excellent | form | interview |

1. _____ : make, get, gain, receive

2. _____ : shape, work, process

3. _____ : interrogation, consultation, audition

4. _____ : important, primary, main

5. _____ : outstanding, perfect, superb, classic,

first-rate

C 우리말은 영어로, 영어는 우리말로 바꾸시오.

1. magistrate   2. 신입, (신입을) 모집하다

3. 공무원   4. resume

5. passionate   6. 은퇴하다

7. 개성, 성격   8. skillful

9. profession   10. 베테랑, 숙련공

Part 6

Society

[사회]

Lesson 1
Society
| 사회

01 accustomed [əkʌ́stəmd] familiar with something and accepting it as normal or usual

a. 익숙해진, 여느 때와 다름 없는, 평범한

accustom v. 익히다, 익숙하게 하다, 길들다 ㅣ unaccustomed a. 익숙하지 않은

Dogs and cats need some time to become accustomed to each other.

개와 고양이는 서로 익숙해지는 데 시간이 조금 필요하다.

---

02 aspect [ǽspekt] a particular part or feature of a situation, a problem, etc.

n. (사물의) 면, 국면, 양상

What we have to consider is the financial aspect.

우리가 고려해야 할 것은 금전적인 측면이다.

---

03 associate [əsóusièit] to make connection between people or things in your mind

v. 연상하다, 어울리다, 제휴하다 연합하다 n. (일 등에서) 동료, 패, 친구

association n. 연상, 제휴 ㅣ associated a. 연합한, 동료의

What do you associate with Christmas?

크리스마스하면 무엇이 연상되세요?

---

04 behalf [bihǽf, -háːf] instead of someone, or as their representative

n. 이익, 원조, 측, 편

on behalf of ~을 대신[대표]하여

The captain accepted the cup on behalf of the Korea.

주장이 팀을 대표하여 우승컵을 받았다.

05 **belong** [bilɔ́ːŋ, -láŋ] to be in the right or suitable place

v. ~에 속하다, ~의 소유물이다
belonging n. 소지품, 소유물

Do not covet something that does not belong to you.

네 것이 아닌 것을 탐하지 마라.

06 **bulletin** [búlətin] an official statement about something important

n. 고시, 게시
bulletin board 게시판

One way to announce something is to post it on the bulletin board.

무언가를 공지하는 방법 중 하나는 게시판에 붙이는 것이다.

07 **carol** [kǽrəl] a Christian religious song sung at Christmas

n. 기쁨의 노래, (종교적) 축가, 캐럴 v. 즐겁게 노래하다, 축가를 부르다

A carol is usually played in downtown from late November to Christmas day.

캐롤은 번화가에서 보통 11월말부터 크리스마스까지 들을 수 있다.

08 **citizen** [sítəzən] a person who has the legal right to belong to a particular country

n. 국민, 시민, 민간인
citizenship n. 시민권, 시민의 자격(신분)

Paying taxes is every citizen's duty.

납세는 모든 국민의 의무이다.

09 civil [sívəl] connected with the people who live in a country or society

a. 시민의, 민간의
civilization n. 문명, 문명 사회, 문명 세계 ǀ **civilian** n. 일반 시민, 민간인

Every citizen has civil **rights and duties.**
모든 시민은 시민의 권리와 의무를 갖고 있다.

10 community [kəmjúːnəti] a group of people who share the same religion, race, job, etc.

n. 공동 사회, 공동체, 집단, 계
communism n. 공산주의 ǀ **communist** n. 공산주의자

A community **consisted of individuals.**
공동체는 개인들로 구성되어 있다.

11 commute [kəmjúːt] to travel regularly by bus, train, car, etc. between your place of work and your home

v. 통근하다, 통학하다 n. 통근, 통학

I live in a suburd and commute **to the city every day.**
나는 교외에 살면서 매일 시내로 통근한다.

12 compete [kəmpíːt] to try to be more successful or better than the others

v. 경쟁하다, 겨루다, 맞서다
competence n. 능력, 적성, 권한 ǀ **competent** a. 유능한, 자격이 있는
competition n. 경쟁, 경기, 시합
competitive a. 경쟁의, 경쟁적인, (가격 등이) 경쟁할 수 있는

No one can compete **with him in soccer.**
축구에서는 그를 따를 자가 없다.

13 complain [kəmpléin] to say that you are annoyed, unhappy or not satisfied

v. 불평하다, 투덜거리다, 푸념하다, 한탄하다
complaint n. 불평, 불만

I've never heard him complain about anything.
나는 그가 불평하는 것을 들어본 적이 없다.

14 comply [kəmplái] to obey a rule, an order, etc.

v. (명령, 요구, 규칙에) 따르다, 응하다, 좇다
compliance n. 응함, 응낙, 추종
compliant a. 유순한, 시키는 대로 하는, 고분고분한

No parents can comply with their children's request.
어떤 부모도 자식의 모든 요구를 들어줄 수는 없다.

15 considerably [kənsídərəbli] much or a lot

ad. 상당히, 꽤, 적지 않게
considerable a. 상당한, 적지 않은 | consideration n. 고려, 배려

Marriage costs a considerably large sum of money.
결혼은 상당히 많은 돈이 필요하다.

16 contribution [kàntrəbjúːʃən] act of giving money or something in order to help

n. 기부, 기증, 기여, 공헌
contribute v. 기부하다, 기증하다, 기여하다 | contributor n. 기부자, 기증자, 기고가

Collecting contributions is an important part of an election.
기부금을 받는 것은 선거에서 중요한 부분 중의 하나이다.

17 **courtesy** [kə́:rtəsi]   polite behavior that shows respect for other people

n. 예의, 공손, 친절
courteous a. 예의 바른, 정중한, 친절한

Whatever the relationship is, courtesy should be maintained.
어떤 관계라도, 예의는 지켜져야 한다.

18 **demonstrate** [démənstrèit]   to protest or support something in public with a lot of people

v. 시위 운동(데모)을 하다
demonstration n. 시위 운동, 데모 ┃ demonstrative a. 시위적인, 예증적인

Demonstrating violently in public places is illegal in Korea. 한국에서 공공장소에서의 폭력적 시위는 불법이다.

19 **different** [dífərənt]   not the same; not like as something or someone

a. ~와 다른, 별개의, 같지 않은
differ v. 다르다, 의견을 달리하다 ┃ difference n. 차이, 다름, 차이점

Customs are different from one country to another.
관습은 나라마다 다르다.

20 **discourage** [diskə́:ridʒ]   to make someone feel less confident or enthusiastic.

V. 낙담시키다, 좌절시키다
discouragement n. 낙담, 낙심, 방해 ┃ discouraged a. 낙담한, 낙심한
discouraging a. 낙담시키는, 실망시키는

Mass unemployment discourages a lot of young Koreans.
대량 실업 사태로 한국의 많은 젊은이들이 좌절한다.

21 donate [dóuneit] to give money, food, clothes, etc. to somebody especially a charity

v. (돈 등을) 기부하다, 기증하다, 증여하다
donation n. 기부, 기증 | donator n. 기부자

Donate your blood regularly, and you will lower your chances of having a heart attack.

규칙적으로 헌혈하라. 그러면 심장병 발병률이 낮아질 것이다.

22 encounter [inkáuntər] to meet someone unexpectedly

v. 만나다, 맞부딪히다 n. 마주침

Many women still encounter prejudice in Korea.

아직도 한국에서는 많은 여성들이 편견에 부딪힌다.

23 equal [íːkwəl] same in size, quantity, value, etc.

a. (지위, 입장 등이) 동등한, 대등한, 균등한, 공평한
equality n. 동등함, 동등, 대등, 균등성
equally ad. 똑같게, 동등하게

All men is equal under the law.

누구나 법 앞에서 평등하다.

24 escape [iskéip] to get away from a place or situation

v. 벗어나다, 도망하다, 탈출하다, 도피하다 n. 탈출, 도망
escaped a. 도망한, 탈주한

Many people want to escape from the same routine.

많은 사람들이 똑같은 일상으로부터 탈출하고 싶어한다.

25 **exclude** [iksklú:d] to prevent someone or something from entering a place or taking part in something

v. 배제하다, 추방하다, 제외시키다
exclusion n. 제외, 배제, 추방 | exclusive a. 배타적인, 독점적인
excluding prep. ~을 제외하고

The window excludes the wind.
창문은 바람을 막아준다.

26 **fashionable** [fǽʃənəbl] following a style that is popular at a particular time

a. 최신 유행의, 유행하는, 유행을 따르는
fashion n. 유행, 유행하는 것, (여성복의) 패션, 풍조, 시류
unfashionable a. 시대에 뒤진, 유행하지 않는

Tanning seems to be fashionable among women this year.
피부 태우기가 올해 여성들 사이에서 유행인 것 같다.

27 **firmly** [fə́:rmli] in a strong or definite way

ad. 단단하게, 견고하게
firm a. 굳은, 단단한, 견고한

Refuse a request firmly when it sounds unjust.
부당한 요청이 있을 때에는 단호하게 거절해라.

28 **handshake** [hǽndʃèik] an act of shaking somebody's hand with your own

n. 악수

A firm handshake means belief and favor.
손을 꽉 쥐는 악수는 믿음과 호의를 의미한다.

29 harmony [háːrməni] a state of peaceful existence and agreement

n. 조화, 일치, 화합, 융화
harmonize v. 조화를 이루다, 어울리다, 화합시키다
harmonious a. 조화된, 균형 잡힌, 사이가 좋은, 화목한

In nature, every creature finds a way to live in harmony**.**
자연의 모든 생명체들은 조화를 이뤄 살아가는 방법을 찾아낸다.

30 homeless [hóumlis] having no home

a. 집 없는 n. 노숙자들

The government provides places to live for homeless **people.**
정부는 집 없는 사람들에게 살 장소를 제공한다.

31 include [inklúːd] to make someone or something part of a larger group or set

v. ~을 (부분, 요소 등으로) 포함하다, 포괄하다
Included a. 함유된, 포함된 | Including prep. ~을 포함하여

The physical looks include **facial expressions and body shapes.**
신체적 외모에는 얼굴 표정과 몸매가 포함된다.

32 indifferent [indífərənt] having or showing no interest in someone or something

a. 무관심한, 냉담한, 개의치 않는
Indifference n. 무관심, 냉담, 개의치 않음

The young should not be indifferent **to politics.**
젊은이들은 정치에 무관심해서는 안된다.

33 **individual** [ìndəvídʒuəl] a person considered separately rather than as a part of a group

n. (집단의 일원으로서의) 개인, 사람 a. 개인의
individualize v. 개성(특성)을 발휘시키다, 개별적으로 취급하다
Individuality n. 개성, 특성, 인격 I Individually ad. 개인적으로, 개별적으로

Each individual **has a unique character and characteristics.**
각 개인은 모두 독특한 성격과 특징을 가지고 있다.

34 **institution** [ìnstətjúːʃən] a large important organization that has a particular purpose

n. 학회, 협회, (공공)시설
institute v. 세우다, 설립하다, 제정하다 I institutional a. 제도상의, 제도적인

City hall plans to found an art institution.
시청에서는 미술 협회를 설립할 계획이다.

35 **join** [dʒɔ́in] to be a part of something or participate in

vt. 참가하다, 결합하다, 가입하다
joint n. 이음매, 이은 자리, 관절 I jointly ad. 공동으로, 연대적으로

Which club do you want to join?
어떤 동아리에 가입하고 싶니?

36 **majority** [mədʒɔ́ːrəti, -dʒɑ́r-] the largest part of a group of people or things

n. 대부분, 대다수, 과반수, 절대 다수
major a. 큰 쪽의, 보다 많은, 대다수의, 과반수의

The majority **of people drive a car every day.**
대다수의 사람들이 매일 차를 운전한다.

37 **movement** [múːvmənt]　a gradual change in what people in society do or think

n. (정치·사회적) 운동, 운동 집단
move v. 움직이다 ｜ movable a. 움직일 수 있는 ｜ movability n. 가동성

He has been involved with the movement for human rights for a long time.
그는 오랫동안 인권 운동에 참여해 왔다.

38 **obey** [oubéi]　to do what you are told or expected to do

v. 복종하다, 순종하다, (명령을) 준수하다
obedience n. 복종, 순종, 충실 ｜ obedient a. 순종하는, 고분고분한, 충실한

Everyone must obey the law without exception.
모든 사람들이 예외없이 법을 준수해야 한다.

39 **possibility** [pàsəbíləti]　an opportunity to do something

n. 가능성, 실현성, 발전의 가능성, 장래성
possible a. 가능한 ｜ possibly ad. 아마, 혹시, 어쩌면

The computer and Internet have infinite possibilities.
컴퓨터와 인터넷은 무한한 가능성을 지녔다.

40 **prejudice** [prédʒədis]　an unreasonable dislike or preference

n. 편견, 선입관, 나쁜 감정, 적대감 v. 편견을 갖게 하다
prejudiced a. 선입견을 가진, 편파적인, 불공평한

Ignorance breeds prejudice.
무지는 편견을 낳는다.

41 **primary** [práimeri, -məri] main; most important; basic

a. 첫째의, 1순위의, 예비의, 근본적인
prime a. 주요한, 으뜸가는, 가장 중요한 | primarily ad. 첫째로, 처음으로, 본래, 우선
primal a. 원시의, 태고의

Health is the primary requisite to success in life.

건강은 성공의 제1의 요건이다.

42 **punctual** [pʌŋktʃuəl] happening or doing something at the arranged or correct time

a. 시간을 잘 지키는, 예정대로의
punctuality n. 시간 엄수, 정확함, 꼼꼼함 | punctually ad. 시간대로, 정각에, 엄수하여

Someone who is always punctual will gain trust.

항상 시간을 잘 엄수하는 사람은 신뢰를 얻을 것이다.

43 **rely** [rilái] to trust or depend on

v. 의지하다, 신뢰하다, 얻다
reliable a. 믿을 수 있는, 의지가 되는, 확실한 | reliant a. 의존하는, 의지하는
reliance n. 의존, 의지 | reliability n. 신뢰도, 확신성

The world we live in today relies heavily on science.

우리가 살고 있는 이 세상은 과학에 크게 의존하고 있다.

44 **ridiculous** [ridíkjuləs] very silly or unreasonable

a. 웃기는, 우스꽝스러운, 바보 같은
ridicule n. 비웃음, 조소, 조롱, 놀림 vt. 비웃다, 조롱하다

Imitating blindly looks ridiculous.

누군가를 무작정 따라 하는 것은 우스꽝스럽게 보인다.

45 sacrifice [sǽkrəfàis]

to give up something that is important or valuable to you in order to get or do something that seems more important

v. 희생하다, 단념하다, 제물을 바치다 n. 제물, 희생

Parents sacrifice **themselves for their children.**

부모들은 그들의 아이를 위해서 어떤 희생이든 한다.

46 society [səsáiəti]

a particular community that shares the same customs, laws, etc.

n. 사회, 지역, 공동체
social a. 사교적인, 사회의 | sociable a. 사교적인, 교제하기를 좋아하는
sociability n. 사교성, 사교적 행사

The family is the basic unit of society.

가족은 사회의 기본 단위이다.

47 stranger [stréindʒər] a person that is unknown or unfamiliar

n. 낯선 사람, 모르는 사람
strange a. 이상한, 야릇한, 묘한 | strangely ad. 이상하게, 기묘하게, 색다르게

Any stranger **who requests financial information should be avoided.**

금융 정보를 요구하는 낯선 사람은 피해야 한다.

48 target [tá:rgit] a result that you try to achieve

n. 목표, 과녁, 표적

He aimed and fired carefully but missed the target.

그는 신중하게 겨냥하고 총을 쏘았지만 목표를 빗나갔다.

49 **tolerance** [tάlərəns]   willingness to allow people to do, say, or believe what they want without criticizing or punishing them

n. 관용, 관대, 용인, 포용력

tolerable a. 참을 수 있는, 포용력 있는 | tolerate v. 관대하게 다루다, 참다, 견디다
toleration n. 관용 | tolerant a. 관대한, 아량이 있는, (의학) 내성이 있는

Our society needs tolerance **for various religions.**

우리 사회는 다양한 종교에 대한 포용력이 필요하다.

---

50 **yearly** [jíərli]   happening once a year or every year

a. 연 1회의, 매년의, 1년간의 ad. 매년

year on year a. 작년 대비, 연도별의 | year round a. 1년 내내, 연중 계속되는

The festival is held yearly **in July.**

축제는 매년 7월에 열린다.

Check up

A 다음의 단어가 본문에서 쓰인 의미를 고르시오.

1. a mountain with a beautiful aspect

ⓐ a particular part of feature of a situation, an idea, a problem, etc.

ⓑ the appearance of a place, a situation or a person

2. a business associate

ⓐ to make a connection between people or things in your mind

ⓑ someone who you work or do business with

3. Whales belong to mammals.

ⓐ to be in the right or suitable place

ⓑ to feel comfortable and happy in a particular situation or people

4. How many people commute to work every day?

ⓐ to travel regularly by bus, train, car, etc. between your place of work and your home

ⓑ to replace one punishment with another that is less severe

5. demonstrate **for lower taxes**

ⓐ **to show something clearly by giving proof or evidence**

ⓑ **to show by your actions that you have a particular quality, feeling or opinion**

B 반대말끼리 연결하시오.

1. different   · encourage

2. discourage ·   · dissonance

3. complain ·   · satisfy

4. exclude ·   · same

5. harmony ·   · include

Lesson 2
Religion

| 종교

01 abbey [ǽbi] a large church with buildings where nuns live or used to live

n. 큰 수도원 (수녀원)

Myung-Dong Abbey **is the biggest church in Korea.**

명동성당이 한국에서 가장 큰 성당이다.

02 Bible [báibl] the holy book of the Christian religion

n. (기독교의) 성서, 성경, 권위 있는 서적
biblical a. 성서의

The witness swore on the Bible.

증인은 성경에 대고 맹세했다.

03 bishop [bíʃəp] a senior priest in charge of the Church

n. (카톨릭) 주교

A bishop **was one of the most powerful positions in the middle ages.**

중세 시대에 주교는 가장 영향력 있는 사람 중의 한 명이었다.

04 bless [blés] to ask for God's favour and protection for people

v. 축복하다, 신의 은혜를 빌다
blessed a. 신성한, 축복받은 I blessing n. 은총, 축복

May God bless **you!**

신의 축복이 있기를!

05 Buddhist [búdist]   a person who has a religion based on the teachings of Buddha

n. 불교도 a. 부처의, 불교도의
Buddha n. 부처님 | Buddhism n. 불교

Sikhs, Christians, and Buddhists are minorities in India.
시크교도, 기독교도, 불교도들은 인도에서는 비주류이다.

06 bury [béri]   to place a dead body in a grave

v. 묻다, 파묻다, 매장하다
buried a. 묻힌 | burial n. 매장

A cemetery is a place where dead people or animals are buried.
묘지는 죽은 사람이나 동물이 묻히는 장소이다.

07 caste [kæst, kɑːst]   a social class of India

n. 카스트 (제도), 배타적 특권 계급

The caste system categorized people into four groups.
카스트 제도는 사람들을 4개의 계급으로 나눈다.

08 cathedral [kəθíːdrəl]   the main church of a district

n. 대성당, 큰 교회당

There are a lot of cathedrals in Korea.
한국에는 많은 성당이 있다.

09 charity [tʃǽrəti] kindness and sympathy towards other people

n. 사랑, 자비심, 자선 (행위)

Mother Teresa did a lot of work for charity.

테레사 수녀는 많은 자선 활동을 했다.

10 chime [tʃaim] to ring; to make a ringing sound, especially to tell you what time it is

v. 종이 울리다, (종, 시계 등) 시간을 알리다

The clock is chiming.

시계가 땡땡 울린다.

11 Christianity [kristʃiǽnəti] the religion that is based on the teachings of Jesus Christ

n. 기독교, 기독교 교파
Christian n. 기독교인 a. 기독교의

Jesus Christ inspired a religion, which is called Christianity

예수는 기독교라고 불리는 종교를 생겨나게 했다.

12 desire [dizáiər] a strong wish to have or do something

n. 욕구, 욕망 v. 몹시 바라다, 욕구하다, 희망하다
desirability n. 바람직함, 바람직한 상황
desirable a. 바람직한, 탐나는, 호감이 가는
desirous a. 원하는, 바라는

Dictators' desire **for absolute power is infinite.**

독재자들의 절대 권력에 대한 욕망은 무한하다.

13 destiny [déstəni] the things which are arranged by fate

n. 운명, 숙명
destined a. 예정된, 운명 지어진 ㅣ destine v. 예정되다, 운명짓다

No one knows their destiny.

아무도 자신의 운명을 모른다.

14 dignity [dígnəti] a calm and serious manner that deserves respect

n. 존엄, 위엄, 품위
dignify v. 장엄하게 하다, 존귀하게 하다

A man of dignity **would never do such a thing.**

위엄있는 사람은 그러한 행동을 절대 하지 않을 것이다.

15 distrust [distrʌ́st] to feel that you cannot trust or believe

v. 믿지 않다, 의심하다 n. 불신(감)
distrustful a. 의심 많은, 믿지 않는, 의심스러운

She distrusted **his motives for wanting to see her again.**

그녀는 자기를 다시 만나고 싶어 하는 그의 동기를 의심했다.

16 divine [diváin] coming from or connected with God or a god

a. 하늘이 내린, 신성한
divinity n. 신, 신성

To err is human, to forgive is divine.

실수는 인간의 본성이고, 용서는 신의 본성이다.

17 Easter [íːstər] a Sunday in March or April when Christians remember the death of Christ and his return to life

n. 부활절(축제)

Easter is just around the corner.

부활절이 곧 온다.

18 evil [íːvəl] anything bad or unpleasant

n. 악 a. 나쁜, 사악한, 불길한
evilly ad. 간악하게, 흉악하게

We need to uproot the evils of our society.

우리는 사회의 악을 근절해야 한다.

19 frock [frɑ́k] a long loose pieces of clothing worn by some Christian monks

n. 원피스, 성직자의 옷, 성직자 신분

Most of the frocks are white or black.

성직자 옷의 대부분은 흰색과 검정색이다.

20 funeral [fjúːnərəl] a ceremony for burying or burning a dead person

n. 장례식, 고별식
funerary a. 장례식의

When the president passed away, a great number of people went to the funeral.

대통령이 서거했을 때 수많은 사람들이 장례식에 갔다.

21 grave [greiv] a place where a dead person is buried

n. 무덤, 묘, 묘석

graveyard n. 묘지 | **gravestone** n. 묘비

His grave is in a remote place.

그의 무덤은 외딴 곳에 있다.

22 grief [griːf] a feeling of great sadness especially when someone dies

n. 큰 슬픔, 비탄, 비통

grieve v. 몹시 슬퍼하다 | **grievance** n. 고충, 불만

Newspapers should not judge whether people's grief is right or wrong.

신문은 사람들의 비통함이 옳은지 그른지에 대한 판단을 해서는 안 된다.

23 heaven [hévən] a place that is believed that good people go after death

n. 천국, 천당, 극락

heavenly a. 천국의, 거룩한, 훌륭한

Heaven helps those who help themselves.

하늘은 스스로 돕는 자를 돕는다.

24 hell [hel] a place where bad people go after death and devils live

n. 지옥

Laziness will make your future a hell.

나태함은 너의 미래를 지옥처럼 만들 것이다.

25 **holy** [hóuli] connected with God or a particular religion

a. 신성한, 성스러운

A saint means a person who lives a holy life.

성인은 신성한 삶을 산 사람을 가리킨다.

26 **hymn** [him] a song of praise, especially sung by Christians

n. (교회의) 찬송가, 찬미가, 성가
hymnal a. 찬송가의, 성가의

A carol is a kind of hymn.

캐롤은 찬송가의 한 종류이다.

27 **idol** [áidl] a person or thing that is loved and admired very much

n. 우상, 숭배물

Different people worship different idols.

다양한 사람들이 다양한 우상을 숭배한다.

28 **mercy** [mə́ːrsi] a kind, forgiving, or generous attitude

n. 자비심, 연민, 연민의 정
merciful a. 자비로운, 인정 많은 ｜ **merciless** a. 잔인한, 무자비한

The rich should show mercy to the poor.

부자들은 가난한 사람들에게 자비를 베풀어야 한다.

29 miracle [mírəkl] an act or event that does not follow the laws of nature

n. 기적, 불가사의한 사람, 사물

miraculous a. 기적적인, 놀랄 만한 I miraculously ad. 기적적으로, 초자연적인

A miracle rarely happens.

기적은 드물게 일어난다.

30 missionary [míʃənèri] a person who is sent to a foreign country to teach people about Christianity

n. 선교자, 전도사

mission n. 전도, 포교

The missionary goes everywhere to convert people to Christianity.

선교사들은 사람들을 기독교로 개종하기 위해 어디든지 간다.

31 monk [mʌŋk] a religious man who lives in monastery

n. 수도사, 수사

Monks give up prides of life.

수도사들은 속세의 영화를 버린다.

32 moral [mɔ́ːrəl, már-] concerned with principles of right and wrong behavior

a. 도덕(상)의, 윤리의 n. 교훈, 품행, 도덕

moralist n. 도덕가, 윤리학자 I morality n. 도덕, 도의, 윤리학

Many fairy tales teach children moral lessons.

많은 동화들이 아이들에게 도덕적인 교훈을 준다.

33 **mourning** [mɔ́:rniŋ] sadness that someone shows and feels because of death

n. (죽음에 대한) 비탄, 애도, 슬픔

mourn v. 슬퍼하다, 한탄하다 | **mournful** a. 슬픔에 잠긴, 애처로운

All of the country was in mourning when the accident has occurred.

그 사고가 일어났을 때 온 나라가 슬픔에 잠겼다.

34 **pilgrim** [pílgrim, -grəm] a person who travels to a holy place for religious reasons

n. 순례자, 성지 참배인

pilgrimage n. 순례 여행, 성지 순례

Pilgrims from England founded the church in Plymouth.

영국에서 온 순례자들이 **Plymouth**에 교회를 세웠다.

35 **pray** [préi] to speak to God in order to ask for help or give thanks

v. 빌다, 간청하다, 기원하다

prayer n. 기도, 기원, 기도하는 사람

We pray to God for forgiveness.

우리는 신에게 용서받기 위해서 기도를 한다.

36 **preach** [príːtʃ] to give a religious talk in a public place, especially in a church during a service

v. 설교하다, 전도하다

preacher n. 설교자, 전도자

Mother Teresa not only preached religion but also lived it.

테레사 수녀는 종교를 전하였을 뿐만 아니라 그것을 실천했다.

37 priest [príːst] a person who is qualified to perform religious duties and ceremonies

n. 성직자, 사제, 신부

A priest hears confessions from people.
신부는 사람들로부터 고해성사를 듣는다.

38 rebirth [riːbə́ːrθ] a second or new birth

n. 부활, 재생, 회복

A funeral consists of prayer for rebirth in paradise.
장례식에는 극락왕생을 비는 기도가 포함되어 있다.

39 religion [rilídʒən] the belief in the existence of a god or gods

n. 종교, 종파, 신앙심
religious a. 종교적인, 신앙심이 깊은

Religion has a great impact on people's lives.
종교는 사람들의 삶에 큰 영향을 미친다.

40 sin [sin] an offence against God or against a religious or moral law

n. (종교적 · 도덕적) 죄, 죄악
sinner n. 죄인, 죄 있는 사람, 불신자 ㅣ sinful a. 죄가 있는, 죄가 많은
sinless a. 죄 없는, 결백한

Telling a lie is a sin.
거짓말하는 것은 죄이다.

41 **solemn** [sáləm] performed in a serious, religious way; holy

a. 신성한, 엄숙한
solemnity n. 장엄, 엄숙, 장중

He spoke in a solemn voice.

그는 엄숙한 목소리로 말했다.

42 **sorrow** [sárou, sɔ́:r-] a feeling of great sadness because something has happened

n. 애도, 슬픔, 비애, 비탄
sorrowful a. 슬퍼하는, 비탄에 잠긴 ㅣ sorrowfully ad. 슬프게

Life has a lot of joys and sorrows.

인생은 기쁨도 많고 슬픔도 많다.

43 **soul** [soul] the spiritual part of a person

n. 영혼, 죽은 자의 망령, 넋
soulful a. 감정이 충만한

Body and soul are not separable.

몸과 마음은 하나다.

44 **spirit** [spírit] the part of a person that includes their mind, feelings and character

n. 정신, 마음, (육체를 떠난) 영혼
spiritual a. 정신의 ㅣ spirituality n. 정신성, 영성

Arts and books enrich our spirit.

예술과 책은 우리의 영혼을 풍요롭게 한다.

45 superstition [sùːpərstíʃən] the belief that cannot be explained by reason or science

n. 미신, 미신적 행위(습관)
superstitious a. 미신의, 미신적인

Superstitions **are often connected with culture and tradition.**
미신은 종종 문화와 전통과 관련되어 있다.

46 taboo [təbúː, tæ-] prohibition for religious reasons

n. (종교상의) 금기, 꺼림

This was considered taboo at that time.
이것은 그 당시에는 금기시되었다.

47 temple [témpl] a building used for the worship of a god or gods

n. 신전, 성당, 절, 사원

Many temples in Korea were destroyed during wars.
한국의 많은 절은 전쟁 중에 파괴되었다.

48 trust [trʌst] the belief that somebody or something is good, sincere, honest, etc.

n. 신임, 신뢰, 신용 v. 신뢰하다, 신용하다
trustful a. 사람을 믿는, 믿음직하게 여기는
trustworthy a. 신용할 수 있는, 믿을 수 있는

Trust **takes a long time to build, but needs a second to lose.**
신뢰를 쌓는 것은 오래 걸리지만, 잃는 것은 순간이다.

49 **vow** [vau] a formal and serious promise

n. 맹세, 서약, (그리스도교) 서원 v. 맹세하다

I am under a vow **not to tell a lie.**

나는 거짓말하지 않겠다고 맹세했다.

---

50 **worship** [wə́ːrʃip] to show respect for God or a god, especially by praying in a religious building

v. 예배하다, 숭배하다 n. 예배, 숭배

People go to church to worship **God.**

사람들은 신을 숭배하기 위해서 교회에 간다.

A 우리말과 같은 뜻이 되도록 빈 칸에 주어진 철자로 시작되는 단어를 쓰시오.

1. He made a solemn v＿＿＿＿＿ not to lose her child again.

   그녀는 다시는 아이를 잃어버리지 않겠다고 굳게 맹세했다.

2. He used to go to a t＿＿＿＿＿ for worship.

   그는 불공을 드리러 절에 가곤 했다.

3. You must not violate a t＿＿＿＿＿ in the city.

   그 지역에서는 금기를 어기면 안 된다.

4. They are afraid of a common s＿＿＿＿＿.

   그들은 흔히 있는 미신을 두려워한다.

5. He delivered s＿＿＿＿＿ speeches, which made people touched.

   그의 장중한 연설이 사람들을 감동시켰다.

B 주어진 표현에 해당하는 단어를 보기에서 고르시오.

pray | mourning | moral | miracle | holy

1. _____ : sorrowful

2. _____ : worship, praise

3. _____ : wonder, phenomenon, marvel

4. _____ : pure, saintly, blameless

5. _____ : ethical

C 우리말은 영어로, 영어는 우리말로 바꾸시오.

1. grief   2. bury

3. 장례식, 고별식   4. bless

5. divine   6. 부처의, 불교도의

7. 존엄, 위엄, 품위   8. distrust

9. 사랑, 자비심, 자선(행위)   10. 무덤, 묘

Lesson 3

World

| 세계

01 **abroad** [əbrɔ́:d] in or to a foreign country

ad. 국외로, 널리

You shouldn't have spent too much money abroad.
너는 해외에서 돈을 너무 낭비해서는 안 되었다.

02 **aid** [eid] to help someone do something

v. 원조하다 n. 도움

It is hard to tell whether we need to aid North Korea or not.
북한을 돕느냐 마느냐 하는 것은 말하기 어려운 문제이다.

03 **billion** [bíljən] the number 1,000,000,000

n. 10억, 막대한 수

Three billion people around the world like soccer.
전 세계 30억의 사람들이 축구를 좋아한다.

04 **border** [bɔ́:rdər] the line that divides two countries or areas

n. 국경, 경계, 국경지방 v. 인접하다
borderer n. 국경의 주민 I border line n. 국경선, 경계선

Crossing the border between the U.S.A. and Mexico is not difficult.
미국과 멕시코 사이의 국경을 넘는 것은 어려운 일이 아니다.

05 common [kάmən] widespread; publicly owned

a. 사회 일반의, 공공의, 일반적인, 보통의
commonly ad. 일반적으로, 보통으로, 통속적으로
uncommon a. 보기 드문, 보통이 아닌 | in common 공동으로, 공통으로

The common cold is a contagious disease.
일반적인 감기는 전염병이다.

06 continue [kəntínjuː] to keep going without stopping

v. 계속하다, 지속하다, 연장하다
continuance n. 계속, 연속 | continual a. 계속적인, 잇따른

Science will continue to develop.
과학은 계속해서 발전할 것이다.

07 countryside [kΛntrisàid] land outside towns and cities

n. 한 지방, 시골

People who live in the countryside tend to be diligent and kind.
시골에 사는 사람들은 부지런하고 친절한 경향이 있다.

08 create [kriːéit] to make something exist that did not exist before

v. 창조하다, 창작하다
creative a. 창조적인, 창의력이 있는 | creation n. 창조
creature n. 창조물, 생물

The air circulation creates wind.
공기 순환이 바람을 만들어 낸다.

09 crowd [kráud] to gather together in large numbers, filling a particular place

v. 군집하다, 꽉 들어차다 n. 군중, 다수
crowded a. 혼잡한, 붐비는, 만원의

Thousands of people crowded **the narrow streets.**

수천 명의 사람들이 좁은 거리를 가득 메웠다.

10 dense [dens] containing a lot of people, things, plants, etc. with little space between them

a. 밀집한, (인구가) 조밀한
density n. 밀도, 농도, 조밀도 ㅣ densely ad. 짙게, 밀집하여, 빽빽하게

A dense **fog rolled over the city.**

짙은 안개가 도시를 뒤덮었다.

11 diminish [dimíniʃ] to become or to make something become smaller, weaker, etc.

v. 줄이다, 감소하다, 손상시키다

If you diminish **sleeping, you will have more time to do something.**

네가 잠을 줄인다면, 무엇인가 할 수 있는 시간이 더 많아질 것이다.

12 domestic [dəméstik] of or inside a particular country

a. 국내의, 국산의, 가정의
domestically ad. 가정적으로, 국내에서
domesticated a. 길들여진, 가정적인

Domestic **and foreign situations affect our economy.**

국내외 정세는 우리 경제에 영향을 미친다.

13　emigrant [émigrənt]　a person who leaves their country to live in another

n. 이민, 이주자 a. 이주하는, 이민의
emigrate v. 이주하다, 이민하다 ❙ emigration n. 이주, 이민

The number of emigrants is increasing.

이민자 수가 증가하고 있다.

14　ethical [éθikəl]　morally correct or acceptable

a. 도덕상의, 윤리상의
ethic n. 윤리, 도덕, 가치 체계 ❙ ethically ad. 윤리적으로, 윤리적 관점에서

Some scientific studies raise ethical questions.

몇몇 과학 연구들은 윤리적인 문제를 불러 일으킨다.

15　ethnic [éθnik]　connected with race or people that share a cultural tradition

a. 인종의, 민족의
ethnically ad. 민족적으로

We should preserve an ethnic heritage.

우리는 민족 유산을 보호해야 합니다.

16　everywhere [évrihwὲər]　in or to every place

ad. 어디나, 도처에

We can read books everywhere.

우리는 어디서나 책을 읽을 수 있습니다.

17 **exist** [igzíst] to be real; to be present in a place or situation

v. 존재하다, 생존하다, 나타나다
existence n. 존재, 실존, 현존 ｜ existent a. 현존하는, 현행의, 실존하는

I think, therefore I exist.
나는 생각한다, 고로 나는 존재한다.

18 **external** [ikstə́ːrnl] connected with foreign countries

a. 외국의, 대외적인
externally ad. 외부적으로, 외부에서

The Koreans were constantly exposed to external **aggressions.**
한국 사람들은 외세의 침략에 끊임없이 노출되었다.

19 **famine** [fǽmin] a lack of food during a long period of time in a region

n. 기근, 굶주림, (물자의) 고갈

Some parts of the world suffer from famine.
세계의 몇몇 지역은 굶주림으로 고통받는다.

20 **foreign** [fɔ́ːrən, fά-] in or from a country that is not your own

a. 외국의, 대외적인
foreigner n. 외국인, 이방인

He is engaged in foreign **trade.**
그는 무역업에 종사하고 있다.

21 **generation** [dʒenəréiʃən] all the people who were born at about the same time

n. 동시대의 사람들, 1세대, 1대
generational a. 세대의 | regeneration n. 갱생, 개혁
degeneration n. 타락, 퇴보, 퇴폐

We must preserve the environment for future generations.
우리는 미래 세대를 위해 환경을 보존해야 한다.

22 **global** [glóubəl] covering or affecting the whole world

a. 세계적인, 세계적 규모의
globally ad. 세계적으로, 전 세계 공통적으로
globalization n. 세계적 규모화, 세계화
globalize v. 세계화하다, 세계적으로 확대하다

The greenhouse effect is a global problem.
온난화 현상은 세계적인 문제이다.

23 **globe** [gloub] the world; a thing shaped like a ball

n. 세계, 지구, 공 모양의 사물

Temperature is getting higher around the globe.
전 세계적으로 온도가 높아지고 있다.

24 **hazardous** [hǽzərdəs] involving risk or danger

a. 모험적인, 위험한, 운에 맡기는
hazard n. 위험, 모험, 위험 요소

Smoking is hazardous to your health.
담배는 건강에 해롭다.

25 human [hjúːmən] a person rather than an animal or a machine

n. 사람, 인간, 인류
humanism n. 인본주의, 인문학
humanly ad. 인간적 관점에서, 인간의 힘으로, 인간답게

Humans **are mammals.**
인간은 포유류이다.

26 humanity [hjuːmǽnəti] people in general

n. 인류, 인간성, 자애, 자비

Nazi deeds were against humanity.
나치의 행동은 반인륜적인 것이었다.

27 ideal [aidíːəl] perfect; most suitable

a. 이상적인, 완전무결한
idealism n. 관념론, 이상주의 | **idealize** v. 관념화하다, 생각하다, 상상하다
ideally ad. 이상적으로, 완벽하게, 관념적으로

Exercise is ideal **for losing weight.**
운동은 체중을 줄이는 데 이상적이다.

28 immigrate [íməgrèit] to come into a foreign country in order to live there permanently

v. 이주해 오다, 귀화하다
immigration n. 이주, 이민 | **immigrant** n. 이주자, 이민자, 입주민

She immigrated **U.S. when she was a baby.**
그녀는 아기였을 때 미국으로 이민했다.

29 **indispensable** [indispénsəbl] too important to be without

a. 없어서는 안 되는, 필수 불가결한

Health is indispensable for happiness.
건강은 행복하기 위해서는 필수적이다.

30 **internal** [intə́:rnl] connected with the inside of a country or something

a. 국내의, 내국의, 내부의
internalize v. 자기 것으로 하다, 내면화하다, 습득하다

An internal disease is hard to find.
내부의 병은 발견하기가 힘들다.

31 **international** [intərnǽʃənl] connected with two or more countries

a. 국제상의, 국제적인

English is an international language.
영어는 국제적인 언어이다.

32 **isolate** [áisəlèit] to separate something or somebody physically or socially

v. 고립시키다, 격리시키다
isolable a. 고립(격리)시킬 수 있는 | **isolated** a. 고립된, 격리된
isolation n. 격리, 분리, 차단, 고독

Depressed people tend to isolate themselves from all relationships.
우울한 사람들은 모든 관계로부터 자신을 고립시키는 경향이 있다.

33 minority [mainɔ́:rəti] the smaller part of a group

n. 소수, 소수당, 소수 민족 a. 소수의

A minority **opinion should be considered as well.**
소수 의견도 존중되어야 한다.

34 modern [mɑ́dərn] belonging to the present time or most recent time

a. 근대의, 현대의, 현대식의
modernize v. 현대화하다, 현대적으로 하다

Modern **technology is a key to solving the food problem.**
현대 과학 기술이 식량 문제 해결의 열쇠이다.

35 national [nǽʃənl] connected with a nation

a. 국가의, 국가적인, 국립의, 애국적인
nation n. 국민, 국가, 민족, 종족
nationality n. 국적, 국민성, 국가적 정서

National **welfare is the purpose of politics.**
국가 복지가 정치의 목적이다.

36 native [néitiv] connected with the place where you were born and have lived for a long time

a. 출생지의, 타고난 n. 원주민, 태어난 사람

Native **Americans had lived there when Columbus found America.**
콜럼버스가 아메리카를 발견했을 때 아메리카 원주민들이 살고 있었다.

37 opportunity [àpərtjúːnəti] a chance to do or get something

n. 기회, 호기

The window of opportunity is open.

기회는 열려 있다.

38 overseas [ouvərsíːz] connected with foreign countries

a. 해외의, 외국의, 외지의 ad. 해외로, 해외에서

We are planning an overseas trip.

우리는 해외여행을 계획하고 있다.

39 population [pàpjuléiʃən] all the people who live in a particular area

n. 인구, 주민의 수, 주민
popular a. 인기 있는, 대중적인 ㅣ populous a. 인구가 조밀한, 붐비는, 많은

Population concentrates in large cities in Korea.

한국의 인구는 대도시에 집중되어 있다.

40 prospective [prəspéktiv] expected to do something or to become something

a. 예상된, 기대되는, 장차의
prospect n. 전망, 조망, 가망

Prospective employees need to qualify themselves for the job.

취업 희망자들은 업무에 걸맞는 자격을 갖출 필요가 있다.

41 race [reis] a group of people who share the same language, history, culture, etc.

n. 인종, 씨족, 혈족, 부류, 집단
racism n. 민족적 우월감, 인종주의 | racial a. 인종상의, 종족의, 민족의
racially ad. 민족적인 측면에서

People of various races live in the USA.

다양한 인종의 사람들이 미국에 살고 있다.

42 region [ríːdʒən] a large area of land, usually without limits or borders

n. 지역, 지방, 지대
regional a. 지역의, 지방의

China is becoming an important region of the global economy.

중국은 세계 경제에서 중요한 지역이 되어가고 있다.

43 reliable [riláiəbl] being trusted to do something well

a. 믿을 수 있는, 의지가 되는, 확실한
rely v. 의존하다, 신뢰하다, 믿다
reliability n. 신뢰할 수 있음, 믿음직함, 신뢰도, 확실성

Friends mean those who are reliable.

친구는 믿을 수 있는 사람을 의미한다.

44 resident [rézədənt] a person who lives permanently in a particular place

n. 거주자 a. 거주하는, 살고 있는, 고유의
residential a. 주거의 | residence n. 주거, 거주, 주소

Only a US resident can get a social security number.

미국 거주자만이 사회 보장 번호를 얻을 수 있다.

45 successive [səksésiv] following immediately one after the other

a. 연속하는, 계속적인, 상속의
succession n. 계승, 상속, 계승자, 상속자 ㅣ succeed v. 뒤를 잇다, 상속(계승)하다

It is likely to rain for successive **days during the rainy season.**
장마철에는 며칠씩 계속 비가 오는 경향이 있다.

46 tribe [traib] a group of people of the same race, language, religion

n. 부족, 종족
tribal a. 종족 특유의, 부족의

Savage tribes **are still out there in some parts of the world.**
세계의 일부 지역에는 아직도 미개한 부족들이 살고 있다.

47 urban [ə́:rbən] connected with a town or city

a. 도시의, 도시 특유의, 도시에 사는
urbanize v. 도시화하다, 도시식으로 하다

London is the UK's biggest urban **zone.**
런던은 영국의 가장 큰 도시 지역이다.

48 useless [júːslis] not useful

a. 쓸모 없는, 무용한, 헛된
use v. 쓰다, 사용하다 ㅣ usage n. 유용성, 실용성
useful a. 쓸모 있는, 유용한, 유익한

All medicines prove useless.
백약이 무효다.

49 **vast** [væst, vɑːst] extremely large in area, size, amount, etc.

a. 광대한, 거대한, 막대한
vastly ad. 광대하게, 막대하게

The Sun provides a vast amount of energy to the Earth.

태양은 지구에 막대한 양의 에너지를 공급한다.

50 **worldwide** [wə́ːrldwaid] affecting all parts of the world

a. 세계적인, 전 세계에 미치는, 세계적으로 유명한

Hangul has a worldwide reputation.

한글은 전 세계적으로 유명하다.

Check up

A 유의어끼리 연결하시오.

1. abroad · · help
2. aid · · boundary
3. border · · popular
4. common · · foreign
5. countryside · · rural

B 단어를 골라 적절히 변형하여 완성하시오.

| crowd | foreign | generation | globe | human |
| minority | native | opportunity | region | tribe |

1. follow the _____ : 대세에 따르다

2. the whole habitable _____ : 전 세계

3. less than _____ : 인간 이하의

4. in the _____ of : ~의 가까이에, 근처에

5. buy _____ : 외국 제품을 사다

6. take an _____ : 기회를 포착하다

7. be in the _____ : 소수(파)이다

8. the _____ of Israel : [성서] 열두 지파(야곱의 열두 아들의 자손)

9. _____ and foreign : 국내외의

10. for _____ : 여러 세대에 걸쳐서

C 다음 영영풀이에 해당하는 단어를 골라 쓰시오.

| urban | useless | vast | successive | resident |

1. extremely large in area, size, amount, etc.

2. connected with a town or city

3. following immediately one after the other

4. not useful

5. a person who lives in a particular place or who has their home there

Lesson 4

Crime & Punishment

죄와 벌

01 accident [ǽksədənt] an unpleasant and unexpected event

n. 사고, 재난, 고장, 재해, 우발 사고
accidental a. 우발적인, 우연한 ㅣ accidentally ad. 우발적으로, 우연히

Many witnesses insisted that the accident **happened on the crosswalk.**
많은 증인들이 그 사고는 횡단보도에서 일어났다고 주장했다.

02 aggressive [əgrésiv] always ready to attack; hostile

a. 공격적인, 침략적인, 공세의
aggression n. 침략, 공격, 침해 ㅣ aggressively ad. 공격적으로, 적극적으로

A good salesman must be aggressive **if he wants to succeed.**
훌륭한 판매원은 성공하려면 매우 적극적이어야 한다.

03 annoy [ənɔ́i] to make someone feel slightly angry and unhappy about something

v. 남을 성가시게 하다, 괴롭히다
annoying a. 성가신 ㅣ annoyance n. 귀찮음, 성가심

I am annoyed **by his frequent visits.**
그 남자가 자꾸 찾아와서 성가시다.

04 arrest [ərést] to take someone to a police station, because the police believe you may have committed a crime

v. 체포하다, 검거하다, 억류하다 n. 체포

You are under arrest.
당신을 체포합니다.

05 assassinate [əsǽsənèit] to murder an important or famous person

v. (정치가 등을) 암살하다, (비열한 방법으로) 훼손하다
assassin n. 암살자, 자객 | assassination n. 암살

The president Kennedy in U.S. was assassinated in 1963.
미대통령 케네디는 1963년에 암살당했다.

06 avoid [əvɔ́id] to keep away or prevent

v. (~이 일어나는 것을) 막다, 예방하다
avoidable a. 피할 수 있는

Some animals have special ways to avoid being eaten.
몇몇 동물들은 잡아먹히지 않기 위한 특별한 방법들을 가지고 있다.

07 blackmail [blǽkmèil] the crime of demanding money from a person by threatening to tell someone else a secret about them

n. 공갈, 갈취, 갈취한 돈 v. 협박하다, 갈취하다

Nuclear weapons are blackmailing the world.
핵무기가 전 세계를 위협하고 있다.

08 bother [bɑ́ðər] to interrupt, worry, annoy or trouble someone

v. 괴롭히다, 귀찮게 하다, 성가시게 하다
bothersome a. 귀찮은, 성가신

I am sorry for bothering you.
귀찮게 해드려서 죄송합니다.

09 **burglar** [bə́ːrglər] a person who enters a building illegally in order to steal

n. (주거침입) 강도

A burglar **walked on the tips of his toes.**

도둑은 발끝으로 가만가만 걸었다.

10 **chase** [tʃeis] to run, drive, etc. after somebody/something in order to catch them

v. 추적(추격)하다 n. 추적, 추격
chaser n. 쫓는 사람, 사냥꾼

The C.S.I. team chased **the suspect.**

과학 수사대는 그 용의자를 추적했다.

11 **clue** [klúː] an object, a piece of evidence or some information that helps the police solve a crime

n. (조사,연구 등의) 단서, 해결의 실마리
clueless n. 단서가 없는, 오리무중의

Someone's sleeping position gives clues **about one's personality.**

사람의 수면 자세는 그 사람의 성격을 파악하는 데 많은 단서를 준다.

12 **crime** [kráim] activities that involve breaking the law

n. 죄, 범죄, 반도덕적 행위

The police are looking for a solution to the crime.

경찰은 그 범죄의 해결책을 찾고 있다.

13 criminal [krímənl] connected with or involving crime

a. 범죄의 n. 범인, 범죄자

He has a criminal record.

그는 전과가 있다.

14 cruel [krú:əl, krúəl] having a desire to cause pain and suffering

a. 잔혹한, 잔인한, 무참한

cruelty n. 잔학, 잔혹, 잔인한 행위

Kids who are cruel to animals are likely to be criminals.

동물을 잔인하게 대하는 아이들은 범죄자가 될 가능성이 있다.

15 cunning [kʌ́niŋ] able to get what you want in a clever way, especially by tricking or cheating someone

a. 교활한, 간사한, 교묘한

cunningly ad. 교활하게, 간사하게

He is as cunning as a fox.

그는 여우처럼 간사하다.

16 deceive [disíːv] to make somebody believe something that is not true

v. 속이다, 기만하다, 현혹시키다

deceivable a. 속일 수 있는 | deceit n. 사기, 기만, 책략

We shouldn't deceive our close friends.

가까운 친구를 속여서는 안된다.

17 deception [disépʃən] the act of deliberately making someone believe something that is not true

n. 속임, 사기, 기만 수단
deceptive a. 속이는, 오해를 사는

Voting deception is one thing that can't be forgiven.

선거 부정은 용서할 수 없는 것이다.

18 despair [dispέər] to lose any hope that a situation will change or improve

vi. 절망하다 n. 절망, 자포자기
desperate a. 절망적인, 가망이 없는 | desperation n. 절망

Well, don't despair. Things will be better.

절망하지 마라. 나아질 것이다.

19 detective [ditéktiv] a person, especially a police officer, whose job is to examine crimes and catch criminals

n. 탐정, 형사
detect v. 발견하다, 간파하다 | detection n. 발각, 간파, 탐지

I am fond of a detective story.

나는 탐정 소설을 좋아한다.

20 doom [dú:m] to make someone or something certain to fail, die, etc.

v. (유죄로) 판정하다, (형을) 선고하다 n. 운명
doomed a. 운이 다한, 불운한 | doomful n. 장래가 어두운, 불길한

A judge doomed a murderer to death.

판사가 살인자에게 사형을 선고했다.

21 **doubt** [dáut] to feel uncertain about something

v. 의심하다, 수상히 여기다, 의혹을 품다
doubtful a. 확신이 없는, 의심스러운 | **doubting** a. 불안한, 의심하는

I doubt that he will be able to do that.
나는 그가 그것을 할 수 있을지 의심스럽다.

22 **evidence** [évədəns] the facts, signs or objects that make you believe that something is true

n. 증거, 물증, 흔적, 증표
evident a. 분명한, 명백한 | **evidentially** ad. 증거에 의해, 증거에 의거하여

The evidence is against the suspect.
증거는 용의자에게 불리하다.

23 **fake** [féik] not genuine

a. 가짜의 v. 위조하다, 속이다 n. 모조품

The genuine ones look fake on me.
진짜도 내가 입으면 가짜 같다.

24 **fault** [fɔːlt] a weakness or failing in character

n. 과실, 허물, 잘못, 비행, 위반
faulty a. 불완전한, 결점이 있는

No man is free from faults.
결점 없는 사람은 없다.

25 forgive [fərgív] to stop feeling angry with someone who has done something wrong

v. 용서하다, 관대히 봐주다, 눈감아 주다
forgiver n. 용서하는 사람, 면제자 ㅣ forgiveness n. 용서, 면제, 탕감
forgivable a. 용서할 수 있는, 용서해도 좋은

Forgive and forget, and you will be free from the past.
용서하고 잊어라, 그러면 과거로부터 자유로워진다.

---

26 fraud [frɔ́ːd] the crime of cheating in order to get money or goods illegally

n. 사기, 기만, 사기 행위, 부정 행위
fraudulent a. 사기의, 부정의

Fraud in finance is increasing these days.
요즘 금융 사기 행각이 늘고 있다.

---

27 happen [hǽpən] to take place, especially without being planned

v. (사건이) 발생하다, 일어나다
happening n. 일, 사건

I am on your side, whatever happens.
무슨 일이 있어도 난 네 편이다.

---

28 hijack [háidʒæ̀k] to use violence or threats to take control of a plane, vehicle, or ship

v. (비행기 등을) 공중 납치하다, (화물 등을) 강탈하다, 털다
hijacking n. 납치 ㅣ hijacker n. 납치 범인

The airplane of flight number 314 was hijacked by terrorists.
편명 314 비행기가 테러리스트들에 의해서 납치되었다.

29 **hostage** [hástidʒ] someone who is kept as a prisoner by an enemy so that the other side will do what the enemy demands

n. 인질, 볼모, 저당, 담보

Pirates held hostages **for money.**

해적들은 돈을 받기 위해 인질들을 억류했다.

30 **imprison** [imprízn] to put someone in a prison or another place from which they cannot escape

v. 교도소에 넣다, 수감하다
imprisonment n. 수감, 투옥

They have imprisoned **an innocent man.**

그들은 무고한 사람을 구속했다.

31 **impulse** [ímpʌls] a sudden strong wish or need to do something

n. 충동, 충동적인 행동
impulsion n. 추진, 충동 | impulsive a. 충동적인, 감정에 끌린
impulsively ad. 충동적으로, 감정적으로

Although she felt an impulse **to cry, she didn't.**

그녀는 울고 싶은 충동을 느꼈으나 그러지 않았다.

32 **incident** [ínsədənt] something that happens, especially unusual or unpleasant

n. 우발적[부수적] 사건, 일어난 일 a. 일어나기 쉬운, 부수적인
incidentally ad. 부수적으로, 우연히
incidental a. 우연히 일어나는, 부수적인, 부차적인

The peaceful meeting ended without incident.

그 평화로운 집회는 사고 없이 끝났다.

33 **kidnap** [kídnæp] to take someone away illegally, especially in order to get money or something else

v. (아이를) 유괴하다, (사람을) 납치하다
kidnapper n. 유괴범 ∣ kidnapping n. 유괴

Some people used to be kidnapped **to North Korea.**
몇몇 사람들은 북한으로 납치되고는 했었다.

34 **lessen** [lésn] to become or make smaller, weaker, less important, etc.

v. 적게 하다, 작게 하다
less a. 보다 적은 ∣ lesser a. 더욱더 작은

The pill lessens **her pain.**
그 알약은 그녀의 고통을 덜어주었다.

35 **murder** [mɔ́:rdər] the crime of killing somebody deliberately

n. 살인, 모살, 살인 사건 v. 죽이다, 살해하다
murderer n. 살인자, 살인범

Murder **can't be justified regardless of reason.**
살인은 어떠한 이유로도 정당화될 수 없다.

36 **panic** [pǽnik] a sudden feeling of great fear that cannot be controlled and prevents you from thinking clearly

n. 돌연한 공포, 공황

Her heart was racing with panic.
그녀의 가슴은 두려움으로 쿵쿵 뛰고 있었다.

37 poison [pɔ́izn] a substance that causes death or harm if it is swallowed or absorbed into the body

n. 독(약), 독물, 해로운 것
poisonous a. 독성이 있는 | **poisoning** n. 중독

One man's meat can be another man's poison.
누군가에게 좋은 것이 다른이에겐 해로운 것이 될 수도 있다.

38 prison [prízn] a building where people are kept as a punishment for a crime

n. 교도소, 감옥, 감방, 구치소
prisoner n. 죄수, 포로, 형사 피고인 | **prison break** 탈옥

Prisoners **eat a piece of bean curd when they are released in Korea.**
한국에서는 출감할 때 죄수들은 두부를 먹는다.

39 punishment [pʌ́niʃmənt] an act or a way of punishing

n. 형벌, 처벌, 징벌, 징계
punish v. 벌하다, 응징하다, 처벌하다 | **punisher** n. 응징하는 사람, 벌하는 사람

Physical punishment **to students is prohibited in our school.**
우리 학교에서는 학생 체벌이 금지되어 있다.

40 regret [rigrét] to feel sorry about something you have done

v. 후회하다 n. (죽음, 불행에 대한) 슬픔, 비탄, 낙담, 유감, 후회
regretful a. 뉘우치는, 애석해하는, 슬퍼하는
regrettable a. 유감스러운, 후회되는

I really regret **to tell you that you are fired.**
당신을 해고하게 되어서 진심으로 유감입니다.

41 **resistance** [rizístəns] dislike of or opposition to a plan, an idea, etc.

n. 저항, 반대, 반항, 적대
resist v. 저항하다, 반항하다
resistant a. 저항하는, 방해하는, 저항력이 있는

Armed resistance **to the police will worsen this situation.**

경찰에 대한 무력 저항은 이 상황을 더 악화시킬 것이다.

42 **robber** [rábər] a person who steals from a person or place

n. 강도, 도둑, 약탈자
robbery n. 강도질, 도둑질, 약탈 I rob v. 강탈하다, 약탈하다, 빼앗다

The police officer caught the bank robbers.

경찰이 은행 강도들을 체포했다.

43 **steal** [stíːl] to take something from a person, shop/store, etc. without permission

v. 훔치다, 무단 차용하다
stealing n. 훔침, 절도

Hunger drives one to steal.

배고프면 도둑질을 하게 된다.

44 **struggle** [strʌ́gl] a hard fight in which people try to obtain or achieve something

n. 투쟁, 몸부림 v. 애쓰다, 몸부림치다
struggling a. 발버둥치는, 애를 쓰는, 기를 쓰는

Evolution is a kind of struggle **for survival.**

진화는 생존을 위한 일종의 몸부림이다.

45 **suicide** [súːəsàid] the act of killing yourself deliberately

n. 자살, 자해
suicidal a. 자포자기한, 자멸적인

Committing suicide **is an inexcusable sin.**

자살은 용서하기 힘든 죄이다.

46 **suspect** [səspékt] to think that something bad has happened or is happening

v. 의심을 하다, 혐의를 걸다 n. 용의자
suspicion n. 의심, 혐의 ǀ suspicious a. 수상한, 의심이 가는

I suspect **they are up to something.**

그들이 뭔가 꾸미고 있는 것 같다.

47 **thief** [θíːf] a person who steals something from another person or place

n. 도둑, 절도
thieve v. 훔치다

The thief **is carrying some bags.**

도둑이 가방 몇 개를 나르고 있다.

48 **trickery** [tríkəri] the use of dishonest methods to trick people

n. 속임수, 사기, 농간
trick v. 속이다, 잔꾀를 부리다 ǀ tricky a. 교활한, 간사한

This contract smells of trickery.

이 계약은 속임수 냄새가 난다.

49 undoubted [ʌ̀ndáutid] beyond doubt or question; evident

a. 의심할 여지가 없는, 진짜의, 확실한

doubt v. 의심하다 ㅣ doubting a. 의심스러운, 불안한

doubtless ad. 의심할 여지 없이, 분명히, 확실히

That the sun rises in the east is an undoubted fact.

해가 동쪽에서 뜬다는 것은 의심할 여지도 없는 사실이다.

50 violence [váiələns] violent behavior that is intended to hurt or kill someone

n. 폭력, 폭행, 강간

violent a. 격렬한, 난폭한, 폭력적인

violently ad. 맹렬하게, 세차게, 폭력적으로

Parents want to shield their children from violence on the streets.

부모들은 자신의 아이들을 거리의 폭력으로부터 보호하기를 원한다.

Check up

A 다음 내용이 설명하고 있는 단어를 〈보기〉에서 고르시오.

> accident ┃ aggressive ┃ assassinate ┃ blackmail ┃ chase

1. angry, and behaving in a threatening way

2. the crime of demanding money from a person by threatening

3. an unpleasant event, especially in a vehicle, that happens unexpectedly

4. after somebody in order to catch him

5. to murder an important or famous person, especially for political reasons

B 단어와 한글 뜻을 알맞게 짝지으시오.

1. clue   •   • 범인, 범죄자

2. deception   •   • 교활한, 간사한

3. cunning   •   • 속임, 사기, 기만

4. detective   •   • 단서, 해결의 실마리

5. criminal   •   • 탐정, 형사

C 다음 빈 칸에 의미상 가장 알맞은 단어를 보기에서 골라 쓰시오.

> violence | thief | suspect | suicide | struggle

1. the prime _____ : 유력한 용의자

2. with _____ : 맹렬히, 격렬하게

3. attempted _____ : 자살미수

4. a common _____ : 좀도둑

5. _____ to one's feet : 간신히 일어서다

D 다음 유의어들을 포함하는 단어를 고르시오.

> steal | punishment | poison | incident | hostage

1. toxin, venom, bane

2. sentence, penalty, retribution

3. prisoner, captive, detainee, prisoner of war

4. happening, event, affair, occasion

5. take, shoplift, poach, embezzle

Lesson 5
Media
| 언론

01 **advertise** [ǽdvərtàiz] to encourage people to buy or to use something

vt. 광고하다, 선전하다
advertisement n. 광고, 선전 ㅣ advertising a. 광고의, 광고에 대한

They plan to advertise **their new product.**
그들은 신제품을 광고할 계획이다.

02 **aerial** [ɛ́əriəl, éiiərial] a piece of equipment to receive and send radio and TV signals

n. 공중선, 안테나 a. 공기의, 대기의

I want to buy the latest receiving aerial.
나는 저 최신 안테나를 사고 싶다.

03 **anchor** [ǽŋkər] a person who reads the news on TV and introduces news reports

n. (뉴스 등의) 종합 사회자

News anchors **use standard language.**
뉴스 앵커들은 표준어를 사용한다.

04 **announce** [ənáuns] to tell people something officially, especially about a decision, plans, etc.

vt. 알리다, 발표하다, 공고하다
announcer n. 아나운서, 방송원, 발표자 ㅣ announcement n. 공고, 발표

Mr. President will announce **a serious statement.**
대통령이 중대 발표를 할 것이다.

05 **article** [ɑ́ːrtikl] a writing about a particular subject in a newspaper or magazine

n. (신문, 잡지의) 기사, 논설

We can learn many things from an editorial article **in the newspaper.**

우리는 신문 사설에서 많은 것을 배울 수 있다.

06 **broadcast** [brɔ́ːdkæ̀st] to send out programs on television or radio

vi. 방송하다, 방송에 나오다
broadcasting n. 방송, 방영 | **broadcaster** n. 방송인, 방송국, 방송 장비

This program will be broadcasted **for about an hour.**

이 프로그램은 약 1시간 동안 방송될 것이다.

07 **cable** [kéibl] a system of broadcasting television programs along wires

n. 유선 TV, 케이블 TV, 굵은 밧줄, 케이블

The road is under construction in order to set up cables.

도로는 케이블 설치를 위한 공사 중에 있다.

08 **cartoon** [kɑːrtúːn] an amusing drawing in a newspaper or magazine

n. (시사) 만화, (신문의) 연속 만화
cartoonist n. 만화가

She specializes in voices for cartoons.

그녀는 만화 영화의 성우이다.

09 celebrity [səlébrəti] a famous person

n. 유명인, 연예인
celebrated a. 유명한, 저명한

It is very difficult for celebrities to guard their privacy.

유명인들은 프라이버시를 지키는 것이 매우 어렵다.

10 censor [sénsər] a person whose job is to examine books, films or movies, etc.

n. (출판물 등의) 검열관 v. 검열하다, 삭제하다
censorable a. 검열에 걸릴 만한 I censorship n. 검열

A government censor removed parts of the book.

정부 당국의 검열관이 책의 일부 대목을 삭제했다.

11 channel [tʃǽnl] a television station

n. (통신) 채널, 주파수대

Thanks to cable TV, there are plenty of channels to pick from.

케이블 TV 덕분에 선택할 수 있는 채널이 많아졌다.

12 circulate [sə́ːrkjulèit] to send goods or information to people

vi. 순환하다 vt. 순환시키다, 퍼뜨리다
circulation n. 발행 부수, 보급 부수 I circulating a. 순환하는, 순회하는

The tap water circulates through pipes.

수돗물은 파이프를 통해 흐른다.

13 code [koud]   a system of words, letters, numbers or symbols that represent a message or record information secretly or in a shorter form

n. 암호, 약호
codec n. (전자) 부호, 부호기 | **coding** n. 부호화, 코딩

This is your new access code for the network.
이것이 네트워크에 접속하기 위한 새 암호이다.

14 column [kάləm]   a part of a newspaper or magazine which appears regularly

n. (신문 등의) 특정 기고란
columnist n. 특별 기고가

I always read her column in the local paper.
나는 항상 지역신문에 실리는 그녀의 칼럼을 읽는다.

15 communication [kəmjùːnəkéiʃən]   ways of sending information, especially using radio, computers, etc.

n. 통신, 교신, 보도 기관
communicate v. 정보, 뉴스 등을 전달하다 | **communicative** a. 통신의, 전달의

The development of technology changes the way of communication. 기술 발전이 통신 방식을 바꾼다.

16 documentary [dὰkjuméntəri]   giving a record of or report on the facts

a. 문서의, (영화, 책 등이) 사실을 기록한 n. 기록물, 기록 영화
document n. 문서, 서류

Documentary programs provide us with a window to look into nature.
다큐멘터리는 우리에게 자연을 알 수 있는 창을 제공해 준다.

17 **edit** [édit]   to prepare a piece of writing, a book, etc. to be published by correcting mistakes, making improvements to it

v. 편집하다, 교정하다
editor n. 편집자, 교정자 | **editorial** a. 편집자의, 사설의, 논설의

Writing is one thing, and editing is another.
글을 쓰는 것과 교정하는 것은 다르다.

18 **entertainment** [èntərtéinmənt]   films, movies, music, etc. used to entertain people

n. 오락, 연예, (책 등의) 읽을 거리
entertain v. 즐겁게 하다 | **entertainer** n. 연예인

Entertainment will be provided tomorrow.
내일 오락 프로그램이 제공될 것이다.

19 **favorite** [féivərit]   best liked; preferred

a. 마음에 드는, 매우 좋아하는, 총애하는
favorable a. 편리한, 좋은 | **favor** n. 호의, 친절, 인기, 평판, 유행

What is your favorite color?
당신이 가장 좋아하는 색은 무엇입니까?

20 **forecast** [fɔ́:rkæst]   a description of what the weather will be like

n. (날씨) 예보 v. (날씨) 예보하다, 예측하다
forecaster n. 기상 통보관, 일기 예보관

A forecast goes wrong too much.
일기 예보가 너무 자주 틀린다.

21 headline [hédlàin] the title of a newspaper article printed in large letters

n. (신문, 기사 등의) 큰 표제, 주요 제목

Catchy headlines **make people pay attention.**

선정적인 제목은 사람들의 관심을 끈다.

22 instead [instéd] in the place of something or somebody

ad. 그 대신에, 그보다도

instead of ~대신에, ~하지 않고

Show me that one instead.

대신 저것을 보여 주세요.

23 issue [íʃuː] an important topic that people are discussing or arguing about

n. 논쟁, 논점, 발행

issuable a. 논쟁이 될 수 있는

The issue **will not disappear until you deal with it.**

네가 그 문제를 해결하기 전까지 그 문제는 사라지지 않을 것이다.

24 journal [dʒə́ːnl] a newspaper or magazine that deals with a particular subject or profession

n. 신문, 정기 간행물

journalism n. 신문 잡지계, 언론계 | journalist n. 저널리스트, 보도기자

He edits a journal **about animals.**

그는 동물에 관한 잡지를 편집한다.

25 **listen** [lísn] to pay attention to someone or something that you can hear

v. 듣다, 귀 기울여 듣다
listener n. 청취자

As long as you listen to the instruction, there is nothing to worry about.
지시에 따르는 한, 걱정할 것이 없다.

26 **magazine** [mǽgəzíːn] a book that is published regularly

n. 잡지, 잡지사
magazinist n. 잡지 편집자, 기자

'Flare' is the most famous magazine in Canada.
'Flare' 는 캐나다에서 가장 유명한 잡지이다.

27 **media** [míːdiə] the main ways that large numbers of people receive information and entertainment

n. 매체

Mass media shouldn't be monopolized.
대중 매체는 독점되어서는 안된다.

28 **message** [mésidʒ] a written or spoken piece of information

n. 통신, 메시지, 전갈, 전언
messenger n. 사자, 전령, (우편) 배달부

If you leave a message, I'll call you later.
메시지를 남겨 주시면 다시 전화하겠습니다.

29 method [méθəd] a particular way of doing something

n. (조직적인) 방법, 방식

Nonviolence was adopted as a method **of social change.**
비폭력은 사회 변화의 방법으로서 채택되었다.

30 nowadays [náuədèiz] at the present time, in contrast with the past

ad. 오늘날에는, 요즈음에는
nowaday a. 오늘날의, 요즈음의

Divorcing is becoming more common nowadays**.**
이혼은 요즈음엔 더 흔해지고 있다.

31 opinion [əpínjən] the belief or views of a group of people

n. 의견, 판단, 평가, 평판
opine v. 의견을 밝히다

Public opinion **is not always right.**
대중의 의견이 항상 옳은 것은 아니다.

32 ordinary [ɔ́:rdənèri] not unusual or different

a. 평상의, 보통의
ordinarily ad. (문장 전체를 수식하여) 보통, 대개, 통상

Flying transportation could be ordinary **in the future.**
미래에는 나는 교통 수단이 일반적인 것이 될 수도 있다.

33 public [pʌ́blik] connected with ordinary people in society in general

a. 공공의, 공적인
publicity n. 공개, 관심, 선전, 주목

This is not a public **health issue.**
이것은 공중보건의 문제가 아니다.

34 publish [pʌ́bliʃ] to produce a book, magazine, CD-ROM, etc. and sell it to the public

v. 출판하다, 발행하다
publication n. 출판, 발행, 출판물

The government will publish **the employment statistics.**
정부는 고용 통계자료를 발행할 것이다.

35 quote [kwout] to repeat the exact words that another person has said or written

v. 인용하다, 예로 들다
quotation n. 인용문, 인용구, 인용

Whatever you quote **from any book, you need to disclose the source.**
어떤 책을 인용하든지 출처를 밝힐 필요가 있다.

36 radio [réidiòu] the activity of broadcasting programs for people to listen to

n. 라디오, 라디오 방송
radio station n. 라디오 방송국

TV has almost replaced radios **since 1990s.**
1990년대 이후 TV가 거의 라디오를 대체했다.

37 reflect [riflékt] to show the image of something or somebody on the surface

v. 반영하다, 반사하다
reflective a. 반사하는 | reflection n. 반영, 반성

You can reflect my opinion into your essay.

내 의견을 네 에세이에 반영해도 된다.

38 remote [rimóut] far away from place where other people live

a. 멀리 떨어진, 원격 조작의
remotely ad. 먼, 먼 옛날의

He lives in the remote country from the city.

그는 도시에서 멀리 떨어진 시골에 산다.

39 replace [ripléis] to be used instead of something or somebody else

v. 되돌리다, 바꾸다, 대체하다
replacement n. 반환, 교체, 교환

After reading a book, replace the book on the shelf.

책을 읽은 후에는 책장에 다시 꽂아라.

40 sensation [senséiʃən] very great surprise, excitement, or interest among a lot of people

n. 세상을 떠들썩하게 하는 것, 감각, 느낌
sensational a. 선풍적 인기의, 눈부신

His appearance created a great sensation.

그의 출현은 대단한 센세이션을 일으켰다.

41 several [sévərəl] more than two but not very many

a. 몇 개의, 수 개의
severally ad. 개별적으로, 단독으로

I have complained several times, but it didn't work.

불평을 몇 번 했지만 효과가 없었다.

42 soap opera [sóup àpərə] a popular television drama series about daily lives and problems

n. 연속 멜로 드라마

A soap opera tends to deal only with the poor or the rich.

드라마는 부자나 가난한 사람들만 다루는 경향이 있다.

43 sponsor [spánsər] a person or company that pays for a radio or television program, or for a concert or sporting event, usually in return for advertising

n. (상업 방송의) 스폰서, 광고주, 보증인

He had a sponsor named Eric Johnson.

그에게는 에릭 존슨이라는 후원자가 있었다.

44 subjective [səbdʒéktiv] based on your own ideas or opinions

a. 주관적인
subject n. 주어, 주인, 주체, 과목 v. 종속시키다, (~을) 받게 하다
subjectively ad. 주관적으로, 주체적으로

The book has too much of the writer's subjective views.

그 책에는 저자의 주관적인 견해가 너무 많이 담겨 있다.

45 **subscribe** [səbskráib] to pay money regularly in order to get newspaper or magazine

v. (신문 · 잡지 등을) 예약 구독하다
subscription n. 예약 구독, 예약 대금 | subscriber n. 예약 구독자

The number of people who subscribe to newspapers are decreasing.
신문 구독자들의 숫자가 감소하고 있다.

46 **survey** [sərvéi] to investigate the opinions, behavior, etc.

v. 조사하다, 검사하다, 사정하다 n. 개관, 조사
surveyor n. 조사자, 감시인

The next morning we surveyed the damage caused by the fire.
그 다음날 아침 우리는 그 화재로 인한 손상을 점검했다.

47 **synchronize** [síŋkrənàiz] to happen at the same time

v. 동시에 일어나다, (음성과 화면을) 일치시키다

The sound track did not synchronize with the action.
(영화의) 사운드 트랙이 동작과 동시에 이뤄지지 않았다.

48 **telegraph** [téligræf, -grà:f] a method of sending messages over long distances, using wires

n. 전신, 전보 v. 전보를 치다
telegraphic a. 전신의, 전송의, 전보의 | telegrapher n. 전신 기사

The invention of the telegraph stopped the Pony Express from delivering mail.
전보가 발명된 후에 조랑말 우편 배달은 멈추었다.

49 **underline** [ʌ́ndərlàin] to draw a line under a word, sentence, etc.

v. 아래에 선을 긋다, 밑줄을 치다, 강조하다

Translate the underlined **parts into English.**

밑줄 친 부분을 영어로 번역하시오.

50 **watch** [wátʃ] to look at someone or something for a time, paying attention to what happens

v. 시청하다, 지켜보다

watcher n. 감시자, 입회인

Many citizens gathered to watch **the funeral.**

많은 시민들이 장례식을 보기 위해 모여들었다.

Check up

A 우리말과 같은 뜻이 되도록 주어진 철자로 시작하는 단어를 쓰시오.

1. They advise investors to w   major economic figures.

그들은 투자자들에게 주요 경제지표에 관심을 기울일 것을 권고했다.

2. Secretary Rice u   the close alliance between the United States and South Korea.

라이스 장관은 한미 간 긴밀한 동맹관계를 강조했다.

3. She found it is easy to s   music with action in the game.

그녀는 게임에서 음악과 행동이 일치되는 것이 쉽다는 것을 알았다.

4. Those who want VOD service have to s   separately.

VOD 서비스를 원하는 사람은 별도로 가입해야 한다.

5. The new invention can be used to r   the ailing cells of patients.

새로운 발명품은 환자의 병든 세포를 대체하는 데 사용될 수 있다.

B 주어진 표현에 해당하는 단어를 보기에서 고르시오.

| quote | publish | ordinary | issue | favorite |

1. _____ : common, fair, average, everyday, routine

2. _____ : issue, release, advertise, print, publicize

3. _____ : matter, question, concern, item

4. _____ : popular, loved

5. _____ : cite, repeat, say, recite, narrate, dictate

C 우리말은 영어로, 영어는 우리말로 바꾸시오.

1. aerial   2. edit

3. circulate   4. celebrity

5. (날씨) 예보, 예보하다   6. 오늘날에는, 요즈음에는

7. announce   8. 공공의

9. 신문, 정기 간행물   10. 원격, 조작의, 멀리 떨어진

Lesson 6
Culture
| 문화

01 **ancestor** [ǽnsestər] a person in your family who lived a long time ago

n. 조상, 선조

Koreans prepare various food for ancestor **worshipping ceremonies.**

한국인들은 조상에게 제사를 지낼 때 다양한 음식을 준비한다.

02 **celebrate** [séləbrèit] to praise something or somebody

v. 축하하다, 경축하다
celebration n. 축하, 찬양 | celebrated a. 유명한, 저명한
celebrity n. 유명한 사람, 명성

In America, people do not celebrate **White Day.**

미국에는 화이트 데이가 없다.

03 **ceremony** [sérəmòuni] a public or religious occasion

n. (종교적 · 국가적 · 사회적) 의식, 행사
ceremonial a. 의식에 사용되는, 예식의 | ceremonious a. 예의바른, 엄숙한

The opening ceremony **will come first, before main event.**

메인 행사 전에 개회식이 열린다.

04 **civilization** [sivəlaizéiʃən] society that is very developed and organized

n. 문명
civilize v. 교화하다, 문명화하다 | civilizable a. 문명화(교화)할 수 있는

Four major civilizations **developed around the world.**

4대 문명이 전 세계에서 발달했었다.

05 claim [kléim] a statement that something is true

n. (권리로서의) 요구, 청구, 주장 v. 요구하다, 주장하다
claimable a. 요구(주장)할 수 있는

I would like to put in a claim for compensation.

나는 보상을 요구하고 싶다.

06 cultural [kʌ́ltʃərəl] connected with the culture of a particular society or group

a. 문화의, 문화적인
culture n. 문화, 문명 | cultured a. 교화된, 교양 있는

Cultural bias is the one problem that has to be solved.

문화적 편견은 반드시 해결되어야 할 문제이다.

07 custom [kʌ́stəm] an accepted way of behaving or of doing things in a society or a community

n. 풍습, 관습, 관례
customary a. 관습상의, 습관적인 | customarily ad. 관례상, 습관적으로

The custom has descended until now.

그 관습은 지금까지 전해져 내려오고 있다.

08 decorate [dékərèit] to make something look more attractive by putting things on it

v. 장식하다
decoration n. 장식(법), 장식물 | decorative a. 장식적인, 화사한
decorator n. (실내) 장식가

Parents prepare special gifts and decorate their houses for Christmas.

크리스마스에 부모들은 특별한 선물을 준비하고 집을 장식한다.

09　**dye** [dai]　to change the color by using liquid or substance

v. 염색하다, 물들이다 n. 염료
dyed a. 물들인, 염색된 ǀ dyer n. 염색업자, 염색소

Teens today want to dye **their hair.**

요즘 십대들은 머리를 염색하고 싶어한다.

10　**especially** [ispéʃəli, es-]　very much; to a particular degree

ad. 특히, 유달리, 유별나게
especial a. 특별한, 특수한

Aspirin is especially **good for headaches.**

아스피린은 특히 두통에 잘 듣는다.

11　**etiquette** [étikit, -kèt]　the formal rules for polite behavior in a society or in a particular group

n. 예의, 예법, 에티켓

Smoking at the table is against etiquette.

식사 중 흡연은 에티켓에 어긋난다.

12　**gap** [gæp]　a big difference between two situations, amounts, groups of people, etc.

n. 차이, 격차, 부족, 결함

The gap **between rich and poor is still considerably widening, and it will be in the future.**

부자와 가난한 사람들의 격차는 아직도 심하고, 앞으로도 그럴 것이다.

13 gather [gǽðər] to collect something

v. 모으다, 모이다, 받다
gathering n. 모임, 집회, 군중, 모임

A rolling stone gathers **no moss.**
구르는 돌에는 이끼가 끼지 않는다.

14 gift [gift] a present; a natural ability

n. 선물, 경품, 타고난 재능
gifted a. 타고난 재능이 있는

Books are the most suitable gifts **for kids.**
책은 아이들에게 아주 좋은 선물이다.

15 habit [hǽbit] a thing that you do often and almost without thinking

n. 버릇, 습관, 관습
habitual a. 습관적인, 버릇이 된 ㅣ habitually ad. 습관적으로, 상습적으로
habituate v. 길들이다, ~에 습관을 들이다 ㅣ habituation n. 습관화

Once smoking becomes a habit, **it hardly goes away.**
일단 흡연이 습관으로 자리 잡으면 끊기가 아주 어렵다.

16 hold [hould] to lift, carry, grab something

v. 들다, 잡다, 쥐다

Hold **on, please.**
(전화를 끊지 말고) 기다리세요.

17 **hospitality** [hɑ̀spətǽləti]   friendly and generous behavior towards guests

n. 환대, 후대
hospitable a. 친절한, 공손한, 극진한

Foreign travelers are impressed because Koreans gave them heartwarming hospitality.

외국 여행자들은 한국인들이 그들에게 보여준 따뜻한 환대에 감동받는다.

18 **housewarming** [hauswɔ́ːrmiŋ]   a party given by someone who has just moved into a new house

n. 집들이

We all look forward to the housewarming **party.**

우리 모두 집들이를 학수고대하고 있어.

19 **infinite** [ínfənət]   without limits

a. 무한한, 무궁한
infinitely ad. 무한히, 무수히
infinity n. 무한대 ㅣ finite a. 한정된, 유한한

You need infinite **patience for this job.**

이 일에는 무한한 끈기가 필요하다.

20 **influence** [ínfluəns]   to have an effect on something or somebody

vt. 영향을 끼치다, 좌우하다 n. 영향, 힘, 작용
influent a. 유입되는, 흘러 들어가는 ㅣ influential a. 영향력이 있는, 유력한

People are influenced **unconsciously by advertising.**

사람들은 무의식적으로 광고에 의해서 영향을 받는다.

21 **inherit** [inhérit] to receive money, property, etc. from somebody when they die

v. 상속하다, 물려받다
inheritable a. 상속할 수 있는 l inheritance n. 상속, 유산
heritage n. 상속 재산, 전통, 문화 유산

He inherited a large fortune from his father.

그는 아버지로부터 많은 재산을 상속받았다.

22 **intend** [inténd] to have a plan, result or purpose in your mind when you do something

vt. ~할 작정이다 vi. 의도하다
intention n. 의향, 의도, 목적, 계획 l intentional a. 고의적인, 계획된
intentionally ad. 고의적으로 l intended a. 의도된

When do you intend to start studying?

당신은 언제 공부를 시작할 작정입니까?

23 **involve** [inválv] to include or affect someone or something

vt. 포함하다, 수반하다
involved a. 복잡한, 뒤얽힌 l involvement n. 연루

Don't involve me in your quarrel.

네 싸움에 나를 끌어들이지 마.

24 **last** [lǽst, lάːst] to continue to exist or to function well

vi. 계속하다, 지속하다 a. 최후의, 끝의
latest a. 최신의, 최근의 l lasting a. 영속하는

That situation will not last for a long time.

그 상황은 오래가지 않을 것이다.

25 manner [mǽnər] the way that something is done or happens

n. 방법, 풍습, 관습
manners n. 예의범절, 테이블 매너 | **mannerly** a. 예절 바른

A certain level of manners is essential in society.

사회에서 일정한 수준의 매너는 필수적이다.

26 mean [míːn] connected to dirty, cruel, unkind behavior

a. 더러운, 상스러운, 비열한
meanly ad. 비열하게, 천하게

You are so mean to do such a thing.

그런 일을 저지르다니 넌 참 못됐구나!

27 memorial [məmɔ́ːriəl] something that is built in order to remind people, event, etc.

n. 기념물, 기념관 a. 기념의
memorable a. 기억할 만한, 인상적인, 주목할 만한
memorably ad. 인상적으로, 눈에 띄게 | **memory** n. 기억, 기억력

The Independence Memorial Hall was built in 1987.

독립기념관은 1987년에 건립되었다.

28 myth [miθ] an idea or story that many people believe, but which is not true

n. 신화, 가공의 인물
mythical a. 상상의, 가공의 | **mythology** n. (집합적) 신화, (널리 퍼진) 그릇된 생각

Most societies have their own creation myths.

대부분의 사회는 그들 나름의 창조 신화가 있다.

29 numerous [njúːmərəs] existing in large numbers; many

a. 다수의, 수많은, 셀 수 없이 많은
numerable a. 셀 수 있는, 계산할 수 있는 ∣ innumerable a. 무수한

There are numerous **restaurants in Korea.**
한국에는 식당이 수없이 많다.

30 odd [ad] strange or unusual

a. 이상한, 기묘한, 홀수의

It was rather odd **that nobody recognized him.**
아무도 그를 알아보지 못했다니 좀 이상했다.

31 oppose [əpóuz] to disagree strongly

v. 반대하다, 대항하다
opposing a. 맞서는, 대항하는 ∣ opposite a. 반대편의, 맞은편의, 정반대의
opposition n. 반대, 저항, 방해

What the opposition should do is to oppose**.**
야당이 해야 하는 일은 반대하는 것이다.

32 origin [ɔ́ːrədʒin, ɑr-] the point from which something starts

n. 기원, 발단, 출신, 태생
originate v. 시작하다, 불러 일으키다 ∣ origination n. 시작, 시초, 발생
originative a. 독창적인, 창의력 있는, 기발한
original a. 최초의, 원시의 n. 원형, 원문

A number of scientists have researched the origin **of the rings of Saturn.**
많은 과학자들이 토성 고리의 기원을 연구해 오고 있다.

33 particular [pərtíkjulər] greater than usual; special

a. 특별한, 특수한, 특정한

We must pay particular attention to this point.

우리는 이 점에 특별한 관심을 기울여야 한다.

34 persist [pərsíst, -zíst] to continue to do something

v. 고집하다, 끝까지 해내다
persistence n. 영속, 종속, 지속성 ǀ persistent a. 고집 센, 완고한

A regime should persist its educational policy.

한 정권은 일관된 교육 정책을 펼쳐야 한다.

35 perspective [pərspéktiv] a particular attitude towards something

n. 견해, 관점, 사고방식

Reading this book will provide you a whole new perspective on life.

이 책을 읽는 것은 너에게 인생에 대한 새로운 시각을 줄 것이다.

36 popular [pápjulər] liked or enjoyed by a large number of people

a. 인기 있는, 대중의, 민중의
popularity n. 인기, 평판 ǀ popularize v. 대중(통속)화하다
popularly ad. 일반적으로, 통속적으로, 평이하게

The former president Mr. Noh is getting very popular after his death.

노무현 전 대통령은 서거 이후에 인기가 올라갔다.

37 rare [rɛ́ər] existing only in small numbers

a. 드문, 진귀한, 희귀한
rarity n. 희귀, 희귀한 것 ㅣ rarely ad. 드물게, 좀처럼 ~하지 않는

A miracle means that it rarely **happens and is unable to be explained.**

기적이라는 것은 거의 일어나지 않고 설명할 수 없다는 것을 의미한다.

38 remind [rimáind] to help somebody remember something

v. 생각나게 하다, 상기시키다, 일깨우다
reminder n. 독촉장, 생각나게 하는 것 ㅣ remindful a. 생각나게 하는

Particular foods, scenes, and even smells remind **me of home.**

특정한 음식, 풍경 그리고 심지어는 냄새도 나로 하여금 집을 생각하게 한다.

39 seldom [séldəm] not often; very rarely or almost never

ad. 드물게, 좀처럼 ~ 않는

He seldom, **if ever, speaks ill of other people.**

그는 좀처럼 남을 헐뜯지 않는다.

40 separate [sépərèit] to take, force or keep apart

v. 가르다, 분리하다, 떼다 a. 갈라진, 따로따로의
separation n. 분리, 이별 ㅣ separately ad. 따로따로, 개별적으로

The kidney's primary role is to separate **waste liquid from the blood.**

신장의 주된 역할은 혈액으로부터 불순물을 걸러내는 것이다.

41 special [spéʃəl] not ordinary or usual

a. 특수한, 특별한, 독특한
specialize v. 특수화하다, 전문화하다 ㅣ specialist n. 전문가

The Special Forces carry out a dangerous plan.
특수부대는 위험한 임무를 수행한다.

42 symbol [símbəl] a person, an object, an event, etc. that represents a more general quality or situation

n. 상징, 기호, 표상
symbolic a. 상징적인, 표상의 ㅣ symbolize v. 상징하다

The tiger is the symbol of Korea.
호랑이는 대한민국의 상징이다.

43 traditional [trədíʃənl] being part of something that have not changed for a long time

a. 전통의, 전통적인, 고풍의
tradition n. 전통, 관례

Shaking hands when you meet someone first time is a traditional custom.
누군가를 처음 만났을 때 악수를 하는 건 전통적인 관습이다.

44 typical [típikəl] having the usual qualities or features of a particular type of person

a. 전형적인, 대표적인

The typical teaching method in English is the grammar translation method.
전형적인 영어 교수 방법은 문법 중심의 번역 수업이다.

45 understand [ʌndərstǽnd] to know or realize the meaning of words, a language, what somebody says, etc.

v. 이해하다, 알아듣다
understanding a. 이해심 있는, 이해력 있는 n. 이해, 이해력
understandingly ad. 이해심을 가지고, 이해심 있게

I can't understand her word at all.
난 그녀의 말을 전혀 이해할 수 없다.

46 unique [juːníːk, ju-] being the only one of its kind

a. 유일무이한, 대신할 것 없는
uniquely a. 독특하게, 특이하게

This is unique feature of our culture.
이것이 우리 문화의 고유한 특색이다.

47 vain [véin] having no result you want or useful effect

a. 헛된, 자만심이 강한
vanity n. 허영심, 자만심 | vainly ad. 헛되이, 공연히
in vain 보람 없이, 헛되이

That appeared to be a vain hope.
그것은 헛된 희망으로 나타났다.

48 various [vέəriəs] several; different

a. 가지각색의, 여러 가지의, 다양한
variety n. 각양각색, 다양성 | vary v. 다르다, 다양하다

People eat pork in various ways.
사람들은 돼지고기를 다양하게 요리해서 먹는다.

49 wedding [wédiŋ] a marriage ceremony

n. 결혼식, 혼례, 결혼 기념일

Their wedding **reception will be held after the** wedding**, so you can't go.**

결혼 피로연은 결혼식 후에 열리니 가면 안 된다.

50 wonderful [wʌ́ndərfəl] very good, pleasant or enjoyable

a. 훌륭한, 굉장한, 경이적인
wonder n. 놀랄 만한 것, 경탄, 기적 v. 놀라다, 이상하게 여기다
wonderfully ad. 놀랄 만큼, 경이적으로

She told us about her wonderful **experiences at that night.**

그녀는 그날 밤의 놀라운 경험에 대하여 우리에게 이야기해 주었다.

A 다음 단어가 본문에서 쓰인 의미를 고르시오.

1. waste one's life in vain pleasures

ⓐ that does not produce the result you want

ⓑ too proud of your own appearance, abilities or achievements

2. a unique copy of an ancient manuscript

ⓐ very special or unusual

ⓑ being the only one of its kind

3. a phonetic symbol

ⓐ an object that represents a more general quality or situation

ⓑ a sign, number, letter, etc. that has a fixed meaning

4. from a historical perspective

ⓐ a particular attitude towards something

ⓑ the art of creating an effect of depth and distance in a picture

5. If a symptom persists, consult your doctor.

ⓐ to continue to do something despite difficulties or opposition

ⓑ to continue to exist

B 알맞은 반대말끼리 연결하시오.

1. oppose   •

2. last   •

3. odd   •

4. particular •

5. involve   •

    • general

    • even

    • approve

    • obviate

    • stop

Part 7

Education

[교육]

Lesson 1
Education

| 교육

01 absent [ǽbsənt] not in a place where somebody should be

a. 결석의, 결근의

absence n. 부재, 불참, 결석, 결근 ㅣ absently ad. 멍하니, 넋을 잃고

Some players were absent yesterday's game because of the slightest injury.

몇몇 선수들은 가벼운 부상 때문에 어제 경기에 불참했다.

02 acknowledge [əknɑ́lidʒ] to accept that something is true

v. 인정하다, 동의하다, 승인하다

acknowledged a. 인정된, 승인된 ㅣ acknowledgment n. 승인, 인정, 사례, 감사

Acknowledge your fault if you want to improve yourself.

스스로를 발전시키고 싶다면 부족함을 인정하라.

03 attend [əténd] to be present at an event

v. 출석하다, (학교에) 다니다

attendance n. 출석, 출근, 참석 ㅣ attendant n. 출석자

I have attended my school since 2007.

나는 2007년부터 학교에 다니고 있다.

04 attention [əténʃən] the act of listening to, looking at or thinking about someone or something carefully

n. 주의, 주목, 주의력

attentive a. 경청하는

Pay attention to what I am talking about.

제가 이야기하는 것에 귀를 기울여 주세요.

05 brilliant [bríljənt] extremely clever or impressive

a. 재능이 뛰어난, 빛나는, 훌륭한

brilliance n. 광명 l brilliantly ad. 찬란하게, 훌륭하게, 뛰어나게

Einstein is a brilliant physicist throughout the physical history. 아인슈타인은 물리학 역사상 훌륭한 물리학자이다.

06 certify [sə́:rtəfai] to state officially, especially in writing, that something is true

v. 증명하다, 인정하다

certification n. 증명, 보증, 증명서 l certified a. 증명된, 보증된

The government certified that the rumor isn't true.

정부는 그 소문이 사실이 아님을 인정했다.

07 compliment [kámpləmənt] a remark that expresses praise or admiration of someone

n. 찬사, 칭찬의 말

complimentary a. 칭찬하는, 경의를 표하는

Compliment can make us laugh at any situation.

칭찬은 어떠한 상황에서도 우릴 웃게 만들 수 있다.

08 comprehend [kàmprihénd] to understand something fully

v. 이해하다, 인식하다

comprehensive a. 이해력이 있는, 포괄적인 l comprehension n. 이해, 이해력

Some students seem not to comprehend the significance of reviewing.

몇몇 학생들은 복습의 중요성을 이해하지 못하는 것 같다.

09 **concentrate** [kánsəntrèit]   to give all your attention to something and not think about anything else

vt. 집중하다
concentration n. 집결, 집중 | concentrated a. 집중된, 밀집된

If you want to get a good score, you have to concentrate **every sentence.**
네가 만약 좋은 점수를 얻고자 한다면 모든 문장에 집중해야 한다.

10 **confident** [kánfədənt]   feeling sure about your own ability to do things and be successful

a. 확신하고 있는, 자신만만한
confidence n. 자신, 확신, 신용 | confidential a. 은밀한, 비밀의, 첩보 기관의

The immune system works best when you feel happy and confident.
면역 체계는 당신이 행복하고 자신감에 차 있을 때 가장 잘 작동한다.

11 **content** [kəntént]   the subject matter of a book, speech, program, etc.

n. (작품, 논문 등의) 취지, 요지, 내용 a. 만족한
contain v. 포함하다, 담다 | container n. 그릇, 용기, 컨테이너

Do not judge a book by it's a cover, but by it's content.
책을 표지로 판단하지 말고, 내용으로 판단하라.

12 **counsel** [káunsəl]   advice given by experts or older people

n. 상담, 의논, 협의 v. 충고[조언]하다
counselor n. 상담역, 고문 | counseling n. 카운슬링, 상담, 조언

Listen to the counsel **of your family.**
가족의 조언에 귀 기울여라.

13 courage [kə́:ridʒ, kʌ́r-] the ability to do something without fear

n. 용기, 담력, 배짱
encourage v. 용기를 북돋우다 | **discourage** v. 낙담시키다

Courage **means that it is different from rashness.**
용기는 무모함과는 다르다.

14 course [kɔ́:rs] a series of lessons or lectures on a particular subject

n. (학습)과정, 교육 과정, 강좌

You will get a graduation certificate after you finish the
four-year course.
4년간의 교육 과정을 마치면 졸업장을 받게 된다.

15 degree [digrí:] the qualification obtained by students who successfully
complete a university or college course

n. 등급, 학위

Almost all young Koreans have university degrees.
대부분의 한국 젊은이들은 대학 졸업장을 가지고 있다.

16 distribute [distríbjuːt] to give things to a large number of people

v. 분류하다, (분류) 배치하다, 배포하다
distributed a. 분포된, 광범위한 | **distribution** n. 분포, 배급, 배포

Distributing **pamphlets is a good way to advertise.**
전단지 배포는 광고의 좋은 방법이다.

17 **education** [edʒukéiʃən] a process of teaching, training and learning

n. 교육, 훈련
educational a. 교육상의, 교육적인 l educated a. 교육받은, 교양 있는

An education is the most important thing for country's future.
국가의 미래를 위해 가장 중요한 것은 교육이다.

18 **endeavor** [indévər, en-] to try very hard to do something

vi. 노력하다, 시도하다 n. 노력

All the things he endeavored were in vain.
그가 기울였던 모든 노력이 허사였다.

19 **enroll** [inróul, en-] make someone to take part in a lesson or school

vt. 입학시키다, 등록하다
enrollment n. 등록, 입학

Universities are forced to enroll handicapped students at the same rate.
대학들은 일정 비율로 장애 학생을 입학시켜야 한다.

20 **entrance** [éntrəns] permission to become a member of a club, society, university, etc.

n. 입학, 입사, 입회
enter v. 들어가다, 입학하다 l éntrant n. 참가자, 신입자, 들어가는 사람

A college entrance examination is truly important in Korea.
한국에서 대입 시험은 매우 중요하다.

21 examination [igzæmənéiʃən] a formal written, spoken or practical test

n. 시험, 성적고사, 검사
examine v. 검사하다, 조사하다 | examinee n. 수험자, 피험자
examiner n. 시험관, 검사관

Adults should have a regular physical examination.

성인들은 정기 검진을 받는 것이 좋다.

---

22 faculty [fǽkəlti] a department or group related departments in a college or university

n. (대학, 고교의) 전 교직원, 교수단, 능력, 재능

Some professors leave the faculty in order to enter politics.

몇몇 교수들은 정치에 입문하기 위해 대학을 떠난다.

---

23 fee [fiː] an amount of money that you pay for professional advice or service

n. 보수, 사례금, 수업료

The delay fee will be added from tomorrow.

내일부터 연체료가 가산됩니다.

---

24 grade [gréid] a mark given in an exam or for a piece of school work

n. 등급, 계급, 성적
gradation n. 단계적 변화 | grading n. 등급 매기기

My grade should have been better than C!

내 성적이 C보다는 좋았어야 했는데!

25 graduate [grǽdʒuèit] to complete a course in education

v. 졸업하다
graduation n. 학위 취득, 졸업

What are you going to do after you graduate?

졸업 후에는 무엇을 할 예정입니까?

26 institution [instətjú:ʃən] a large important organization that has a particular purpose

n. (학교, 병원, 교회 등) 공공시설
institute vt. 제정하다, 설립하다

Child-care institutions **take care of children who are in need.**

보육원은 도움이 필요한 아이들을 돌본다.

27 instruct [instrʌ́kt] to teach someone something, especially a practical skill

v. 가르치다, 교육하다
instruction n. 교수, 교육, 교훈 I instructor n. 강사, 교사

We must do as they instructed.

우리는 그들이 지시한 대로 해야 한다.

28 lead [líːd] to go with or in front of a person or an animal to show the way

v. 지도하다, 지휘하다, 인솔하다
leader n. 지도자, 선도자, 인솔자 I leading a. 주요한, 지도하는, 인도하는

The act of learning will lead **you to a better life.**

배움이 당신을 더 나은 삶으로 이끌 것이다.

29 lecture [léktʃər] a talk to teach about a particular subject

n. 강의, 강연 v. 강연하다, 설교하다
lecturer n. 강연자, 훈계자, 강사

The teacher bores us with his lecture, so most students don't like him.

그 선생님의 수업은 지루해서 대부분의 학생들은 그를 좋아하지 않는다.

30 lesson [lésn] something that is intended to be learned

n. 수업, 연습, 교훈, 학과, 과업

I have a lesson in art history tomorrow.

난 내일 미술사 수업이 있어.

31 license [láisəns] permission to do something

n. 면허, 인가, 면허증
licensed a. 인가된, 허가된, 면허를 받은

Driver's license and registration, please.

운전 면허증과 차량 등록증을 제시해 주세요.

32 major [méidʒər] to specialize in

v. 전공하다 n. 전공 a. 큰 쪽의, 주요한

He majored in English education and Korean education.

그는 영어 교육과 국어 교육을 전공했다.

33 **memorize** [méməràiz] to remember something exactly

v. 기억하다, 암기하다
memory n. 기억, 기억력 | memorial n. 기념물, 기념일, 기념비

If you want to be a good actor, memorize all of your lines.
좋은 배우가 되고 싶다면 너의 대사를 전부 외워라.

34 **mentor** [méntɔːr, -tər] an experienced person who advises and helps someone with less experience over a period of time

n. 좋은 지도자, 스승, (지도) 교사

Whether or not you have a mentor in puberty is an important matter.
청소년기에 좋은 스승을 가지느냐 아니냐는 중요한 문제이다.

35 **nerd** [nə́ːrd] someone who only interested in computers and other technical things

n. 얼간이, 멍텅구리, 컴퓨터만 아는 괴짜

A computer nerd differs from a computer game addict.
컴퓨터 광과 게임 중독자는 다르다.

36 **perceive** [pərsíːv] to notice or become aware of something

v. 이해하다, 깨닫다
perception n. 지각, 인지 | perceptive a. 통찰력 있는, 지각할 수 있는

Women can perceive small changes in other people's appearance.
여성들은 다른 사람의 조그마한 외적 변화들을 알아차릴 수 있다.

37 praise [préiz]   words that show approval of or admiration for someone or something

n. 칭찬, 찬양 v. 칭찬하다
praiseworthy a. 칭찬할 만한, 기특한, 훌륭한 | appraise v. 값을 매기다, 평가하다

Praise stimulates students to work hard.

칭찬은 학생들을 자극하여 열심히 공부하게 한다.

38 present [préznt]   being in a particular place

a. 출석한, 참석한
presence n. 참석, 출석

My teacher will start when all students are present.

모든 학생들이 출석하면 선생님은 수업을 시작할 것이다.

39 pupil [pjú:pəl]   a person who is being taught

n. 학생, 제자, 문하생
pupilary a. 학생의, 미성년기의

Seoul National University has about 20,000 pupils.

서울대학교의 학생 수는 대략 2만 명 정도이다.

40 raise [réiz]   to lift or move something to a higher level

v. 향상시키다, 올리다
raised a. 높인, 높아진

In the past women were expected to raise their children after marriage.

과거에 여성들은 결혼 후에 아이들을 양육할 것으로 기대되었다.

41 **readily** [rédəli] quickly and without difficulty

ad. 쾌히, 기꺼이, 손쉽게
ready a. 준비가 된 I readiness n. 준비가 되어 있음

If something has to be done, do it readily.

어차피 해야 한다면, 기꺼이 해라.

42 **register** [rédʒistər] to record a name on an official list

v. (입학, 수업 등에) 등록하다
registration n. 등록, 등록된 기록 I registered a. 등록된

Students have to register for classes by the specified date.

학생들은 정해진 날짜까지 수강 신청을 마쳐야 한다.

43 **scholarship** [skάlərʃip] an amount of money given to someone by an organization to help pay for their education

n. 장학금 (제도), 학문
scholar n. 장학생, 학생, 학자 I scholarly a. 학문적인, 학술적인, 학구적인

A scholarship is given on the basis of financial need and academic ability.

장학금은 재정적인 필요와 학문적 자질을 기준으로 주어진다.

44 **significant** [signífikənt] large or important; enough to have an effect or to be noticed

a. 중요한, 의미 있는, 뜻깊은
significance n. 중요, 중요성 I significantly ad. 의미 있게, 의미심장하게

A significant difference between men and women is their way of talking.

남성과 여성의 큰 차이점은 말하는 방식에 있다.

45 solution [səljúːʃən] a way of solving a problem

n. (문제 등의) 해결, 해석, 설명
solve v. 해결하다

One solution for the traffic problem is to make sky-taxis.
교통체증을 해결하는 한 가지 방법은 하늘을 나는 택시를 만드는 것이다.

46 specialize [spéʃəlàiz] to become an expert in a particular activity, field of study, etc.

v. 전공하다, 전문으로 삼다
specialized a. 전문화된 I specialty n. 전문

My dream is to specialize in English literature at Stanford.
내 꿈은 스탠포드에서 영문학을 전공하는 것이다.

47 submit [səbmít] to give a document, proposal, etc.

v. (과제, 서류 등을) 제출하다, 제시하다

Please fill this form out and submit it to an attendant.
이 서류를 작성해서 승무원에게 제출해 주세요.

48 summary [sʌ́məri] a short statement that gives only the main points of something, not the details

n. 요약, 개요, 일람
summarize v. 요약하다, 개괄하다

A summary shouldn't be too long or too short.
개요는 너무 길거나 짧아서는 안된다.

| 49 | syllabus [síləbəs] | a list of the topics, books, etc. that students should study in a particular subject at school or college |

n. (강의의) 요강, 요목, 개략

Make sure you look through syllabus **of this class before you register.**

이 수업을 신청하기 전에 반드시 강의 요강을 살펴 보세요.

| 50 | tuition [tjuːíʃən] | the act of teaching |

n. 수업, 수업 지도, 수업료

tuitional   a. 교수(지도)용의

An anonymous businessman will pay the tuition **fees for poor students.**

익명의 한 사업가가 가난한 학생들을 위해 수업료를 대납할 것이다.

A 알맞은 유의어끼리 연결하시오.

1. absent   •   • come

2. acknowledge •   • nonexistent

3. attend   •   • comprehend

4. brilliant   •   • intelligent

5. understand •   • accept

B 보기에서 알맞은 단어를 골라 관용어를 완성하시오.

> compliment | concentrate | content | counsel | courage
> degree | endeavor | entrance | fee | graduate

1. keep one' s own _____ : 자기 생각을 남에게 털어놓지 않다

2. orange juice _____ : 농축 오렌지 주스

3. at a pin's _____ : (부정적) 정말 얼마 안 되는 가치도

4. to some _____ : 약간은, 어느 정도는

5. a doubtful _____ : 빈정대는 칭찬

6. a _____ fellowship : 대학원의 연구 장학금

7. do one's best _____ : 전력을 다하다

8. _____ free. : 무료 입장

9. Dutch _____ : 술김에 내는 용기

10. to one's heart's _____ : 마음껏, 실컷

C 다음 영영풀이에 해당되는 단어를 골라 쓰시오.

instruct	license	nerd	perceive	significant

1. a person who is boring, stupid and not fashionable

2. to notice or become aware of something

3. to tell somebody to do something, especially in a formal or official way

4. large or important enough to have an effect or to be noticed

5. to give somebody official permission to do

Lesson 2

Academy

| 학문

01 **absolute** [ǽbsəlùːt] definite and without any doubt or confusion

a. 절대적인, 완전한, 전면적인
absolutely ad. 완전히, 절대적으로

You must have absolute proof.

확실한 증거가 있다.

02 **abstract** [ǽbstrækt] based on general ideas and not on any particular real person, thing or situation

a. 추상적인 n. 추상 vt. 추출하다, 끌어내다
abstracted a. 넋 잃은, 멍한 | abstraction n. 추상

We cannot easily understand the mean of abstract paintings.

우리는 추상화의 의미를 쉽게 이해할 수 없다.

03 **academy** [əkǽdəmi] a school or college for special training

n. 학원, 전문학교, 협회, 학회
academic a. 학원의, 대학의

The academy was modeled after a British public school.

그 학교는 영국의 사립학교를 모델로 만들어진 학교이다.

04 **accurate** [ǽkjurət] correct and true in every detail

a. 정확한
accuracy n. 정확 | accurately ad. 정확히

My information is more accurate than you have.

나의 정보는 네가 가진 것보다 더욱 정확하다.

05 ambiguous [æmbígjuəs] having more than one possible meaning

a. 두 가지 이상의 뜻으로 해석할 수 있는, 모호한
ambiguity n. 모호, 애매함

Her account was deliberately ambiguous.

그녀는 설명을 일부러 모호하게 했다.

06 assume [əsúːm] to think or accept that something is true but without having proof of it

v. 사실이라고 보다, 가정하다, 맡다, 취하다

I assume you have proof of this.

이것에 대한 증거를 네가 가지고 있을 거라 생각한다.

07 astronomy [əstrɑ́nəmi] the scientific study of the sun, moon, stars, planets, etc.

n. 천문학
astronomical a. 천문의 | astronomer n. 천문학자

The professor is devoted to astronomy.

그 교수는 천문학에 전념하고 있다.

08 biology [baiɑ́lədʒi] the scientific study of the life and structure of plants and animals

n. 생물학
biologic a. 생물학의 | biologist n. 생물학자

My son got A in biology.

나의 아들은 생물학에서 A학점을 받았다.

09 category [kǽtəgɔːri] a group of people or things with particular features in common

n. 범주 , 부분
categorize v. 분류하다

It falls into three categories.

세 범주로 구분된다.

10 coherent [kouhírərənt] talking in a way that is clear and easy to understand

a. 논리 정연한, 응집성의, 일관성 있는
coherence n. 일관성, 일치, 응집

What he says is not coherent.

그의 말은 논리 정연하지 못하다.

11 conceive [kənsíːv] to form an idea, a plan, etc. in your mind

v. 상상하다, 생각하다, 품다
conception n. 개념 ｜ conceivable a. 상상할 수 있는

I could not conceive **that he would do such a thing.**

그가 그런 일을 하리라고는 생각지 못했다.

12 concrete [kánkriːt] definite and specific

a. 구체적인 n. 콘크리트

The sentence she told is a concrete **example.**

그녀가 말한 문장이 구체적인 예이다.

13 confuse [kənfjúːz] to make somebody unable to think clearly or understand something

v. 혼동하다, 어리둥절하게 하다
confusion n. 혼동, 혼란, 혼미, 당황 | confusing a. 혼란스러운

I always confuse him with his brother.
나는 항상 그를 그의 형과 혼동한다.

14 criticize [krítisàiz] to express disapproval of someone or something

v. 비평하다, 비난하다
criticism n. 비평 | critical a. 비판적인, 매우 중요한

It's not my place to criticize.
나는 비난할 처지가 못된다.

15 define [difáin] to say or explain what the meaning of a word or phrase is

v. 정의를 내리다, 한정되다
definite a. 분명히 한정된, 명확한 | definition n. 정의

You have to define his position.
너는 그의 임무를 분명하게 규정해야 한다.

16 describe [diskráib] to say what somebody or something is like

v. 묘사하다, 칭하다
description n. (기술)서술적 묘사 | descriptive a. 기술적인

Words cannot describe the scene.
말로는 그 광경을 설명할 수 없다.

17 **effort** [éfərt] the physical or mental energy that you need to do something

n. 노력
effortless a. 힘들지 않는, 노력하지 않는

I made an effort **to help him.**

나는 그를 돕기 위해 노력했다.

18 **encyclopedia** [insàikləpíːdiə] a book or CD, or set of these containing facts about many different subjects

n. 백과사전
encyclopedic a. 백과사전적인, 해박한, 박학의

She copied the paragraph from the encyclopedia.

그녀는 백과사전에서 그 단락을 복사했다.

19 **explain** [ikspléin] to tell somebody about something in a way that makes it easy to understand

v. 설명하다
explanation n. 설명 | **explainable** a. 설명할 수 있는

Can you explain **to me how you solve this problem?**

이 문제를 어떻게 풀었는지 설명해 줄 수 있나요?

20 **extreme** [ikstríːm] very great in degree

a. 극도의, 과격한 n. 극단, 극단적인 것
extremely ad. 극단적으로, 매우

I dislike extreme **sports.**

난 극한 스포츠를 좋아하지 않는다.

21 fulfill [fulfíl] to carry out or perform a task, promise, etc.

v. 수행하다, 이행하다, 완료하다
fulfillment n. 이행

I was really good because the company fulfilled the requirements.

그 회사가 조건을 충족시켰기 때문에 나는 매우 기뻤다.

22 guess [ges] to try and give an answer or make a judgement about something without being sure of all the facts

v. 짐작하다, 추측하다 n. 추측

If you guess what comes next, let me know.

네가 다음에 올 것이 무엇인지를 짐작할 수 있다면 내게 말해라.

23 ignorant [ígnərənt] lacking knowledge or information about something

a. 무지한
ignore v. 무시하다 | **ignorance** n. 무시

People who are ignorant can't make this business successful.

무지한 사람들은 이 사업을 성공적으로 만들 수 없다.

24 incoherent [inkouhíərənt] not expressed or organized clearly

a. 비논리적인, 일관성이 없는

Find and rewrite the sentences that are incoherent.

일관성이 없는 문장들을 찾아서 다시 쓰시오.

25 **infer** [infə́ːr] to reach an opinion or decide that something is true on the basis of information that is available

v. 추론하다
inference n. 추론, 추론의 결과, 추정

I infer that my proposal has been accepted.

나의 제안이 받아들여졌다고 생각한다.

26 **insight** [ínsait] the ability to see and understand the truth about people or situations

n. 통찰, 통찰력

He has amazing insight about the future.

그는 미래에 대한 뛰어난 통찰력을 가지고 있다.

27 **inspire** [inspáiər] to give somebody the desire, confidence or enthusiasm to do something well

v. 고무하다, 불어넣다, 영감을 주다
inspiration n. 영감 | inspiring a. 고무적인

I was surprised to hear that my story inspired them.

내 이야기가 그들에게 영감을 주었다는 이야기를 듣고 놀랐다.

28 **intellectual** [intəléktʃuəl] connected with a person's ability to think in a logical way

a. 지적인, 지성을 가진
intellect n. 지력, 지성

He infringed intellectual property rights.

그는 지적 재산권을 침해했다.

29 interpret [intə́:rprit] to explain the meaning of something

v. 해석하다, 통역하다
interpretation n. 해석, 통역 | interpreter n. 무시

I had to interpret the passage to them.

나는 그들에게 그 구절을 해석해 주어야 했다.

30 laboratory [lǽbərətɔ:ri] a room or building used for scientific research, experiment, testing, etc.

n. 실험실
laboratorial a. 실험실의

You must wear the white gown when you enter the laboratory.

실험실에 들어갈 때에는 흰 가운을 입어야 한다.

31 novel [nɑ́vəl] a story book about imaginary people and events

n. 소설 a. 새로운
novelty n. 진기함, 신기로움

I like reading novels especially Kim Jin Myeong's.

나는 소설, 특히 김진명 소설을 좋아한다.

32 outcome [áutkʌm] the result or effect of an action or event

n. 결과, 성과, 결론

The outcome I had through my experiment has issued for more than a month.

내 실험을 통해 얻은 결과는 한 달 이상 이슈가 되고 있다.

33 physics [fíziks] scientific study of forces such as heat, light, sound, etc.

n. 물리학

physicist n. 물리학자

Physics is used practically in our life.

물리학은 우리의 삶에 실용적으로 사용된다.

34 predict [pridíkt] to say that something will happen in the future

v. 예언하다

prediction n. 예보, 예언 ㅣ predictable a. 예측할 수 있는

She predicts from pure conjecture.

그녀는 순전히 추측에 의해 예언한다.

35 presume [prizú:m] to suppose that something is true, although you do not have actual proof

v. 가정하다

presumption n. 추정

We must presume all of them to be innocent until the court will be closed.

재판이 종결될 때까지 우리는 그들 모두를 결백하다고 생각해야 한다.

36 prime [práim] main; most important

a. 제1의, 주요한 n. 전성기, 초기

His prime concern is the peace of the world.

그의 주요한 관심사는 세계 평화이다.

37 **prose** [próuz]   a piece of writing that is not poetry

n. 산문
prosaic a. 산문적인, 무미건조한

Her prose **is far too mannered and self-conscious.**
그녀의 산문은 너무 지나치게 작위적이고 자의식에 차 있다.

38 **psychology** [saikáːlədʒi]   the scientific study of the mind and how it influences behaviour

n. 심리학 , 심리
psychological a. 심리학의, 심리적인

I cannot understand his psychology.
그의 심리를 모르겠다.

39 **pursue** [pərsúː]   to do something or try to achieve something over a period of time

v. 쫓다, 추구하다, 종사하다
pursuit n. 추적, 추구

You have to pursue **your ultimate purpose in your life.**
너는 너의 인생의 궁극적인 목적을 추구해야 한다.

40 **recite** [risáit]   to say a poem, piece of literature, etc. that you have learned, especially to an audience

n. 읊다, 낭독하다
recital n. 발표회, 연주회

The woman will recite **some poems for us tonight.**
오늘 밤 그녀가 몇 개의 시를 낭독해 줄 것이다.

41 **refer** [rifə́:r] to mention or speak about someone or something

v. 알아보도록 하다, 위탁하다, 참고하다, 문의하다
reference n. 참조, 문의 | **referent** a. 언급한, 관계있는

If you want, you can refer to the other books from here.

네가 원한다면 여기에 있는 다른 책들을 참고해도 된다.

42 **remarkable** [rimá:rkəbl] unusual or surprising in a way that causes people to take notice

a. 주목할 만한, 놀랄 만한
remark v. ~에 주의하다, 말하다 n. 주의, 의견, 논평, 비평
remarkably ad. 두드러지게

It's remarkable to see such clean streets.

그렇게 깨끗한 거리를 보게 되다니 놀랄 만한 일이다.

43 **seminar** [sémənà:r] a meeting where a group of people discuss a problem or topic

n. 세미나

It's a one-day business management seminar.

그것은 하루 일정의 사업 경영 세미나이다.

44 **statistics** [stətístiks] a collection of information shown in numbers

n. 통계, 통계학
statistically ad. 통계상으로

We can make the result list of a survey easily by statistics.

우리는 통계학을 통해 여론 조사의 결과 목록을 쉽게 작성할 수 있다.

45 text [tékst] the main printed part of a book or magazine, not the notes, pictures, etc.

n. 본문

textbook n. 교과서 ǀ textual a. 본문의, 원문대로의

What is stated in the text?

본문에서 언급된 내용은 무엇인가?

46 translation the process of changing something that is written or
[trænsléiʃən, trænz-] spoken into another language

n. 번역

translate v. 번역하다 ǀ translator n. 번역가

Reading the translation version is not better than original version.

번역본을 읽는 것은 원본을 읽는 것보다 낮지 않다.

47 verse [və́:rs] writing that is arranged in lines, often with a regular rhythm or pattern of rhyme poetry

n. 운문 v. 시를 짓다

Mr. Kim quoted a verse.

Mr. Kim은 시구 한 소절을 인용했다.

48 vision [víʒən] the ability to see

n. 시력, 상상력, 통찰력, 환영

visual a. 시력의 ǀ visible a. 명백한, 눈에 보이는

She has a vision sometimes.

그녀는 가끔 환영이 나타난다.

49 **wisdom** [wízdəm] good sense and judgement, based especially on your experience of life

n. 지혜, 현명
wise a. 현명한 | wisely ad. 현명하게

He had the wisdom to refuse the company's suggestion.

그는 현명하게도 그 회사의 제안을 거절했다.

50 **zoological** [zòuəládʒikəl] connected with the science of zoology

a. 동물학의
zoology n. 동물학 | zoologist n. 동물학자

He is interested in the subjects ranging from accounting to zoology.

그는 회계학에서 동물학에 걸친 과목들에 관심이 있다.

Check up

A 다음 내용이 설명하고 있는 단어를 〈보기〉에서 골라 그 기호를 쓰시오.

> absolute | abstract | accurate | ambiguous | category

1. theoretical, ideal, ideological, conceptual

2. double, uncertain, enigmatic, indeterminate

3. true, right, close, correct, straight

4. class, heading, league, bracket, classification

5. complete, direct, implicit, infinite

B 단어와 한글 뜻을 알맞게 짝지으시오.

1. coherent ·   · 상상하다, 생각하다

2. conceive ·   · 구체적인

3. concrete ·   · 비평하다, 비난하다

4. criticize ·   · 논리 정연한, 응집성의

5. fulfill ·   · 다하다, 이행하다

C 다음 빈 칸에 의미상 가장 알맞은 단어를 보기에서 골라 쓰시오.

> guess | ignorant | insight | laboratory | presume

1. have another _____ coming : 착각하고 있다

2. gain an _____ into : ~을 간파하다, 통찰하다

3. a _____ animal : 실험용 동물

4. blissfully _____ : 모르는 게 약인, 몰라서 행복한

5. You _____ : 주제넘구나, 건방지구나

D 영영풀이에 알맞은 단어를 고르시오.

> prose | psychology | pursue | recite | remarkable

1. to say a poem, piece of literature, etc.

2. the scientific study of the mind and how it influences behavior

3. writing that is not poetry

4. to do something or try to achieve something over a period of time

5. unusual or surprising in a way that causes people to take notice

Lesson 3
Languages
| 언어

01   **abbreviation** [əbrì:viéiʃən]   a short form of a word

n. 생략, 약어
abbreviate v. 단축하다, 생략하다 | **abbreviated** a. 단축된, 짧게 한

You have to make it clear that this abbreviation means.

너는 이 약자들이 무슨 뜻인지 분명히 해두어야 한다.

02   **absurd** [əbsə́:rd]   completely ridiculous, not logical and sensible

a. 불합리한, 어리석은
absurdity n. 부조리, 어리석은 일

He must be silly to hear his absurd words.

그의 불합리한 말을 들어보면 그는 바보임에 틀림없다.

03   **biography** [baiágrəfi]   the story of a person's life written by somebody else

n. 전기
biographic a. 전기의

Helen Keller's biography inspired me so strongly.

헬렌켈러의 전기는 나에게 강하게 영감을 불어넣어 주었다.

04   **character** [kǽrəktər]   all the qualities and features that make a person, groups of people, and places different from others

n. 성격, 특성, 특질, 특색
characteristic a. 특색 있는, 독특한 | **characterize** v. 특성을 기술하다

This is a quaint town with a lot of character.

이곳은 많은 특성을 지닌 고풍스런 마을이다.

05 clause [klɔ́:z] a group of words that includes a subject and a verb, and forms a sentence or part of a sentence

n. 절, 조항

That is not a clause because it doesn't include a subject and a verb.

저것은 주어와 동사가 포함되어 있지 않기 때문에 절이 아니다.

06 climax [kláimæks] the most exciting or important event or point in time

n. 최고조, 클라이맥스
climactic a. 최고조의, 클라이맥스의

The tension built up to a climax.

긴장이 최고조로 달했다.

07 complicated [kámpləkèitid] difficult to understand or deal with; complex

a. 복잡한
complicate v. 복잡하게 하다

She can't understand the complicated sentences.

그녀는 복잡한 문장을 이해하지 못한다.

08 context [kántekst] the situation in which something happens and that helps you to understand it

n. 문맥
contextual a. 문맥상의, 전후 관계의

He cites a passage out of context.

그는 문맥을 무시하고 하나의 단락을 인용한다.

09　**dialect** [dáiəlèkt]　the form of a language that is spoken in a particular area

n. 방언

dialectal　a. 방언의, 방언 특유의

You'd better not speak dialect in public broadcasting.

공중파 방송에서는 사투리를 쓰지 않는 것이 나을 것이다.

10　**emphasize** [émfəsaiz]　to give special importance on something

v. 강조하다

emphasis　n. 강조

He emphasized that he was a former agent.

그는 전직 요원이었다는 것을 강조했다.

11　**entitle** [intáitl]　to give somebody the right to have or to do something

v. 자격을 주다, ~의 호칭을 주다

entitlement　n. 권리, 수급원리

He is entitled to check the sanitation condition of the restaurants.

그는 식당의 위생 상태를 점검할 자격이 있다.

12　**epic** [épik]　a long poem about the actions of great men and women or about a nation's history

n. 서사시

It'll be helpful for you to comprehend the history to read epics.

서사시를 읽는 것은 네가 역사를 이해하는 데에 도움이 될 것이다.

13   essay [ései]   a short piece of writing on a particular subject

n. 수필

I have homework to write an essay **about the industry.**
나는 산업에 대한 수필을 쓰는 숙제가 있다.

14   explicit [iksplísit]   clear and easy to understand

a. 명백한
explicable a. 설명할 수 있는 ǀ explication n. 설명, 해설

I thought it was very explicit**.**
굉장히 명백하다고 생각했다.

15   express [iksprés]   to show or make known a feeling, an opinion, etc. by words, looks or actions

v. 표현하다, 자기가 생각하는 바를 말하다
expression n. 표현, 표현법, 표정 ǀ expressive a. 표현적인, 나타내는

She expresses **herself in good English.**
그녀는 유창한 영어실력으로 자신을 표현한다.

16   feature [fí:tʃər]   something important, interesting or typical of a place or thing

n. 특징, 얼굴 생김새   v. 특색으로 삼다
featured a. 특색으로 한

Her best feature **is pretty.**
그녀의 가장 큰 특징은 귀여움이다.

17 **fiction** [fíkʃən] a type of literature that describes imaginary people and events, not real ones

n. 소설, 꾸민 이야기
fictional a. 꾸며낸

She likes the science fiction movies very much.
그녀는 공상 과학 영화를 매우 좋아한다.

18 **gerund** [dʒérənd] a noun in the form of the present participle of a verb

n. 동명사 (문법)

A gerund can play a role of a subject in the sentence.
동명사는 문장에서 주어의 역할을 할 수 있다.

19 **gesture** [dʒéstʃər] a movement that you make with your hands, your head or your face to show a particular meaning

n. 몸짓

In English, a gesture is important.
영어에서 제스처는 중요하다.

20 **illustrate** [íləstrèit, ilʌ́streit] to use pictures, photographs, diagrams, etc. in a book

v. 설명하다, 삽화를 넣다
illustration n. 삽화, 일러스트 ǀ illustrator n. 삽화가

I will illustrate the rules of this game.
나는 이 경기의 규칙을 설명할 것이다.

21 **imply** [impái] to suggest that something is true, without saying this directly

v. 포함하다, 의미하다, 암시하다
implication n. 함축, 포함, 암시

He found out what this sentence implies quickly.

그는 이 문장이 암시하는 것을 빠르게 찾아냈다.

22 **impress** [imprés] to produce a strong, and usually favorable impression on someone

v. ~에게 인상을 주다, 감동시키다
impressive a. 강한 인상을 주는 | impression n. 인상

She impressed me as a scholar.

그녀는 학자 같은 인상을 주었다.

23 **initial** [iníʃəl] happening at the beginning

a. 처음의 n. 머리글자
initiate v. 시작하다

The necklaces which were made of the initials of one's name were popular few years ago.

이름의 머리글자로 만들어진 목걸이가 몇 년 전에 인기가 있었다.

24 **letter** [létər] a message that is written down or printed on paper and usually put in an envelope and sent to somebody

n. 편지, 글자

Parking lot is marked by a letter "P" on the map.

주차장은 지도에서 "P" 자로 표시된다.

25 **literal** [lítərəl] being the basic or usual meaning of a word or phrase

a. 글자 그대로의 , 문자 그대로의
literally ad. 문자 그대로

She thought the meaning out of the literal meaning.

그녀는 글자 그대로의 뜻을 넘어선 뜻을 생각했다.

26 **literature** [lítərətʃər, -tʃùər] pieces of writing that are valued as works of art, especially novels, plays and poems

n. 문학, 문헌
literary a. 문학의 ǀ literate a. 학식이 있는

Literature is a mirror of society.

문학은 사회상을 반영한다.

27 **logic** [ládʒik] a way of thinking or explaining something

n. 논리학, 논리
logical a. 논리학의 ǀ logically ad. 논리적으로

I fail to see the logic behind his argument.

나는 그의 주장에 담긴 논리를 알 수 없다.

28 **paragraph** [pǽrəgræf, -grɑ̀:f] a section of a piece of writing

n. 절, 단락

Most passages include about three paragraphs in the test.

시험에서는 대부분의 글이 대략 세 개의 단락을 포함하고 있다.

29 passage [pǽsidʒ] a short section from a book, piece of music, etc.

n. 구절, 통행, 통로, 여행
pass v. 지나가다, 추월하다, 통하다, 지나다 , 통과하다

You have to read each following passage and answer the questions in one minute.

너는 다음 글을 읽고 1분 안에 질문에 대답해야 한다.

30 pattern [pǽtərn] a regular arrangement of lines, shapes, colours, etc. as design on materials, carpets, etc.

n. 무늬, 형, 양식

She found the different patterns between two novels.

그녀는 두 소설 간의 다른 양상을 발견했다.

31 peculiar [pikjúːljər] strange or unusual

a. 기묘한, 특이한
peculiarity n. 특색 | peculiarly ad. 특히, 기묘하게

Language is peculiar to mankind.

언어는 인간 고유의 것이다.

32 plot [plɑt] the series of events which form the story of a novel, play, film or movie, etc.

n. 구성, 줄거리, 음모 v. 몰래 꾸미다

A plot is the collection of continuous events in a work of literature.

줄거리란 문학작품에 있는 연속적인 사건들의 모음이다.

33 prominent [prámənənt] important or well known

a. 현저한, 두드러진
prominence n. 두드러짐, 현저함

She is prominent in the whole class to see her writing.

그녀가 쓴 글을 보면 그녀는 반 전체에서 두드러진 면모를 보인다.

34 proverb [právə:rb] a well-known phrase or sentence that gives advice or says something that is generally true

n. 속담, 격언
proverbial a. 속담의

There is an old proverb that haste makes waste.

서두르면 일을 그르친다는 속담이 있다.

35 punctuation [pʌ̀ŋktʃuéiʃən] the marks used in writing that divide sentences and phrases

n. 구두, 구두점, 구두법
punctuate v. ~에 구두점을 찍다

You made a mistake about punctuation.

너는 구두점에 실수를 범했다.

36 rhyme [ráim] word that has the same sound or ends with the same sound as another word

n. 운, 압운 v. 시를 짓다, 운이 맞다

What is the rhyme for 'simple'?

'simple' 과 운이 맞는 단어는 무엇인가?

37 **romantic** [rouméntik] connected or concerned with love or a sexual relationship

a. 낭만적인
romance n. 사랑, 연애

He married for romantic love.

그는 열렬한 연애를 해서 결혼했다.

---

38 **satire** [sétaiər] a way of criticizing a people's behaviors or ideas using humor to show their faults or weaknesses

n. 풍자

This story should be read as a satire.

이 이야기는 풍자로 해석되어야 한다.

---

39 **saying** [séiiŋ] a well-known phrase or statement that expresses something about life; a proverb or maxim

n. 말하기, 속담

'Rome was not built in a day.' is one of sayings.

'로마는 하루 아침에 지어지지 않았다.'는 속담 중 하나이다.

---

40 **sense** [sens] the physical abilities of sight, smell, hearing, touch, and taste

n. 감각, 의식 v. 느끼다
sensitive a. 민감한 | sensible a. 분별 있는, 느낄 수 있는
sensual a. 관능적인, 관능주의의

She lost a sense of taste for a while.

그녀는 잠시 미각을 잃었다.

41 sentence [séntəns]   a set of words expressing a statement, a question or an order, usually containing a subject and a verb

n. 문장, 판결   v. 판결하다

Can you answer me in one sentence?

내 질문에 한 문장으로 대답할 수 있겠니?

---

42 sentiment [séntəmənt]   a feeling or an opinion, especially one based on emotions

n. 감정
sentimental a. 감정적인

All of the audience echo his sentiment.

모든 관객이 그의 감정에 공감한다.

---

43 speech [spíːtʃ]   a formal talk that a person gives to an audience

n. 말, 연설
speechless a. 말문이 막힌, 말을 못하는

You'd better get speech **therapy.**

너는 언어 치료를 받는 게 좋겠다.

---

44 synonym [sínənìm]   a word or expression that has the same or nearly the same meaning as another in the same language

n. 동의어

A synonym **can make students confused.**

동의어는 학생들을 혼란스럽게 만들 수 있다.

45 **theme** [θiːm]   the subject or main idea in a talk, piece of writing or work of art

n. 주제

The theme of the poem is stated in the title.

그 시의 주제는 제목에 나와 있다.

---

46 **title** [táitl]   the name of a book, poem, painting, piece of music, etc.

n. 표제, 제목
titled   a. 직함이 있는

What would you like to make another title of '*The little mermaid*'.

'인어공주' 의 다른 제목으로 무엇을 만들고 싶니?

---

47 **tongue** [tʌŋ]   the soft part in the mouth that moves around, used for tasting, swallowing, speaking, etc.

n. 혀, 말
tongueless   a. 혀가 없는, 말을 안하는

He has a nasty tongue, so almost everyone doesn't like to talk to him.

그는 입이 거칠어서 거의 모든 사람들이 그에게 말하기를 싫어한다.

---

48 **utter** [ʌ́tər]   to make a sound with your voice

v. 입 밖에 내다, 발언하다
utterance   n. 입 밖에 냄, 발언, 최후, 죽음

You shouldn't utter the secret, promise me.

너는 비밀을 누설해서는 안 된다, 약속해.

49 version [və́:rʒən, -ʃən] a form of something that is slightly different from an earlier form or from other forms of the same thing

n. 번역, 판

He read that novel in English version.

그는 저 소설을 영문판으로 읽었다.

---

50 wit [wit] the ability to say or write things that are both clever and amusing

n. 지혜, 기지, 재치

Wit gives zest to conversation.

기지는 대화의 재미를 더해 준다.

Check up

A 단어와 한글 뜻을 알맞게 짝지으시오.

1. wit •　　　　• 동의어

2. utter •　　　　• 풍자

3. theme •　　　　• 주제

4. synonym •　　　• 입 밖에 내다, 발언하다

5. satire •　　　　• 지혜, 기지

B 보기에서 알맞은 단어를 골라 관용어를 완성하시오.

| rhyme | punctuation | proverb | prominent | plot |
| pattern | passage | logic | literal | initial |

1. pass into a _____ : 속담이 되다, 소문거리가 되다

2. _____ against a person's life : ~을 죽일 음모를 꾸미다

3. without _____ or reason : 분별이 없는, 전혀 까닭 모를

4. deductive _____ : 연역 논리학

5. run to _____ : 틀에 박혀 있다

6. _____ marks : 구두점

7. the _____ stage : 초기, 제1기

8. in the _____ sense of the word : 그 단어의 뜻 그대로

9. _____ of arms : 시합, 치고 받기; 논전

10. _____ features : 눈에 띄는 용모

C 다음 영영풀이에 해당되는 단어를 골라 쓰시오.

| impress | imply | illustrate | fiction | feature |

1. to suggest that something is true, without saying this directly

2. a type of literature that describes imaginary people and events

3. to feel admiration

4. something important, interesting or typical of place or thing

5. to use picture, photographs, diagrams, etc. in a book, etc.

Lesson 4
History
|역사

01 **acquire** [əkwáiər] to gain something by your own efforts, ability or behavior

v. 취득하다, 얻다
acquisition n. 획득 l acquisitive a. 획득하려는, 소유욕이 많은

My son acquired **a bad habit. I'm so worried about that.**
내 아들이 나쁜 버릇이 들어서 매우 걱정이 된다.

02 **ancient** [éinʃənt] belonging to a period of history that is thousands of years in the past

a. 고대의

It's mysterious to build such a building without any machine in ancient **age.**
고대 시대에 어떠한 기계도 없이 그러한 건물을 지었다는 것은 신비한 일이다.

03 **archaeology** [à:rkiálədʒi] the study of cultures of the past, and of periods of history by examining the remains of buildings and objects found in the ground

n. 고고학

Archaeology **helps us to know about past time better.**
고고학은 우리가 과거에 대해 더 잘 알 수 있도록 도와준다.

04 **broad** [brɔːd] wide; including many different kinds of things or people

a. 폭이 넓은, 널따란
broaden v. 넓히다

I'm looking for men who have broad **views.**
견문이 넓은 사람들을 찾고 있다.

05 century [séntʃəri] a period of 100 years

n. 1세기, 100년
centurial a. 100년의, 1세기의

They are the documents from the 17th century.

그것들은 17세기에 만들어진 서류이다.

06 cherish [tʃériʃ] to love someone or something very much and take care of them well

v. 소중히 하다, 품다

We will love and cherish **each other as we live the rest of our happy lives as a couple.**

우리는 부부로 서로 사랑하고 아껴가며 남은 삶을 행복하게 살아가겠습니다.

07 chronology [krənálədʒi] the order in which a series of events happened

n. 연대순 배열, 연대기, 연표, 연대학
chronic a. 장기간에 걸친 ǀ chronicle n. 연대기

The book includes a chronology **of his life and work.**

그 책은 그의 생활과 일에 대한 일대기를 포함하고 있다.

08 colonize [kálənaiz] to take control of an area or a country that is not your own, especially using force, and send people from your own country to live there

v. 식민지로 개척하다, 식민지를 만들다

North America was colonized **by the British and French.**

북아메리카는 영국과 프랑스의 식민지였다.

09 colony [kάləni] a country or an area that is governed by people from another more powerful country

n. 식민지
colonial a. 식민지의 I colonist n. 해외 이주민

Almost all countries tried to make their own colonies in the past time.
과거에 거의 모든 나라들은 그들만의 식민지를 만들려고 노력했었다.

---

10 conquer [kάŋkər] to take control of a country or city and its people by force

v. 정복하다
conquest n. 정복 I conqueror n. 정복자

The general hoped that he would conquer all over the world.
그 장군은 전 세계를 정복하기를 원했다.

---

11 contemporary [kəntémpərèri] relating to the present time

a. 같은 시대의, 현대의

This library has a large collection of contemporary literature.
이 도서관에는 현대문학 작품이 많다.

---

12 decade [dékeid] a period of 10 years, for example 1910 to 1919

n. 10년 (특히 1910년~1919년이나 1990년~1999년과 같은 기간을 가리킴)

This is a crime that happened over a decade ago.
이것은 10년 전에 있었던 사건이었다.

13 **depression** [dipréʃən] the state of feeling very sad and without hope

n. 우울증, 의기소침, 움푹한 땅, 불경기
depress v. 낙담시키다, 우울하게 하다 I depressed a. 의기소침한

He was in a state of total depression.

그는 심한 우울증에 걸린 상태였다.

14 **deserve** [dizə́:rv] be entitled to or be worthy of a reward or punishment

v. 할 만하다, ~할 가치가 있다

A hard worker deserves **good pay.**

열심히 일하는 사람은 많은 급료를 받을 만하다.

15 **dwell** [dwel] to live somewhere

v. 살다
dwelling 주거지 I dweller n. 거주자

I hope we all dwell **in the peaceful world.**

우리 모두가 평화로운 세계에서 살기를 희망한다.

16 **dynasty** [dáinəsti] a series of rulers of a country who all belong to the same family

n. 왕조
dynastic a. 왕조의, 왕가의 I dynast n. 왕, 군주

The liquor was banned for a while in the Joseon Dynasty **period.**

조선 왕조 시대에 잠시 동안 주류가 금지됐었다.

17 empire [émpaiər] a group of countries or states that are controlled by one ruler or government

n. 제국

It is interesting to study about Roman Empire.

로마제국을 공부하는 것은 흥미롭다.

18 epoch [épək, épɑk] a period of time in history, especially one during which important events or changes happen

n. 신기원, 중요한 사건
epochal a. 신기원의, 획기적인

We have to try to move into a new epoch.

우리는 새로운 시대로 들어가려고 노력해야 한다.

19 era [íərə, érə] a period of time in history that is known for particular event, or for particular qualities

n. 연대

Almost all of Asia countries have had its era of colonial period.

거의 모든 아시아 국가들에게는 식민지 시대가 있었다.

20 establish [istǽbliʃ, es-] to start or create an organization, a system, etc. that is meant to last for a long time

v. 설립하다, 제정하다
establishment n. 설립 | established a. 확립된

Alfred Novel established the Novel Prize.

알프레드 노벨이 노벨상을 제정했다.

21 eventually [ivéntʃuəli] at the end of a period of time or a series of events

ad. 결국, 드디어, 마침내
eventual a. 최후의

My father passed the exam eventually **in spite of his old age.**

아버지는 많은 나이에도 불구하고 결국 그 시험에 통과했다.

22 exploit [iksplɔ́it] to treat a person or situation as an opportunity to gain an advantage for yourself

v. 개척하다, 개발하다, 착취하다
exploitation n. 개척, 개발, 착취

Alternative energy should be exploited **immediately.**

대체 에너지는 즉시 개발되어야 한다.

23 factor [fǽktər] one of several things that cause or influence something

n. 요인
fact n. 사실, 실제

Make sure that you have to focus on an important factor.

너는 중요한 요인에 집중해야 한다는 것을 명심해라.

24 feast [fíːst] a thing, or an event that brings great pleasure

n. 축하연, 즐거워하는 것

The feast **will be held after the ceremony for about two hours.**

약 2시간 동안의 의식이 끝나면 축하연이 열릴 것이다.

25 goddess [gádis] a female god

n. 여신

People in Hawaii thought the Hula made the goddesses **happy.**

하와이 사람들은 홀라춤이 여신을 행복하게 한다고 생각했다.

26 great [gréit] very large

a. 큰, 위대한 ad. 훌륭히
greatly ad. 크게, 위대하게 | greatness n. 거대함, 위대함

Working together is a great **start for relationships.**

함께 일하는 것은 인간 관계를 맺기 위한 좋은 출발이다.

27 hero [híərou] a person, especially a man, who is admired by many people for doing something brave or good

n. 영웅, 주인공
heroic a. 영웅의 | heroine n. 여걸, 여주인공

He is known as a great hero.

그는 위대한 영웅으로 알려져 있다.

28 history [hístəri] all the events that happened in the past

n. 역사 , 역사책 , 경력
historical a. 역사상의 | historic a. 역사의

You don't have to memorize all of the heroes in history.

역사에 나오는 모든 영웅들을 기억할 필요는 없다.

29 imperial [impíəriəl] connected with an empire

a. 제국의, 황제의

They were sent to Rome by the imperial **order.**

그들은 황제의 명령에 의해 로마로 보내졌다.

30 invent [invént] to produce or design something that has not existed before

v. 발명하다, 날조하다

invention n. 발명, 발명품

Edison is the most famous all over the world for inventing **something.**

에디슨은 무엇인가를 발명하는 데 있어 전 세계에서 가장 유명하다.

31 kingdom [kíŋdəm] a country ruled by a king or queen

n. 왕조

This is the end of a kingdom.

이것이 왕국의 말로이다.

32 legend [lédʒənd] a story from ancient times about people and events, that may or may not be true

n. 전설

legendary a. 전설의

According to legend, **the bear became a woman.**

전설에 따르면 곰이 여자가 되었다.

33 lose [luːz] to be unable to find something or somebody

v. 잃다, 지다, 지치다
loss n. 분실, 유실 | lost a. 잃어버린

Your complaining makes me lose my temper.
네 불평이 나를 화나게 만든다.

34 millennium [miléniəm] a period of 1,000 years, especially as calculated before or after the birth of Christ

n. 천년 간, 천년 왕국, 황금 시대, 천년제
millennial a. 천년 간의, 천년 왕국의

In many schools, millennium buildings had been built.
많은 학교에서 밀레니엄 빌딩들이 지어졌다.

35 mythical [míθikəl] existing only in ancient myths

a. 신화의
myth n. 신화 | mythology n. 신화

Hercules is my favorite mythical hero.
헤라클레스는 내가 가장 좋아하는 신화 속의 영웅이다.

36 orient [ɔ́ːrient] the eastern part of the world

n. 동양
oriental a. 동양의

I realized that I'm interested in the orient through my major.
나는 전공을 통해서 내가 동방 제국에 관심이 있다는 것을 깨달았다.

37 patriot [péitriət]　a person who loves his or her country and who is ready to defend it against an enemy

n. 애국자
patriotic a. 애국자의 | **patriotism** n. 애국심

There are much more people who insist themselves patriots than you thought.

네가 생각하는 것보다 자기가 애국자라고 주장하는 사람은 훨씬 더 많다.

38 period [píəriəd]　a particular length of time

n. 기간, 시대
periodical a. 정기 간행의 n. 정기 간행물 | **periodic** a. 정기적인

I had trouble living without income in that period.

나는 그 당시에 수입 없이 살아가는 데에 어려움을 겪었다.

39 pioneer [pàiəníər]　a person who is important in the early development of something, and whose work or ideas are later developed by other people

n. 개척자, 선구자

He was a pioneer who was abead of his time.

그는 시대를 앞서간 선구자였다.

40 prehistory [pri:hístəri]　the period of time in history before information was written down

n. 유사 이전, 선사 시대, 선사학
prehistoric a. 유사 이전의

Studying Korean prehistory is difficult but interesting.

한국의 선사시대를 공부하는 것은 어렵지만 재미있다.

41 primitive [prímətiv] belonging to a very simple way of life that existed in the past and does not have modern industries

a. 원시의 , 미개의

At survival camp, we learned how to make fire in the primitive way.

서바이벌 캠프에서, 우리는 원시적인 방법으로 불을 피우는 법을 배웠다.

42 pyramid [pírəmìd] ancient stone buildings with four triangular sloping sides

n. 피라미드

Pyramid is the symbol of the ancient Egypt.

피라미드는 고대 이집트의 상징이다.

43 ruin [rú:in] to damage something so badly that it loses all its value, pleasure, etc.

v. 파멸시키다 n. 폐허, 파멸
ruined a. 파멸한, 멸망한

An oil spill ruins fishing business in the pertinent area.

기름 유출은 그 지역의 어업을 망친다.

44 settle [sétl] to put an end to an argument or a disagreement

v. 놓다, 진정시키다, 해결하다, 자리를 잡다
settled a. 고정된 | settler n. 이주자, 개척자

She settled a disordered brain.

그녀는 흐트러진 머리 속을 진정시켰다.

45 **settlement** [sétlmənt] the process of people making their homes in a place

n. 정착, 이민

The process of a settlement to the west America was adversity in a row.

미 서부지역으로의 이주 과정은 고난의 연속이었다.

46 **shaman** [ʃɑ́:mən, ʃéi-, ʃǽ-] a priest or priestess in shamanism

n. 무당, 주술사

Shamans are usually the local religious leader.

주술사들은 보통 한 지역의 종교 지도자들이다.

47 **shelter** [ʃéltər] a structure built to give protection, especially from the weather or attack

n. 피난처, 방공호 v. 보호하다
sheltered a. 보호된, 지켜지고 있는, 세상의 풍파로부터 격리된

It's that guy from the animal shelter.

동물 보호소에 왔던 사람이야.

48 **slave** [sléiv] a person who is legally owned by other people and is forced to work for them

n. 노예
slavery n. 노예 제도 | slaver n. 노예 상인, 노예 소유자

Many Africans were kidnapped and became slaves.

많은 아프리카 사람들이 납치되어 노예가 되었다.

| 49 | sphinx [sfíŋks] | an ancient Egyptian image of a lion with a human head, lying down |

n. 스핑크스

The sphinx is very famous in the world as you know.

네가 알고 있는 것처럼 스핑크스는 세계에서 매우 유명하다.

| 50 | wander [wándər] | to walk slowly around or to a place, often without any particular sense of purpose or direction |

v. 돌아다니다, 빗나가다

wanderer n. 돌아다니는 사람 | wandering a. 돌아다니는

He has wandered to find his missing brother for a few days.

그는 잃어버린 남동생을 찾기 위해 며칠째 돌아다니고 있다.

Check up

A 다음 단어가 본문에서 쓰인 의미를 고르시오.

1. broad shoulders

ⓐ wide

ⓑ general; not detailed

2. cherish a resentment against a person

ⓐ to love somebody very much and want to protect them or it

ⓑ to keep an idea, a hope or a pleasant feeling in your mind for a long time

3. what can be called the humanitarian colonization of Africa

ⓐ to take control of an area or a country that is not your own, especially using force, and send people from your own country to live there

ⓑ [biology] to live or grow in large numbers in a particular area

4. He wants to conquer the world.

ⓐ to take control of a country or city and its people by force

ⓑ to become very popular or successful in a place

5. A magazine on modern and contemporary Korean art is to be published in the winter.

ⓐ belonging to the same time

ⓑ relating to the present time

B 알맞은 반대말끼리 연결하시오.

1. lose   •   • poor

2. ancient   •   • narrow

3. great   •   • occident

4. broad   •   • win, gain

5. orient   •   • modern

Lesson 5

Arts

| 예술

01 active [ǽktiv] always busy doing things, especially physical activities

a. 활동적인, 활발한, 적극적인, 의욕적인

activity n. 활동, 운동 ｜ activate v. 활동적으로 하다

Guide dogs help their owners to live as active lives.

맹도견들은 주인이 활동적인 삶을 살도록 돕는다.

02 admire [ədmáiər] to respect somebody for what they are or for what they have done

v. 감탄하다, 탄복하다

admiration n. 감탄 ｜ admiring a. 감탄하는

admirable a. 감탄할 만한

We admire her for her tact.

그녀의 재치에 감탄하고 있다.

03 art [á:rt] the use of the imagination to express ideas or feelings, particularly in painting, drawing or sculpture

n. 예술, 미술, 기술

Some people believe that art is long but life is short.

어떤 사람들은 예술은 길고 인생은 짧다는 말을 믿는다.

04 artistic [a:rtístik] connected with art or artists

a. 예술적인, 예술의

artist n. 예술가

She realized that she had an artistic temperament.

그녀는 자신이 예술가적 자질이 있다는 것을 깨달았다.

05　**aspire** [əspáiər] to have a strong desire to achieve or to become something

v. 열망하다
aspiration n. 포부 ǀ aspiring a. 포부가 있는, 대망을 품은

Some people always aspire after further knowledge.
어떤 사람들은 항상 더 많은 지식을 열망한다.

06　**attract** [ətrǽkt] to make someone interested in something

v. 끌다, 유인하다
attraction n. 끌어당김, 매력 ǀ attractive a. 사람의 마음을 끄는

We attracted the best talented foreign employees for their advanced management.
우리나라는 선진 경영기법을 위해 외국인 인재를 유치했다.

07　**audience** [ɔ́ːdiəns] the group of people who have gathered to watch or listen to something

n. 청중, 관중
audient a. 듣는, 경청하는

That will continue a great mood with a large audience.
많은 관중과 함께 좋은 분위기가 될 것이다.

08　**chorus** [kɔ́ːrəs] part of a song that is sung after each verse

n. 합창, 합창곡, 합창단

The chorus was singing "The Ode to Joy".
그 합창단은 "환희의 송가"를 노래했다.

| 09 | **classic** [klǽsik] | accepted or deserving to be accepted as one of the best or most important of its kind |

a. 고전의, 일류의, 최고 수준의
classical a. 고전적인 | **classically** ad. 고전적으로

People think that classical music is boring and difficult.

사람들이 고전 음악은 지루하고 어렵다고 생각한다.

| 10 | **comment** [kάment] | something that you say or write which gives an opinion on |

n. 논평, 비평, 비판

His comment was very cynical.

그의 논평은 매우 냉소적이었다.

| 11 | **craft** [kræft, kra:ft] | an activity involving a special skill at making things with your hands |

n. 기능, 공예
crafty a. 교활한 | **craftman** n. 공예가, 숙련공

The craft experts will help us finish this work.

공예 전문가들이 우리가 이 작업을 마칠 수 있도록 도울 것이다.

| 12 | **cubism** [kjú:bizm] | a 20th century style of art, in which objects and people are represented by geometric shapes |

n. 입체파, 큐비즘
cubist n. 입체파 화가

It is called cubism and a kind of artistic styles.

그것은 입체파라고 불리고, 예술 양식 중의 하나이다.

13 **exhibit** [igzíbit]   to show something in a public place for people to enjoy or to give them information

v. 전시하다, 출품하다 n. 전시, 전람
exhibition n. 전시 | **exhibitor** n. 출품자, 영화관 경영자

Various paintings of six modern artists were exhibited.

6명의 현대 미술화가의 다양한 작품들이 전시되었다.

14 **famous** [féiməs] known about by many people in many places

a. 유명한, 멋진, 뛰어난
fame n. 유명, 명성 | **famously** ad. 뛰어나게, 유명하게

I have a famous **appetite to surprise you.**

나는 너를 놀라게 할 만한 왕성한 식욕을 가지고 있다.

15 **film** [film]   a story that is told using sound and moving pictures, shown at a cinema or on television

n. 얇은 막, 필름, 영화

I like to see movies and discuss those films **with others.**

나는 영화를 보고 그 영화들에 대해 다른 사람들과 토론하는 것을 좋아한다.

16 **genius** [dʒíːnjəs, -niəs]   someone who has great intelligence, skill or artistic ability

n. 천재, 특수한 재능

She is a genius **to think of that.**

그것을 생각해내다니 그녀는 천재구나.

17 genre [ʒɑ́:nrə] a particular type or style of literature, art, film or music that you can recognize because of its special features

n. 유형, 형식, 풍속화, 풍속화법, 종류, 양식

We all know how the story ends in a romantic comedy genre movie.

우리 모두는 로맨틱 코미디 영화의 결말이 어떤지 안다.

18 genuine [dʒénjuin] real; not false

a. 진짜의, 진품의
genuinely ad. 진정으로

A genuine leather product is much more expensive than synthetic one.

진짜 가죽 제품은 인조 가죽 제품보다 훨씬 비싸다.

19 glory [glɔ́:ri] fame, praise or honor that is given to somebody because they have achieved something important

n. 영광, 영화
glorious a. 영광스러운

He came home a rich man, covered in glory.

그는 부유한 사람이 되어 영예롭게 귀향했다.

20 harmony [hɑ́:rməni] a state of peaceful existence and agreement

n. 조화
harmonious a. 조화된 | harmonic a. 화음의 | harmonize v. 조화시키다

Harmony is the most important element in chorus.

조화가 합창에서 가장 중요한 요소이다.

21 illusion [ilú:ʒən] something that seems to exist but in fact does not

n. 환각

illusory a. 사람을 미혹하는, 착각의, 가공의, 실체가 없는

She has been tired of her continuous illusion.

그녀는 계속되는 환각에 지쳐왔다.

22 imagine [imǽdʒin] to form a picture in your mind of what something might be like

v. 상상하다, ~라고 생각하다

image n. 상, 닮은 사람 | **imagination** n. 상상

imaginary a. 상상의 | **imaginable** a. 상상할 수 있는

I can't imagine he was a prince in his former life.

그가 전생에 왕자였다는 것이 상상이 안 된다.

23 imitate [íməteit] to copy somebody or something

v. 모방하다, 모사하다

imitation n. 모방, 모조 | **imitated** a. 본뜬, 모조의

He is good at imitating other's voice.

그는 목소리 흉내를 잘 낸다.

24 ingenious [indʒí:njəs] marked by, showing or having skill, originality and inventive cleverness

a. 재간이 많은, 독창적인

ingenuity n. 발명의 재주

She is ingenuous to solve the problem so quickly.

문제를 그렇게 빨리 해결하다니 그녀가 참 재주가 많다.

25 **instrument** [ínstrəmənt] a tool or device used for a particular task, especially for delicate or scientific work

n. 기계, 기구, 악기
instrumental a. 수단이 되는, 기구의, 기악의

I can play a lot of instruments. A violin is one of them.

나는 많은 악기를 연주할 수 있다. 바이올린이 그 중 하나이다.

26 **master** [mǽstər] a man who has people working for him, often as servants in his home

n. 주인, 선생, 자유로이 구사할 수 있는 사람 v. 지배하다

My master always drove me crazy.

내 주인은 항상 날 미치게 몰아갔다.

27 **masterpiece** [mǽstərpìːs, máːs-] an extremely good painting, novel, film, or other work of art

n. 명작

The book is regarded as a masterpiece of his writings.

그 책은 그의 작품들 중에 걸작으로 간주된다.

28 **most** [móust] the largest in number or amount

a. 가장 큰, 대개의 n. 최대량, 최대액, 최대 한도, 대개의 사람들, 대부분
mostly ad. 대개, 주로

Most people dislike the president nowadays.

요즘 대부분의 사람들은 대통령을 좋아하지 않는다.

29 **museum** [mjuːzíːəm]   a building where important cultural, historical, or scientific objects are kept and shown to the public

n. 박물관

The exhibition runs until April 8th at Deasang Art museum at Seoul Arts center.

이번 전시회는 서울 예술센터 내 대상미술관에서 4월 8일까지 계속된다.

30 **orchestra** [ɔ́ːrkəstrə]   a large group of people who play various musical instruments together, led by a conductor

n. 오케스트라, 관현악단

The orchestra was playing our song.

오케스트라가 우리 노래를 연주하는 중이었다.

31 **painter** [péintər]   person whose job is painting buildings, walls, etc.

n. 화가, 페인트공

I want to be either a painter or teacher.

나는 화가나 선생님 중에 하나가 되고 싶다.

32 **passion** [pǽʃən]   a very strong feeling of love, hatred, anger, enthusiasm, etc.

n. 열정, 격렬한 감정, 정열
passionate a. 열렬한, 정열적인

Although he is 95 years old, his passion for art will go on.

그가 95세이긴 하지만 예술에 대한 그의 열정은 계속될 것이다.

33 **passive** [pǽsiv] accepting what happens or what people do without trying to change anything or oppose them

a. 수동적인, 무저항의

Being too passive **in everything means getting few chances to do something.**

모든 일에 너무 수동적이면 기회를 얻기 어렵다.

34 **perfect** [pə́:rfikt] having everything that is necessary

a. 완전한, 정확한 v. 완성하다

perfection n. 완전 ǀ perfectly ad. 완전히 ǀ imperfect a. 불완전한

She has a perfect **talent that fits her role.**

그녀는 그녀의 역할에 맞는 완벽한 재능을 가지고 있다.

35 **perform** [pərfɔ́:rm] to do something, such as a piece of work, task or duty

v. 이행하다, 실행하다, 연주하다

performer n. 실행자, 연기자 ǀ performing a. 실행할 수 있는

performance n. 공연, 성과, 성능, 수행

A parents role is not easy to perform.

부모 역할은 어렵다.

36 **pleasure** [pléʒər] a feeling of enjoyment

n. 즐거움

pleasant a. 즐거운 ǀ pleased a. 좋아하는, 만족스러운

please v. 기쁘게 하다, 남의 마음에 들다

It is a pleasure **to have time with you.**

당신과 함께 할 수 있어서 기쁩니다.

37 portrait [pɔ́ːrtrit, -treit] a painting, drawing or photograph of a person, especially of the head and shoulders

n. 초상
portray v. 그리다, 묘사하다

I've seen the portrait of Vincent van Gogh in Europe.

유럽에서 고흐의 초상화를 본 적이 있다.

38 reality [riǽləti] the true situation and the problems that actually exist in life

n. 진실
real a. 진실의, 진짜의 | realize v. 실감하다, 이해하다

That story is popular because it is closer to reality in our lives.

그 이야기는 우리의 현실과 가깝기 때문에 인기가 있다.

39 rehearsal [rihə́ːrsəl] a time when all the people in a play, concert etc. practice before a public performance

n. 리허설
rehearse v. 연습하다

Every singer is in rehearsal now.

모든 가수가 지금 리허설 중이다.

40 revival [riváivəl] a case of something being brought back into use or existence

n. 재생
revive v. 소생하다, 소생하게 하다

Its revival function hasn't worked since last week.

재생 기능이 지난주부터 작동이 되지 않는다.

41 **sculpture** [skʌ́lptʃər] an object made out of stone, wood, clay, etc. by an artist

n. 조각
sculptured a. 조각된, 깎아 만든, 조각같이 잘 다듬어진
sculpt v. 조각하다

Her sculpture is a head out of the marble.
그녀의 조각은 대리석으로 만들어진 두상이다.

42 **simulation** [sìmjuléiʃən] the process of simulating something or the result of simulating it

n. 가장, 흉내, 모의 실험
simulate v. 흉내내다 ㅣ simulated a. 모조의, 모의 실험의

A flight simulation will be a good experience for students who want to be a pilot.
모의 비행은 파일럿이 되고 싶은 학생들에게 좋은 경험이 될 것입니다.

43 **sketch** [skétʃ] a simple picture that is drawn quickly and does not have many details

n. 스케치 v. 스케치하다

Going to sketch to a park in spring is a pleasant thing.
봄에 공원으로 그림을 그리러 나가는 것은 기분 좋은 일이다.

44 **soloist** [sóulouist] a person who plays an instrument or performs alone

n. 독주자, 독창자
solo n. 독창, 독주

The soloist in the evening concert will be Korean pianist Baek Gun-Woo.
저녁 연주회의 독주자는 한국인 피아니스트 백건우씨이다.

45 specific [spisífik] detailed and exact

a. 독특한, 특수한, 구체적인
specify v. 일일이 열거하다 I specification n. 명세, 상술

These symptoms are specific to liver disease.

이러한 증상은 특히 간 질환에 나타나는 증상이다.

46 symmetry [símətri] the exact match in size and shape between two halved, parts or sides of something

n. 대칭
symmetrical a. 대칭적인

Symmetry is very important in art.

예술에서 대칭은 매우 중요하다.

47 tragic [trǽdʒik] making you feel very sad, usually because someone has died or suffered a lot

a. 비참한, 비극의
tragedy n. 비극

It was tragic that they all perished.

그들 모두가 사망한 것은 비극적인 일이었다.

48 tune [tʃúːn] a series of musical notes that are sung or played in a particular order

n. 곡조, 어조, 가락, 장단

Traditional tune of Korean folk songs is normally sad.

한국 민속 음악의 곡조는 대개 슬프다.

49 **versatile** [vɔ́ːrsətl] able to do many different things

a. 다재다능한, 만능의, 변덕스러운

He has a versatile disposition.

그는 변덕스러운 기질을 가지고 있다.

50 **worth** [wɔ́ːrθ] having a value in money, etc.

a. ~의 가치가 있는 n. 가치, 값어치
worthy a. 가치 있는, 훌륭한 ǀ worthless a. 가치 없는, 무익한

For you, it might be worth working at the bank.

은행에서 일하는 것은 너에겐 가치 있는 일일 것이다.

Check up

A 다음 내용이 설명하고 있는 단어를 〈보기〉에서 골라 그 기호를 쓰시오.

---

worth │ versatile │ specific │ pleasure │ perfect

---

1. valuable, worthy

2. special, limited, specified, circumstantial

3. delight, joy, privilege, treat, pride

4. skilled, variable, mobile, varied

5. excellent, terrific, wonderful, fantastic

B 단어와 한글 뜻을 알맞게 짝지으시오.

1. passive   •   • 독창적인, 재능 있는

2. passion   •   • 환각

3. masterpiece •   • 수동적인

4. ingenious   •   • 열정, 열애

5. illusion   •   • 명작, 작품

C 다음 빈 칸에 의미상 가장 알맞은 단어를 보기에서 골라 쓰시오.

| harmony | glory | genius | famous | exhibit |

1. one's good ＿＿＿＿＿ : 사람에게 붙어 다니는 수호신

2. go to ＿＿＿＿ : 죽다, 승천하다

3. ＿＿＿＿ last words : (비꼼) 그렇고 말고

4. on ＿＿＿＿ : 진열되어

5. the ＿＿＿＿ of the spheres : 천체의 화성 (천체의 운행으로 생기는 음악)

D 영영풀이에 알맞은 단어를 고르시오.

| craft | comment | classic | chorus | aspire |

1. accepted or deserving to be accepted as one of the best or most important

2. something that you say or write which gives an opinion on or explains something

3. part of a song that is sung after each verse

4. an activity involving a special skill at making thing with your hands

5. to have a strong desire to achieve or to become something

|부록|

Answers

Part 1 Daily Life 일상생활

Lesson 1 Family 가족

A

1 ① 2 ②
3 ② 4 ①
5 ①

B

1 acquaintance – stranger
2 adult – juvenile
3 ancestor – descendant
4 mutual – non-reciprocal
5 tender – tough

Lesson 2 Shelter 주거

A

1 decorated 2 neighbor
3 suburb 4 vacant
5 lease

B

1 accommodate
2 antique
3 displace
4 handy
5 resident

C

1 건축
2 comparison
3 destruct

4 공급하다, 비치하다
5 개선하다, 향상시키다
6 pave
7 자리잡게 하다, 정착시키다
8 terrace
9 occupy
10 빌리다, 임대하다

Lesson 3 Clothes 의류

A

1 appropriate 2 casual
3 custom 4 vogue
5 tidy

B

1 alter 2 attract
3 brand 4 match
5 charm 6 fasten
7 shrink 8 tight
9 length

C

1 widens 2 cost
3 coordinates 4 sews
5 fit

Lesson 4 Something to eat 음식

A

1 ⓔ 2 ⓒ
3 ⓐ 4 ⓑ
5 ⓓ

B

1 appetite − 식욕
2 caffeine − 카페인
3 chef − 요리사
4 edible − 먹을 수 있는
5 protein − 단백질

C

1	stir	2	thirst
3	kettle	4	nutrition
5	ripe		

D

1	essential	2	handful
3	rare	4	blend
5	contain		

Lesson 5 **Fitness** 건강

A

1	ⓑ	2	ⓔ
3	ⓐ	4	ⓑ
5	ⓓ		

B

1	ⓑ	2	ⓒ
3	ⓐ	4	ⓒ
5	ⓓ		

Lesson 6 **Interests & Exercises** 취미와 운동

A

| 1 | ⓒ | 2 | ⓑ |
| 3 | ⓑ | 4 | ⓔ |

B

| 1 | awesome | 2 | field |
| 3 | fair | 4 | face |

Lesson 7 **Journey** 여행

A

1	diffident	2	enthusiastic
3	unpack	4	plan
5	unwilling	6	view
7	disarrange	8	cruise
9	negate	10	rational

B

1	ⓑ	2	ⓐ
3	ⓒ	4	ⓓ
5	ⓕ	6	ⓔ
7	ⓖ	8	ⓗ

Part 2 **Nature** 자연

Lesson 1 **Nature** 자연

A

1	ⓓ	2	ⓔ
3	ⓐ	4	ⓒ
5	ⓑ		

B

1 conserve − 보존하다, 보호하다
2 create − 창조하다, 만들다
3 crisis − 위기, 결정적 단계
4 daybreak − 새벽
5 decay − 썩다, 쇠퇴하다

C

1	eclipse	2	depend
3	distinct	4	drastic
5	disappear		

D

1 extinct   2 indistinct
3 inevitable   4 remain
5 source

Lesson 2 **Weather & Geography** 날씨와 지리

A

1 ⓐ   2 ⓑ
3 ⓐ   4 ⓐ
5 ⓑ

B

1 freeze – boil
2 harsh – fine
3 vertical – horizontal
4 typical – atypical
5 indicate – contraindicate

Lesson 3 **Environment & Contamination** 환경과 오염

A

1 accumulated   2 aerial
3 avail   4 damp
5 decayed

B

1 disgusting
2 dusty
3 echo
4 investigation
5 marsh

C

1 안개
2 parallel
3 destruct
4 오염, 공해

5 흙무더기, 고문, 제방, 방죽
6 stain
7 noise
8 증기, 수증기
9 과수원
10 wilderness

Part 3 **Science** 과학

Lesson 1 **Technology** 기술

A

1 amend   2 automatic
3 bind   4 cling
5 coffin

B

1 ditch   2 microscope
3 paved   4 screw
5 commence   6 handy
7 split   8 equip
9 cork   10 construction

C

1 telegraph   2 weave
3 transform   4 toil
5 wireless

Lesson 2 **Medical Science** 의학

A

1 ⓒ   2 ⓔ
3 ⓒ   4 ⓓ
5 ⓐ

B

1 ⓑ   2 ⓐ
3 ⓓ   4 ⓓ
5 ⓑ

Lesson 3 Aerospace 우주과학

A

1 ⓑ   2 ⓐ
3 ⓒ   4 ⓒ
5 ⓐ

B

1 crater   2 rotate
3 dense   4 heaven

Lesson 4 Computer 컴퓨터

A

1 access   2 appropriate
3 delete   4 insert
5 particular

B

1 component   2 frequent
3 proceed   4 respond
5 virtual

C

1 appropriate − inappropriate
2 complex − simple
3 connect − disconnect
4 appear − disappear
5 input − output

Part 4 Politics 정치

Lesson 1 Government 정부

A

1 ⓑ   2 ⓐ
3 ⓐ   4 ⓑ
5 ⓑ

B

1 attend − miss
2 central − peripheral
3 control − unrestraint
4 corrupt − straight
5 enforce − exempt

Lesson 2 Law 법률

A

1 accused   2 ban
3 confess   4 evidence
5 illegal

B

1 blame   2 basis
3 compensate   4 court
5 ban

C

1 제한하다   2 convict
3 deny   4 발견하다
5 벌금   6 guilty
7 identify   8 불법의
9 합법적인   10 obey

Lesson 3 Thought 사상

A

1	advocate	2	argue
3	aware	4	communism
5	compromise		

B

1	swear	2	recognition
3	prejudice	4	suppose
5	fancy	6	grant
7	faith	8	purpose
9	mental	10	sympathy

C

1	expose	2	determine
3	critical	4	emphasis
5	dispute		

Lesson 4 War & Peace 전쟁과 평화

A

1	ⓑ	2	ⓓ
3	ⓔ	4	ⓐ
5	ⓒ		

B

1 casualty – 불의의 재난, 부상자
2 civilian – 일반 국민, 인간의
3 compulsory – 의무적인, 강제적인
4 defeat – 패배, 좌절
5 disarm – 무장 해제하다

C

1 discipline
2 emergency
3 enemy
4 disguise
5 drift

D

1 triumph
2 surrender
3 poverty
4 hostile
5 honorable

Part 5 Economy 경제

Lesson 1 Economy 경제

A

1	ⓒ	2	ⓑ
3	ⓑ	4	ⓐ
5	ⓒ		

B

1	employ	2	estimate
3	income	4	durable
5	deal		

C

1	노동력	2	purchase
3	warrant	4	통계치
5	slight	6	possess
7	경감하다	8	실직한
9	다국적의	10	consumption

Lesson 2 Agriculture 농업

A

1	ⓐ	2	ⓐ
3	ⓑ	4	ⓐ
5	ⓑ		

B

1 weed − cultivated plant
2 sterile − fertile
3 lack − have
4 generous − stingy
5 feed − starve

Lesson 3 Industry 산업

A

1 absorb   2 alternative
3 architecture   4 collapsed
5 efficient

B

1 efficient   2 crucial
3 interior   4 design
5 expand

C

1 나머지, 잉여금   2 swift
3 계획, 음모   4 sector
5 관세   6 recession
7 이익, 이득   8 prevail
9 독점   10 merge

Lesson 4 Trade 무역

A

1 adjusts   2 arrived
3 certificate   4 circulation
5 confirmed

B

1 delivered   2 freight
3 engagement   4 contract
5 holiday   6 exchange
7 invitation   8 load
9 delay   10 demanding

C

1 notification   2 necessary
3 protest   4 postpone
5 negotiate

Lesson 5 Finance 금융

A

1 bankrupt   2 approximate
3 debt   4 deliberate
5 charge

B

1 deposit − 예금액, 예금
2 endow − 기부하다, 증여하다
3 expire − 만기가 되다, 기간이 끝나다
4 guarantee − 담보, 보증
5 impose − (세금, 벌 등을) 부과하다

C

1 loan   2 interest
3 rate   4 lease
5 owe

D

1 signature   2 sum
3 withdraw   4 refund
5 thrift

Lesson 6 Occupation 직업

A

1 ⓓ   2 ⓐ
3 ⓓ   4 ⓑ
5 ⓐ

B

1 earn   2 form
3 interview   4 chief
5 excellent

C

1	행정 장관	2	recruit
3	official	4	이력서
5	열정적인	6	retire
7	personality	8	솜씨 좋은
9	직업	10	veteran

Part 6 Society 사회

Lesson 1 Society 사회

A

1	ⓑ	2	ⓑ
3	ⓐ	4	ⓐ
5	ⓑ		

B

1 different − same
2 discourage − encourage
3 complain − satisfy
4 exclude − include
5 harmony − dissonance

Lesson 2 Religion 종교

A

1	vow	2	temple
3	taboo	4	superstition
5	solemn		

B

1	mourning	2	pray
3	miracle	4	holy
5	moral		

C

1	슬픔	2	묻다, 매장하다
3	funeral	4	축복하다
5	신성한	6	Buddhist
7	dignity	8	의심하다
9	mercy	10	grave

Lesson 3 World 세계

A

1 abroad − foreign
2 aid − help
3 border − boundary
4 common − popular
5 countryside − rural

B

1	crowd	2	globe
3	human	4	region
5	foreign	6	opportunity
7	minority	8	tribes
9	native	10	generations

C

1	vast	2	urban
3	successive	4	useless
5	resident		

Lesson 4 Crime & Punishment 죄와 벌

A

1	aggressive	2	blackmail
3	accident	4	chase
5	assassinate		

B

1 clue − 단서, 해결의 실마리
2 deception − 속임, 사기, 기만

3 cunning − 교활한, 간사한
4 detective − 탐정, 형사
5 criminal − 범인, 범죄자

C

1 suspect 2 violence
3 suicide 4 thief
5 struggle

D

1 poison 2 punishment
3 hostage 4 incident
5 steal

Lesson 5 Media 언론

A

1 watch 2 underlined
3 synchronize 4 subscribe
5 replace

B

1 ordinary 2 publish
3 issue 4 favorite
5 quote

C

1 공기의, 안테나 2 편집하다
3 순환하다 4 유명인
5 forecast 6 nowadays
7 알리다, 공표하다 8 public
9 journal 10 remote

Lesson 6 Culture 문화

A

1 ⓐ 2 ⓑ
3 ⓐ 4 ⓐ
5 ⓑ

B

1 oppose − approve
2 last − stop
3 odd − even
4 particular − general
5 involve − obviate

Part 7 Education 교육

Lesson 1 Education 교육

A

1 absent − nonexistent
2 acknowledge − accept
3 attend − come
4 brilliant − intelligent
5 comprehend − understand

B

1 counsel 2 concentrate
3 fee 4 degree
5 complement 6 graduate
7 endeavors 8 entrance
9 courage 10 content

C

1 nerd 2 perceive
3 instruct 4 significant
5 license

Lesson 2 Academy 학문

A

1 abstract 2 ambiguous
3 accurate 4 category
5 absolute

B

1 coherent – 논리 정연한, 응집성의
2 conceive – 상상하다, 생각하다
3 concrete – 구체적인
4 criticize – 비평하다, 비난하다
5 fulfill – 다하다, 이행하다

C

1 guess 2 insight
3 laboratory 4 ignorant
5 presume

D

1 recite 2 psychology
3 prose 4 pursue
5 remarkable

Lesson 3 Languages 언어

A

1 wit – 지혜, 기지
2 utter – 입 밖에 내다, 발언하다
3 theme – 주제
4 synonym – 동의어
5 satire – 풍자

B

1 proverb 2 plot
3 rhyme 4 logic
5 pattern 6 punctuation
7 initial 8 literal
9 passage 10 prominent

C

1 imply 2 fiction
3 impress 4 feature
5 illustrate

Lesson 4 History 역사

A

1 ⓐ 2 ⓑ
3 ⓐ 4 ⓐ
5 ⓑ

B

1 lose – win, gain
2 ancient – modern
3 great – poor
4 broad – narrow
5 orient – occident

Lesson 5 Arts 예술

A

1 worth 2 specific
3 pleasure 4 versatile
5 perfect

B

1 passive – 수동적인
2 passion – 열정, 열애
3 masterpiece – 명작, 작품
4 ingenious – 독창적인, 재능 있는
5 illusion – 환각

C

1 genius 2 glory
3 famous 4 exhibit
5 harmony

D

1 classic 2 comment
3 chorus 4 craft
5 aspire